The Readers' Advisory Guide
to
Nonfiction

ALA READERS' ADVISORY SERIES

· ·

Serving Teens through Readers' Advisory

The Horror Readers' Advisory:
The Librarian's Guide to Vampires,
Killer Tomatoes, and Haunted Houses

The Science Fiction and Fantasy Readers' Advisory:
The Librarian's Guide to Cyborgs, Aliens, and Sorcerers

The Mystery Readers' Advisory:
The Librarian's Clues to Murder and Mayhem

The Readers' Advisory Guide to Genre Fiction

The Romance Readers' Advisory:
The Librarian's Guide to Love in the Stacks

The Short Story Readers' Advisory:
A Guide to the Best

Neal Wyatt

The Readers' Advisory
Guide
to
Nonfiction

American Library Association

Chicago   2007

Composition by ALA Editions in Janson Text and Helvetica Condensed using InDesign CS2.

The paper used in this publication meets the minimum requirements of American National Standard for Information Sciences—Permanence of Paper for Printed Library Materials, ANSI Z39.48-1992. ∞

Library of Congress Cataloging-in-Publication Data
Wyatt, Neal.
　　The Readers' Advisory guide to nonfiction / Neal Wyatt.
　　　　p. cm. — (ALA readers' advisory series)
　　Includes bibliographical references and index.
　　ISBN-13: 978-0-8389-0936-2 (alk. paper)
　　ISBN-10: 0-8389-0936-1 (alk. paper)
　　1. Readers' advisory services—United States. 2. Public libraries—Reference services—United States. 3. Public libraries—United States—Book lists. 4. Books and reading—United States. 5. Reading interests—United States.　I. Title.
　　Z711.55.W93 2007
　　025.5′4—dc22　　　　　　　　　　　　　　　　　　　　　　　2006102318

ISBN-13: 978-0-8389-0936-2
ISBN-10: 0-8389-0936-1

Printed in the United States of America

11　10　09　08　07　　5　4　3　2　1

For my father

CONTENTS

Appendixes

ACKNOWLEDGMENTS

This book was born in the back of a taxi. Joyce Saricks and I were traveling from the convention center during an ALA conference when she asked me if I had ever thought of writing a book. I owe Joyce so very much. Not only did she suggest me as the author of this book to her editor at ALA Editions, she talked me through the early stages of deciding to write it and shared useful advice about the process. She read the first subject chapter when it was in draft form and supplied valuable input to make it, and thus the rest of the chapters, better. She read, in a mad dash at the end, almost the entire book and again supplied me with great advice and wonderful editing.

Deep and heartfelt thanks also go to Nancy Pearl. Nancy was in the middle of writing *More Book Lust: Recommended Reading for Every Mood, Moment, and Reason* when I began thinking about this book, and she went on to write *Book Crush: For Kids and Teens—Recommended Reading for Every Mood, Moment, and Interest* while I was wrestling with this manuscript. During that time, when she had so much to do, Nancy was endlessly generous in talking with me about titles, reacting to ideas, offering improving suggestions and edits, and sharing advice.

There are many other people whom I would like to acknowledge and thank: my mother, who has read every chapter and has, from her viewpoint as an avid reader, cheered the book along with great enthusiasm and excitement—a better in-house editor could not be hoped for; my brothers, who have suffered endless conversations about "The Book" and have offered suggestions of their favorite titles along with large doses of encouragement; Ginger Armstrong, my colleague and great friend, who has been a support, sounding board, critic, and cheerleader; Ann Theis, colleague and the creator of Overbooked.org, who offered title suggestions and heaps of encouragement; all my other colleagues but especially Rebecca Neas, Teresa Puckett, and Carol Wise; Duncan Smith, the genius behind *NoveList*, who read much of the manuscript and supplied great comments and suggestions; Della

Coulter, also of *NoveList*, who helped me think through the history chapter; Cathleen Towey for her support, good wishes, and friendship; Brian Kenney, editor in chief of *School Library Journal*, and Osbely Tala for their support and encouragement; Corinne Hill and Diane Zabel for their endless enthusiasm; all the folks at *Library Journal* for their support and encouragement and for letting me write "Wyatt's World" every week and edit "The Reader's Shelf" each month; the editorial staff at *Booklist*, who have helped me so much to think from the reader's perspective; Katie Mediatore Stover, who sparked the idea of readers' advisory Mad Libs; Georgine Olson, who sparked the idea for the 1–3 annotation and taught me how to just look at a book; Professor Jean Preer, for teaching me so well and for making me the librarian I am; Lia and Cole Gayle—just because; and Lisa Clemmer Brooks, my peanut butter and jelly friend, who shared the joys and fears of writing over dinners and phone calls and made it all seem possible even while her world was getting impossibly scary—here's to Chris, serving heroically in Iraq.

And finally, my deepest thanks go to my editor, Laura Pelehach. Laura made writing this book a joy. She was endlessly supportive and reassuring and provided insightful and improving comments all the way through the process. Laura, thank you.

INTRODUCTION

Welcome to the world of nonfiction—a heady, vibrant, and often overwhelming realm inhabited by various types of readers, writers, and reasons for reading; a world of uncharted territory we are only now beginning to explore. Consider this book both a map and an invitation. My hope is that it will start to chart the landscape that is nonfiction and entice librarians and readers into its many wondrous locales.

To undertake the journey of nonfiction, it is vital to keep in mind that not every reader chooses a book for the same reason, and there is no particular standard a book has to meet to become beloved by a reader. This book does not distinguish between readers or the directions in which they wish to travel, be they reading for pleasure, leisure, or learning. And it does not exclude books that are not story-centric. It is a map to the extravagantly rich world of nonfiction. I hope all readers and all librarians find it to hold wonderful books they cannot wait to read next—which to me will always be the central motivating point of readers' advisory service.

Traditionally, we have thought about readers' advisory service as a fiction-only enterprise. For the most part, we have been unwilling to cross the Dewey divide and enter the nonfiction side of our stacks to find great readable books for our patrons. When readers ask us to suggest books, when we pull books for our sure-bet carts, even—to a large extent—when we make book displays, we tend to concentrate on fiction. Standard reference tools such as *Genreflecting; NoveList; Now Read This; What Do I Read Next?* and the host of genre books by ALA Editions and Libraries Unlimited have all focused on fiction. Even as we employ that standard opening readers' advisory invitation—"Tell me about a book you have recently read and enjoyed"—we expect to hear a fiction title as the reply. I suspect many of us would be surprised if the patron's response was *The Elegant Universe: Superstrings, Hidden Dimensions, and the Quest for the Ultimate Theory,* by Brian Greene. And, if that had been the response, it is possible that we might have led the patron back to the reference desk, away from the books, and asked what question she wanted answered (all the time wondering just what superstrings were).

Most of the work in readers' advisory service, and all of our best tools, have focused on fiction. The people who reinvigorated modern readers' advisory work did so using fiction—perhaps because that is what most of the readers' advisory community reads or perhaps because, before now, few of us really thought about nonfiction when we thought about suggesting books. After all, nonfiction is so specialized. It's almost like a tool—a light sort of reference book, if you will. Once most of us enter the world of reading for pleasure—heady, voracious, give-me-an-hour-and-let-me-read reading—we are reading fiction. When most of us think about reading, I hazard to guess that we are thinking about novels. Novels are, in the vast majority, the source of book group selections, movies, Oprah picks, and most major literary awards. Novels fuel our dreams and memories. They are what we choose to read while waiting in the doctor's office or flying across the country. So fiction seems to rule our landscapes, and the Dewey divide has come to define the working boundary of our suggestion repertoire: on one side are the books we consider readable, and on the other side are the books we consider an extension of the reference department.

We forget that as kids we read a mix of fiction and nonfiction, more likely either evenly divided or more weighted toward nonfiction. All the dinosaur books, all the Eyewitness books, all the books on icky gross things that we loved to read about or look at were nonfiction. The joy of discovery was not delineated by fiction and nonfiction. We found that joy in the pages of a book—*any* book—we loved. My godchildren's favorite book is *Guinness World Records*. They can spend hours showing me something weird or gross or unbelievable (but it must be true!). They don't really know the difference between fiction and nonfiction yet. They will learn that in school. They will subtly, like all of us before them, be taught to see fiction as pleasure and nonfiction as homework help.

Yet, all hope is not lost for them or for us. Slowly, wonderful books, books that read like the very best of novels, have made their way into the collective mind of the public. What makes them even better is that they are real. Books like *The Perfect Storm: A True Story of Men against the Sea*, by Sebastian Junger, and *Into Thin Air: A Personal Account of the Mt. Everest Disaster*, by Jon Krakauer, have stepped up to compete with blockbuster fiction thrillers. Books like *Seabiscuit: An American Legend*, by Laura Hillenbrand, and *The Devil in the White City: Murder, Magic, and Madness at the Fair That Changed America*, by Erik Larson, have come along and exposed the reading population to the idea that nonfiction can be as compelling and readable as fiction. Readers want more ways to find these types of books, and readers' advisory librarians, having read and loved these books as well, also want more.

And thus, simmering along for a half dozen years now has been the idea of offering readers' advisory service in nonfiction. We started out suggesting adventure thriller types of nonfiction, true stories that read almost the same as a novel. We have progressed to big biographies and big historical epics, noted more for their authors than their topics. We have added in, here and there, bit by bit, books of funny essays and some titles that seem to catch the fleeting interest of the public. Notable readers' advisory figures have begun to talk about nonfiction with the same enthusiasm and care they have always given to fiction. In the third edition of her landmark *Readers' Advisory Service in the Pubic Library*, Joyce Saricks weaves nonfiction into her explanations of how readers' advisory service works.[1] Nancy Pearl, in both *Book Lust: Recommended Reading for Every Mood, Moment, and Reason* and *More Book Lust: Recommended Reading for Every Mood, Moment, and Reason*, mixes nonfiction titles into her addictive lists of reading suggestions.[2] In 2006 the venerable *Genreflecting* model was finally applied to nonfiction in Sarah Statz Cords's *The Real Story: A Guide to Nonfiction Reading Interests*.[3] Slowly, online readers' advisory tools are beginning to include nonfiction or have plans to do so. Programs at both the state and national levels have also followed the trend and are now addressing nonfiction readers' advisory topics. The time is ripe for all of us to broaden our repertoire of suggestions and help open the world of nonfiction to readers. This book seeks to bridge the Dewey divide and explore nonfiction; to highlight its complexity and order, its grand books and key authors, its appeal to readers; to demonstrate how to suggest it and how to work with nonfiction in a readers' advisory context.

In chapters 1 and 2 of this book, I set out the conceptual groundwork for nonfiction readers' advisory service, introduce methods of working with nonfiction, and offer suggestions for incorporating these theories into your readers' advisory service.

The core of this book, chapters 3–11, examines prominent nonfiction subject areas in terms of these concepts. Each chapter introduces a nonfiction subject, discusses what readers particularly enjoy in the subject area, and explores the major appeals of the subject. These chapters also offer discussions of the types of books most common in the subject range, their differences, and appeals. Lists of key authors and title suggestions are included within the discussion of each type. A benchmark title to read and suggest for each type of nonfiction writing is also provided, with reasons why a librarian should read the title and why patrons may want to do so as well. Additional read-alike and read-around title suggestions are included within the benchmark annotations. A discussion of resources for finding titles and a list of key awards in the subject area conclude each chapter.

The book itself concludes with a chapter on learning and marketing your collection, a chapter on whole collection readers' advisory service, and several appendixes to provide more tools to help you on your journey into the realm of nonfiction readers' advisory service.

NOTES

1. Joyce G. Saricks, *Readers' Advisory Service in the Public Library*, 3rd ed. (Chicago: American Library Association, 2005).
2. Nancy Pearl, *Book Lust: Recommended Reading for Every Mood, Moment, and Reason* (Seattle: Sasquatch Books, 2003); and *More Book Lust: Recommended Reading for Every Mood, Moment, and Reason* (Seattle: Sasquatch Books, 2005).
3. Sarah Statz Cords, *The Real Story: A Guide to Nonfiction Reading Interests* (Westport, Conn.: Libraries Unlimited, 2006).

1

A READERS' ADVISORY APPROACH
TO NONFICTION

The world of nonfiction is huge. Readers' advisory librarians need a way to view the overall landscape and a method of understanding why a reader would enjoy one title more than another. This chapter provides a foundational approach to nonfiction. It addresses its two functional divisions and introduces a method in which all nonfiction titles can be considered from a readers' advisory point of view. Think of it as the compass guiding you along the map of nonfiction. It shows you the way and reassures you that you are on the right path.

To start, it is helpful to define the world of nonfiction this book addresses and to explore the naming conventions of this body of literature. Although several terms and concepts are linked to nonfiction, little consensus exists over which term to use or even what books to include. Early on, some of the authors who were part of the development of one type of writing referred to it as "new journalism," "literary journalism," or "immersion journalism." "Creative nonfiction" became a new catchword when Lee Gutkind used the phrase to name his groundbreaking literary journal. Librarians have not yet settled on a term, calling it "narrative nonfiction," "popular nonfiction," "literary nonfiction," or "readable nonfiction" or describing it as the nonfiction readers pick up as part of their leisure or pleasure reading, or nonfiction that "reads like a novel."

I am not certain that we need to name nonfiction or work so hard to define what it is and is not. As a profession, librarians love to classify. Even those of us who took one look at MARC and ran toward the reference desk and collection development department as fast as we could love to bring order to the chaos of bibliography. We like to name things, too. We have genres and subgenres. We use descriptors like "cozy" and "noir." We attempt to make distinctions between thriller and suspense. We talk about factual writing, instructional writing, and narrative writing, as if we assume that all our patrons speak our language or that even our own professional community always collectively understands what we mean. And this drive to order and arrange things, classify them so we can say this is included and this is not, is futile in any case. Readers don't follow an orderly system when choosing what to read. They make their choices according to a chaotic whorl of interests based on an ever-changing set of reasons and moods.

Yet we need some borders to our map of nonfiction so we can get our bearings and guide readers in the directions they wish to travel. To do that, this book divides the nonfiction world into two divisions of purpose: task books and nontask books. Task books are those readers want to use for some task-oriented function. These are the books readers turn to when they want to learn to knit, build a fence, or do some fact-specific research. For the most part, I do not consider these how-to-ish and reference-ish books here. In contrast, readers turn to nontask books for all sorts of other reasons, including pleasure, recreation, story, escape, exploration, and learning. Readers choose them for many of the same reasons they choose fiction, but also for reasons that are particular to nonfiction.

The first thing to do in offering nonfiction readers' advisory service is to find out what the reader needs. Readers who want task-based nonfiction need a good librarian with a well-crafted catalog and a well-developed collection to help them find what they are after. Readers who want nontask-based nonfiction need readers' advisory assistance.

When readers' advisory service is needed, we must discern what elements influence a reader's reaction to a title. Four intertwining aspects shape this response: the work's narrative context, subject, type, and appeal. These elements have to be considered individually, but they act in concert as we consider both a reader's response to a title and the inherent qualities of a title itself.

In this chapter, and still more in the subject chapters that make up the bulk of this book, I demonstrate the intertwining nature of these elements and give many examples to show how the approach works when applied to nonfiction titles. Learning how to work with this foundational approach is the critical skill of nonfiction readers' advisory service.

The Narrative Context

Narrative is a fancy word for "story," and story is important. It offers readers understanding, comfort, and a way to contextualize life. Narrative authors use the devices of storytelling, such as character, dialogue, setting, plot, and scene building, to tell their story. These devices are not limited to novels; they are present in all types of writing including plays, poetry, and many forms of nonfiction. But even though story is important and the devices of narrative can enrich reading, a work does not have to be narrative to offer understanding, comfort, or contextualization. Not all nonfiction that is deeply enjoyed by readers is highly narrative.

Narrative exists on a continuum. Some nonfiction writers employ many narrative devices to shape their works into compelling page-turning reading. Others use only some narrative devices in their work, and still others use hardly any of these devices at all, opting instead for fact-based writing.

At the most narrative end of the continuum are books that do indeed read like fiction. *The Perfect Storm* is an example of this type of book. It is highly narrative and tells a gripping, cannot-put-it-down story. On the other end of the continuum are nonfiction books such as *The Elegant Universe*, which explains a particular theory through a complex tour of science. This book does not rely on many narrative devices, yet it provides an illuminating reading experience that is just as pleasurable to some as books like *The Perfect Storm* are to others.

Nonfiction books do not have to read like novels to work in a readers' advisory context. There are many other reasons to enjoy a title than the force of its story. Just how much narrative is needed depends on the reader. The concept of narrative is one of the first aspects about a title to consider in a readers' advisory context. It helps readers' advisory librarians gain a quick and broad understanding of the kind of book a reader is seeking.

Narrative provides a hook for readers to pull themselves through a title. Some readers need a strong driving narrative to keep them reading. These readers are most happy with highly plotted fiction or highly narrative nonfiction. They are less happy with meandering, unfocused works, be they fiction or nonfiction. Other readers, such as those who read for character or language, do not need as highly narrative a work and can deeply enjoy novels without a clear story focus or nonfiction that is less narrative in its drive.

The narrative hook does not have to work on the micro level, played out in a plot that builds chapter by chapter; instead, it can work as an overriding "story" contained within the book. *The Elegant Universe* has a narrative hook that stretches throughout the entire book, guiding the reader along through the explanation of the very small to what readers hope will be a gradual understanding of string theory. *The Perfect Storm* has a narrative hook that builds chapter by chapter in a continuous swell that pushes readers rapidly toward the end of the story.

The continuum on which narrative exists is wide. Here are three examples of nonfiction. The first is very narrative, the second is somewhere in the middle of the continuum, and the third is much less narrative.

High on the Narrative Continuum

From *Black Hawk Down*, by Mark Bowden[1]

Nelson watched dumbstruck as the chopper fell.

"Oh, my God, you guys, look at this," he shouted. "Look at this!"

Waddell gasped, "Oh, Jesus," and fought the urge to just stand and watch the bird go down. He turned away to keep his eyes on his corner.

Nelson shouted, "It just went down! It just crashed!"

"What happened?" called Lieutenant DiTomasso, who came running.

"A bird just went down!" Nelson said. "We've gotta go. We've gotta go right now!"

Word spread wildly over the radio, voices overlapping with the bad news. There was no pretense now of the deadpan military cool, that mandatory monotone that conveyed *everything under control*. Voices rose with surprise and fear:

—*We got a Black Hawk going down! We got a Black Hawk going down!*

—*We got a Black Hawk crashed in the city! Six One!*

—*He took an RPG!*

—*Six One down!*

—*We got a bird down, northeast of the target. I need you to move on out and secure that location!*

—*Roger, bird down!*

It was more than a helicopter crash. It cracked the task force's sense of righteous invulnerability. The Black Hawks and Little Birds were their trump card in this God-forsaken place. The choppers, more than their rifles and machine guns, were what kept the savage mobs at a distance. The Somalis *couldn't* shoot them down!

But they had seen it, the chopper spinning, falling, one of the D-boys hanging on with one hand, both feet in the air, riding it down.

In the Middle of the Narrative Continuum

From *Sea of Glory: America's Voyage of Discovery, the U.S. Exploring Expedition, 1838–1842*, by Nathaniel Philbrick[2]

Poinsett, with the help of outgoing secretary of the navy Paulding, arranged for the Expedition's collection to be directed to Washington, where he secured space in the newly built Patent

Office Building. He then hired a curator and staff to begin the job of unpacking the Expedition's crates and preparing the specimens for display. But as soon as Wilkes arrived in Washington, he realized that the Institute had made a mess of the collections. Prior to being shipped to the United States, each crate of specimens had been carefully catalogued using a color-coded number and letter system that keyed the objects to the scientists' field notes. Since the Institute's curator was without the catalogue lists, he had no way of determining what was in each crate unless he opened it up and looked inside. Soon the Expedition's collections were in chaos. Titian Peale was horrified to find that a taxidermist had combined the skins of a male and female bird of the same species into a single bird. James Dana discovered that some of the more delicate marine organisms he had collected had been taken out of their bottles of preservative, dried, and then stuck with pins.

Even though the Institute's curator was fired in September and Charles Pickering was brought on to supervise the collection, Wilkes and the scientists remained leery. For his part, Senator Tappan believed that the Expedition's collection should remain a government-subsidized entity unto itself, and he secured the necessary funding from Congress for that. Pickering began to reassemble the Expedition's scientists in Washington. Soon they were unpacking the collections and preparing the objects for exhibition in the Patent Office's huge, 265-foot-long Great Hall.

Pickering provided an early and much-needed rallying point for the Expedition's scientists, but he had little interest in being the head of what was rapidly becoming the country's first national museum. Pickering was a scientist, not a curator. It wasn't the objects themselves that were important, he insisted, it was the knowledge that could be derived from those objects. In Pickering's view, the Expedition's greatest achievements were yet to come since a scientist's true role was not simply to collect and exhibit objects, but to study them. In July, Pickering resigned as superintendent of the collection so that he could continue researching the book he was planning to write about the races of man.

Low on the Narrative Continuum

From *Road to Reality: A Complete Guide to the Laws of the Universe,* by Roger Penrose[3]

In particular, let us consider the remarkable fact, asserted at the end of §9.7, that any continuous function f defined on the unit circle in the complex plane can be represented as a hyperfunction. This assertion effectively states that any continuous f is the sum of two parts, one of which extends holomorphically into the interior of the unit circle and the other of which extends holomorphically into the exterior, where we now think of the complex plane completed to the Riemann sphere. This assertion is effectively equivalent (according to the discussion of §9.2) to the existence of a Fourier series representation of f, where f is regarded as a periodic function of a real variable. For simplicity, assume that f is real-valued.

Using these examples as a reference, we can see that highly narrative works entice the reader into the story and actually help some readers become engaged in the work. Moderately narrative titles mix story with facts and ask more of readers than to simply read for the story itself. Less narrative works, on the other hand, offer few of the elements of narrative and provide readers enjoyment for totally different reasons. The narrative context of a work, and the reader's reaction to that level of narrative, is a major consideration when offering nonfiction suggestions to readers. The reader's mood and level of interest influence where a book needs to fall on the narrative continuum, as do a book's subject, type, and appeal aspects. When working with a reader, it is important to ascertain what levels of narrative the reader typically needs before considering titles to suggest.

Subject

The *subject* element allows readers' advisors to manage the huge scope of nonfiction. Melvil Dewey charted the subject divisions of nonfiction more than a hundred years ago, and we have been taught to see the collective body of nonfiction based on his subject-oriented system. From a readers' advisory perspective, this general division works well, if not perfectly. My recurring fantasy about libraries is that at night, after everyone goes home, the books come to life and mingle in a fabulous cocktail party. Finally, the poor biographies, languishing in exile during the day, get to join their compatriots. Still, despite whatever small flaws the Dewey system has, it does order the landscape of possible subjects and offers both the reader and the readers' advisory librarian a common place to start a conversation.

This book is organized into eight subject chapters, with a ninth chapter covering a litany of additional subjects in brief. The categories were selected on the basis of their popularity with readers, the fact that there is a sufficient body of nontask-based writing in the area to support readers' advisory efforts, and because the subjects work well in a readers' advisory context. In a sense, this book is built around the ideal nonfiction collection, a collection I doubt many of us have either the funding or the shelf space to acquire and house. It is important for each of us to relate what we know and can offer to our own collection, so I urge you to investigate your collections and see for yourself what you have and, perhaps, what you need to weed or acquire. Appendix A of this book is a resource titled "How to Build a Nonfiction Subject Guide" that can help you study your library's holdings and build nonfiction subject guides based on your own collection.

In fiction readers' advisory service, we have been taught not to pay too much attention to the subject of the book because, in the end, subjects do not work as well as appeal points when suggesting fiction books to readers. But we all know fiction readers who get on jags and want to read all the novels we have on Marie Antoinette or some other specific topic. When readers do that, they are not really reading for appeal, but simply to feed their obsession. They enjoy some books more than others, based on how those books match the appeal aspects they typically read for, but it does not really matter. They are now reading based on subject, and our job is to simply feed the need. (But feed it well! When you do encounter a reader who is on a jag, be as expansive in your suggestions as possible and offer both fiction and nonfiction titles as well as all the other materials your library offers including movies and music. See chapter 13 for more on whole collection readers' advisory service.)

With nonfiction, however, subject does matter a great deal. It measures the initial degree of interest a reader has in a title. In fact, subject is usually the strongest pull readers feel toward a book in the beginning—unless they already know the author, in which case the main pull is typically a mix of author and subject. Many readers approach nonfiction simply because of the subject, and it becomes the focus of their title selection decisions. They enjoy reading books on World War I or on football, travel adventures, or grisly serial killers.

There is, however, a limit to the usefulness of subject in even nonfiction readers' advisory work. From a practical point of view, there is a limit to the number of books available on any one subject. Although there can appear to be an endless stream of titles on a given subject, that is not really the case, and this is never more apparent than when you face a reader who has read all the books on that subject in your collection. Subjects do get exhausted, and the more specialized the subject is, the more quickly both you and the reader will reach the end of available titles.

In any case, as strong as the initial draw of subject may be, in the end it is not what keeps a reader reading a book—that is a combination of how closely the book fits the type or pattern the reader is seeking, how the narrative nature of the book matches her reading needs, and all the appeal aspects she consciously or unconsciously enjoys when reading. Readers go to a book because of its subject, but they stay for everything else. Subject is helped along by other factors a reader enjoys. Readers who liked *T. rex and the Crater of Doom*, by Walter Alvarez, may enjoy another detective story about dinosaur extinction, but the degree to which they enjoy it is also based on how well it matches the type of book *T. rex* is, its narrative nature, and the other points they liked: the clarity of language, the entertaining approach, the explanation of concepts, the details provided.

Additionally, readers do not want just any book on World War I or football; they want the book that focuses on the subject in the way they want to experience it. There are World War I books that address military battles, or the huge personalities of the war, or the social shifts the war caused. There are football books on the heroes and villains of sport, or on what it means to play the game, or on the fans who support their teams with rabid dedication.

Subject is of vital importance. It is the first spark that leads a reader to a title and can help guide readers' advisory librarians when making suggestions. But it goes only so far. Though it can get readers' advisory librarians to the right spot on the shelves, it cannot help us pull the right book off the shelf. We also need to know the types of books available within each subject and use them in combination with narrative and appeal to help readers find the books they are seeking.

Type

Memoir, biography, letters, and essays are all *types* of nonfiction; novels and short stories are types of fiction. When we offer fiction readers' advisory service, we often simply assume that a reader wants a novel. It is different with nonfiction, where we have a bit more to work through. We need to find out how much story is needed (narrative context) and what a reader wants to read about (subject), but we also need to find out what kind of book on that subject the reader wants. And that consideration is classified as type.

In fiction, especially in individual genres, we expect books to follow certain patterns. In romance there is a happy ending, in mysteries there is a solution to the crime, and to a great extent we read for such patterns. Although it is not a direct parallel, it might be useful to think of nonfiction types as working like fiction genres. Just as there are cozy mysteries, police procedurals, and noir mysteries, there are investigative science books, explanatory science books, and literary science books. Just as readers ask for Regency romances or chick lit, they also tend to ask for works we can classify as history in retrospect or journeys, escapes, and adventures.

Readers themselves may or may not know to call the works they want by these type terms, but we as readers' advisory librarians must be able to recognize their requests as desires for history in retrospect or exciting journeys, escapes, and adventures so that we know what type of book they are looking for, what subject areas of the collection will fit their needs, and what appeal aspects are applicable.

Our shelves are full of many different types of nonfiction books, and each provides a different reading experience. We expect something different from *Night*, by Elie Wiesel, than we do from *Band of Brothers: E Company, 506th Regiment, 101st Airborne from Normandy to Hitler's Eagle's Nest*, by Stephen Ambrose, even though both are generally about World War II and the experiences of individuals caught up in the horror of war. *Night* is a memoir—a personal testament to the nightmare of the Holocaust. *Band of Brothers* is a history of war title. The two are different types and thus offer different reading experiences. Conversely, *Heat: An Amateur's Adventures as Kitchen Slave, Line Cook, Pasta-Maker, and Apprentice to a Dante-Quoting Butcher in Tuscany*, by Bill Buford, and *Next Man Up: A Year behind the Lines in Today's NFL*, by John Feinstein, provide relatively similar reading experiences because they are both works of reporting. Buford is reporting on the topic of food and the personalities of the cooking world, Feinstein is reporting on football and the personalities of an NFL team, but the two books are of a similar type and thus give a similar reading experience. This does not mean that they make good read-alikes for each other. The subjects alone could be too disparate. But for a reader who wants insider looks at different subjects, these two books, because they share a type, could indeed work together.

Beyond memoirs and reporting, there are other types of nonfiction, some particular to an individual subject and some that seem to be present in almost all areas of nonfiction. The more you consider nonfiction, the more you see the differences among the books, even books on the same general subject. Readers of nonfiction can be in the mood to read historical biography or narrative cookbooks. Type offers readers that variance of mood and perspective.

Type strongly affects the tone, pace, language, detail, story line, mood, and narrative nature of a book. It is an aspect of nonfiction that readers read for, so it is vital to understand that there are differences between types of nonfiction. It is so important that each subject chapter of this book includes explanations of the nonfiction types associated with the given subject, and the titles are arranged by type and not, for the most part, by their particular narrow subject.

Appeal

Appeal is the last of the four intertwined aspects used when working with readers. In *Readers' Advisory Service in the Public Library*, Joyce Saricks does an excellent job explaining the concept of appeal, and I suggest her book to all readers' advisory librarians for whom appeal is a new concept. Briefly, however, appeal is a way to capture what a reader likes about a book. At its most basic, appeal terms translate why a reader enjoyed a book into a language that can be applied to a wide range of other title possibilities.

Readers' advisory librarians serve as translators between books and readers. We listen to what readers tell us about a book they enjoyed, we translate what the readers say into appeal terms, and we suggest other titles that contain those elements. We use the concept of appeal to capture the feel of a book and to amplify the plot and subject headings of titles to provide readers with information they can use to decide if they are in the mood for that particular type of reading experience.

The broad and adaptive framework of appeal underpins the entire system of fiction readers' advisory service. With nonfiction, the various elements that constitute appeal are intertwined with a title's narrative nature, subject, and type, and all of these aspects work together to make up the total reading experience. Understanding these elements, recognizing them, and learning how to articulate them is fundamental to nonfiction readers' advisory service.

In working with nonfiction there are at least eight appeal elements to consider: pacing, characterization, story line, detail, learning/experiencing, language, setting, and tone.

Pacing

Pacing is a way of describing how a book moves through the story arc. It has two facets: the feel of the pace when the book is read and the speed at which the story unfolds.

All books have a pace that affects the feel of reading. Books can seem fast or slow, measured or leisurely. *Black Hawk Down: A Story of Modern War,* by Mark Bowden, moves quickly and is a gripping read. *Pilgrim at Tinker Creek,* by Annie Dillard, unfolds at a leisurely, almost meditative pace. *Zarafa: A Giraffe's True Story, from Deep in Africa to the Heart of Paris,* by Michael Allin, unfolds at a measured pace, neither fast nor slow.

In fiction, pace is typically affected by how quickly readers get to know the characters and understand the basic direction of the story and by such factors as how the story is constructed and the amount of description and dialogue included. In nonfiction, pace is similarly affected by these aspects. But, it is also affected by the amount of fact and theory the reader has to process and how the author incorporates and presents those elements. Books like *The Elegant Universe,* by Brian Greene, read differently from books like *The Perfect Storm,* by Sebastian Junger, simply because Greene has a great deal of factual information to explain. Junger has less, and he works what he does have more seamlessly into his story. It takes time to process fact-based writing. Therefore, nonfiction books full of factual detail, those with a great deal of back story or theory that needs to be explained first, and those dealing with several different theories tend to read more slowly than those that are not as fact based or research oriented.

The perception of pace is also affected by the knowledge readers bring to the book and their interest in the topic. A reader who has no idea about basic scientific theory will find reading a book about superstrings and quarks much more difficult and will interpret the pace as slower than a reader who knows a great deal about these topics. Similarly, readers who could care less about football will experience a biography about a famous coach much differently from a reader obsessed with the sport.

The second aspect of pace is the speed at which the story unfolds and how quickly the reader understands where the book is going. This aspect is directly related to the narrative nature of the title. Books that are highly narrative tend to unfold more directly than titles that are less narrative. Strong narrative drive not only acts as a hook to pull the reader through the book, it also acts as a map to give direction to the reading experience. Readers vary on how quickly they need to understand what a book is about and where it is heading. This is a measure of the level of certainty and competence they like to feel when reading. Some readers are perfectly comfortable wandering around lost in a book, trusting that the author is going to make sense eventually or slowly come to a conclusion; others need to understand everything all at once or have books that are more end oriented. Books such as *Longitude: The True Story of a Lone Genius Who Solved the Greatest Scientific Problem of His Time,* by Dava Sobel, offer the reader more explanation and scientific handholding than books like *Consilience: The Unity of Knowledge,* by Edward O. Wilson. Also, *Longitude* works toward a conclusion, whereas *Consilience* is much less end oriented. Books such as *Arctic Dreams,* by Barry Lopez, and *Red: Passion and Patience in the Desert,* by Terry Tempest Williams, do not require an understanding of any theories going in, but they do require a willingness to wander with the writer. They do not provide a narrative that rushes toward a conclusion, as does Piers Paul Read in his gripping true adventure tale *Alive: The Story of the Andes Survivors.*

The less sure a reader is about what is happening, where a book is heading, or how something works, the more disconnected and therefore slow the book feels. And this, of course, connects directly back to the narrative context of a book and illustrates how all the aspects work together.

Knowing the pace of a title is important; readers prefer, sometimes always and sometimes as the mood strikes them, certain types of pacing and narrative flow. Realizing that the experience of pace differs from reader to reader—depending on what they need in terms of narrative drive and in terms of what they already know about any given subject—is key to working with this aspect of appeal.

Characterization

Character is a driving element for many nonfiction readers, and there is a great deal of character development for readers to enjoy: historical figures in biographies, the author as main character in memoirs, intriguing researchers in science books, and all the rest of the characters who populate the pages of nonfiction. Many readers find these characters to be more interesting than fictional characters because they are real, and that sense of reality adds a fascinating layer to nonfiction works.

As in fiction, character and pace work together in nonfiction. Nonfiction characters tend either to be quickly defined and remain relatively constant or to be slowly revealed as they develop over the life of the story. Compare Joseph J. Ellis's *American Sphinx: The Character of Thomas Jefferson,* with its slow layering of the formation of Jefferson, to the cocky, sure, and up-front self-characterization of Anthony Bourdain in his wickedly funny *Kitchen Confidential: Adventures in the Culinary Underbelly*. The longer it takes a reader to understand the character, the slower the pace seems to be. Some readers love to get to know the character over a long period, while others find that frustrating and need more immediacy and certainty in their reading. They need to know who is good or bad, who to root for, and who to dislike right away. Getting to know the characters quickly tends to create a more rapidly paced reading experience, since neither the reader nor the author needs to spend much time explicating character.

Another aspect of appeal that is character focused but also affects pace is how the characters are animated. Is the story about their actions or about thoughts, theory, or concepts? True adventure and true crime tend to read more quickly than many science books because their story is more narrative and the characters are acting through the story. With many science books, on the other hand, the development of the story is more internal, and the characters or the author are thinking through the book. The more active the nature of the main character, the faster paced a book seems.

Other character aspects of appeal involve the types and number of characters in a book, secondary characters, and repeating characters. Characters can be either single-set or large-cast. If single-set, one set of characters is the main focus, as is typical with memoir. If large-cast, the focus of the story is divided among groups of characters, such as in *1776*, by David McCullough, or *1968: The Year That Rocked the World*, by Mark Kurlansky, in which any number of characters may be onstage at any given time. Some readers enjoy the broader landscape; others do not like leaving one set of characters for another or having to keep up with a large number of players.

Secondary characters have a significant role in a story but are not the main characters. In many true adventure and travel books, intriguing, funny, and just plain odd characters interact with or cause trauma to the main characters' lives or travels. In *A Year in Provence*, by Peter Mayle, for example, the no-show builders, the wonderfully exclusive villagers, and freeloading friends all combine to add richness and depth to the story. Intriguing secondary characters also can be found in biographies and many other types of books. For example, part of the appeal of *Undaunted Courage: Meriwether Lewis, Thomas Jefferson, and the Opening of the American West*, by Stephen Ambrose, is the scale of the expedition and all the other people involved in the journey west. Though they are not as strongly drawn or present as Ron and Hermione in the Harry Potter books, secondary characters do add richness and depth to many nonfiction titles and can also add layers to the story as the author breaks away from the main story line to detail other story threads. For example, in his riveting *Ship of Gold in the Deep Blue Sea*, Gary Kinder intertwines the story of the passengers and crew of the SS *Central America* and the biography and treasure hunt of Tommy Thompson. Some readers love to get to know secondary characters because they add to the richness of the work; others prefer not to break away from the main story and characters for someone else.

Whereas fiction books have series characters (those books that continue in multiples and feature the same set of characters), nonfiction books have repeating characters that are treated by many different authors. Don't underestimate the effect of individual character appeal on your readers. Different authors often address the same person from varying points of view, whether they be American heroes such as Washington, Jefferson, and Lincoln or assorted royalty, villains, and epic personages. Readers, especially history and biography readers, can become vested in the character they have come to know through their reading and continually look for more books on their subject. Readers find the various takes on a character intriguing, familiar, comforting (or perversely frustrating). Additionally, there is always a new interpretation of a character, so readers have a backlist to work through and something to look forward to as long as the character they read about is a popular topic.

Other things to think about include the reader's interaction with the characters. Are the characters there to be identified with or observed? Memoir readers almost always want to connect in some way to the subject of the book (which, in such an odd juxtaposition, is often the author of the book), and true adventure readers get vicarious thrills out of many of the escapades of the characters. True crime readers often say that they want to figure out the motivations of the criminals, and many biography readers want to observe and understand the character. The reading experience changes depending on how the reader responds to the character. If the reader is supposed to observe the characters, standing apart from them, either because of some psychological barrier imposed by the author or because of the nature of the character, then the reading experience is different from one in which the reader feels engaged with the character. Hand in hand with this element is the question of whether the characters are meant to be sympathized with or viewed objectively. The first draws the reader into the story; the other creates a more distant reading experience.

14

Finally, unique to nonfiction is the question of the reader's trust and engagement with the author and the authorial voice. A great deal of nonfiction is someone else's story. Biographies are about someone other than the author, as are most history books; many food, sports, and science books; and most true crime books. Readers need to trust that writers know what they are talking about and have sufficient knowledge, insight, and understanding to be a reliable voice on the topic. Still, a great deal of nonfiction is in fact about the author. All memoirs are about the author in at least some way, as are many true adventure and travel books. For these books, the reader must be able to engage with the author on at least some minimal level. The reader's trust in the author or relationship to the author as character is critical. It is as important in nonfiction as the reader's ability to identify with character is in genre fiction. In suspense, for example, if a reader does not like the hero or share the hero's excitement, fear, or tension, then the book falls flat. Similarly, if a reader cannot identify with an author when expected to do so or does not trust the authorial voice, the book simply does not work.

Story Line

Story line is key in nonfiction because it so strongly affects a reader's response. Although story line is a hard appeal element to conceptualize, it is actually fairly easy to recognize. When readers' advisory librarians talk about story line, we are not simply talking about the plot of a book. As odd as it may seem, many readers do not read for plot. They read for a combination of other appeal elements. This is of added importance in types of nonfiction where plot can be tenuous at best. This is a critical point to understand. It is why narrative exists on a continuum and why readers can read a wide range of books within that continuum. Plot does not matter as much as we think. Although it is useful to be able to talk about the plot of a book, what is more useful is to be able to talk about the whole mix of elements that explicate the story line.

Story line in nonfiction addresses many of the issues of subject, type, and narrative nature. It is within story line that those separate and vital issues of nonfiction are interwoven with appeal. Though it is important to be able to articulate the basic plot or story of a book to readers, there are other more important concerns. Among them are the effects of story line on the narrative nature of the book, the intent of the author and the focus of the story, and how the subject is treated by the author.

STORY LINE AND NARRATIVE NATURE

The narrative continuum is measured out in the appeal aspect of story line. It is where the reader experiences narrative context. *The Majic Bus: An American Odyssey,* by Douglas Brinkley, the story of a bus full of college students traveling around the country to learn history in context, is more highly narrative than *De Kooning: An American Master,* by Mark Stevens and Annalyn Swan, which is an illuminating study of a man and his art. Both are wonderful examples of nonfiction, but they do not fall on the same point on the continuum—because they have different story line approaches and thus different narrative features.

Story line has a strong influence on the narrative nature of a work, and readers' advisory librarians should be aware of its overarching effects. Some readers need highly narrative books and some do not. Story line is one of the places where that need is measured. Because highly narrative nonfiction books tell a strong story, they tend to be the easiest books to suggest to readers looking to transcend the Dewey divide. They are great to introduce in book discussion groups and to include on booklists and in displays. More fact-based nonfiction books have less narrative drive to them. Fans of these books do not find story line to be an overriding factor in how they choose or enjoy titles.

THE INTENT OF THE AUTHOR AND THE EFFECT ON STORY LINE AND TYPE

All books are written with a specific intent and focus. We can see this most clearly when we compare authors. Both Anthony Bourdain and Mark Kurlansky write books about food, but they do not write books with the same intent, nor do they have the same focus.

Mark Kurlansky is a historian with an eye to the minute and its role in the huge. He is concerned, among other things, with the broad historical implications of food on culture. His writing is literary, clear, and evocative, and his work is descriptive and educating. Anthony Bourdain is a chef, an opinionated, sharp writer concerned with his experiences and his take on food. He is focused on the immediate, on his relationship with food and his take on making it. He is funny and snide, and utterly engaging, but he is not trying to write the same kind of book as Kurlansky.

Thinking about the author's intent removes us from the need to judge a book on the basis of any criteria other than those internal to the book. Mark Kurlansky is not better than Anthony Bourdain; he is just different. We can talk to readers about them both and talk about their intents rather than about our opinions of their titles. This is vital in offering readers' advisory service that embraces the reader's tastes and desires as the sole focus of the service.

All the intertwined aspects of nonfiction readers' advisory service allow us to talk about books without judgment. For example, there is no implied judgment in "fast paced" or "leisurely paced," "food oriented" or "basketball oriented." It does seem, though, that we tend to judge on story line. We tend to view literary works as more worthy than popular works, or highly narrative and imaginative works as more readable than fact-based titles. This is a disservice to our patrons and to the authors. Story line removes that instinct to judge and lets us simply talk about the book in its most pure form—that is, what the author intended to create.

Many narrative nonfiction books have the intent of educating us, of expanding our collective knowledge. Many authors do this in a popular way, such as Nathaniel Philbrick in his amazing *In the Heart of the Sea: The Tragedy of the Whaleship* Essex, and many do it more formally, like Roger Penrose in his illuminating *The Road to Reality: A Complete Guide to the Laws of the Universe.* Nonfiction authors write with many different intents. Some seek to educate, some to be funny or in general to entertain, some to expose something, to report, to persuade, to focus on an issue, or to explore and present new findings.

Story line works in tandem with type in this regard; many of the different book types are directly related to the intent and focus of the author. Books of a particular type are more suitable for some intents and focus than others. Seeing how story line affects type and being able to work with these two aspects to aid readers are critical to offering nonfiction readers' advisory service. Jeff MacGregor's *Sunday Money: Speed! Lust! Madness! Death! A Hot Lap around America with NASCAR* has a different intent and focus than Ted Leeson's *The Habit of Rivers.* Both men write about sports, but they write very different types. The revved-up reporting of MacGregor stands in stark contrast to Leeson's lyrical memoir-ish musings. Similarly, Thomas L. Friedman, author of *The World Is Flat: A Brief History of the Twenty-first Century,* is not writing with the same intent or focus as any of the political commentators, left or right, that publish opinion-oriented polemics.

STORY LINE AND SUBJECT

Story line provides a place in the appeal construct to consider how the subject is approached. Subjects tend to either be sole-focus or used as a vessel to collect a range of other subjects to muse on. In highly collective books it can sometimes be hard to decide just what the subject is. *Arctic Dreams,* by Barry Lopez, for example, is about a whole range of topics, including animals, landscape, first peoples, geology, and personal interaction. Though some readers find the various topics fascinating, others are frustrated that there is no direct story line. *Under the Tuscan Sun,* by Frances Mayes, on the other hand, is about the main character's life, and though it bobs and weaves throughout her story, it is always her story.

Another element of nonfiction that can affect readers' response is the nature of the work itself. *Possible Side Effects,* by Augusten Burroughs, or *A Girl Named Zippy: Growing Up Small in Mooreland Indiana,* by Haven Kimmel, are straight-line stories; they create an easy-to-follow linear narrative that is meant to be experienced by the reader. Other books, such as *A Brief History of Time,* by Stephen Hawking, are dense and fact based; they assume a basic reading knowledge of the subject and are written in such a way that the reader must pay attention and devote both time and effort to reading the work. These more layered works are meant to be navigated by the reader, they circle back on themselves, they pose questions, and they present facts that need to be assimilated.

Additionally, some nonfiction is not very subject oriented at all, whereas other titles are all about the subject. History is usually completely about the subject, as is science and biography. But travel, cooking, memoir, and true adventure can often be more about the story than about the subject. Just as readers respond differently to high-narrative versus less-narrative works or to one type of nonfiction rather than another, they respond to books according to what the author is doing with the subject. *Home Cooking: A Writer in the Kitchen,* by Laurie Colwin, is really more about Laurie Colwin and her thoughts on food than about food itself. She is dealing with the subject of food much more obliquely than Mark Kurlansky does in *Salt: A World History,* and Kurlansky is dealing with food more obliquely than Michael Pollan in *The Omnivore's Dilemma: A Natural History of Four Meals.*

Story line is a multifaceted aspect of appeal. Though it may be easier to fall back on a brief plot summary when talking to a reader, it is not truly helpful. But the opportunity to blend all four aspects of nonfiction—narrative context, subject, type, and appeal—is endlessly helpful. When you do this, you open up the book for the reader in ways they always appreciate.

Detail

The detail element of appeal describes the sumptuousness and interior life of the book in terms of the level of description and background in the story. Details are the canvas on which the book is set; they bring out a richness in the book and create a backdrop to the reading experience.

Detail can be anything: battle movements and weaponry in a war memoir, descriptions of clothing in a lush period biography, the deliberations of layout when designing Central Park, the measurements of iron needed to build the transcontinental railroad. Details help enliven the work. In some books the details are important, and their lack would ruin the pleasure of reading. *Tender at the Bone: Growing Up at the Table,* by Ruth Reichl, would not be the same reading experience if Reichl did not detail food and place as she does. Her descriptions of the dripping yet rough rind of cheese and her explanations of how that cheese is made make the book come alive in a sensual feast. Likewise, the details of clothing, battles, weather, and towns in David McCullough's *1776* make the book so much richer for their presence.

In nonfiction, detail also extends to the visual content of the book and the way it augments the text. Maps (well drawn and clear), informative charts, illustrations, photographs, letters, family trees, floor plans, bibliographies, recipes, good and useful indexes, footnotes, and appendixes—all these "value-added" items also count as detail.

Readers who like detail notice its absence and tend to enjoy books according to the amount of detail present. For them, details add a reason for reading beyond all the other appeal elements.

Learning/Experiencing

Reading nonfiction, even highly narrative nonfiction, is a different experience than reading fiction. Part of the biggest difference is the nonfiction author's intent to turn fact into a teachable moment. I would never venture that readers of fiction do not read, in part or in whole, to learn and experience. Indeed, the best part of reading for many, be it fiction or nonfiction, is the escape into other experiences and the things we learn from books. It is, however, a particular and notable part of nonfiction that many authors set out to teach readers and many readers pick up a book to learn.

Certainly almost all task-based nonfiction is about learning. Readers learn to make a webpage, build a water garden, plan a trip, and endless other things inside the pages of such books. In nontask-based nonfiction they learn as well, and the degree to which they approach a book intent on learning and the degree to which they learn in a clear, helpful way is another measure of reader enjoyment of a title.

Books as highly narrative as *The Perfect Storm* teach readers both what it feels like to drown and the physics of a boat getting crushed by a wave. Books such as *Endless Forms Most Beautiful: The New Science of Evo Devo and the Making of the Animal Kingdom,* by Sean B. Carroll, teach readers about evolutionary developmental biology. *Carnivorous Nights: On the Trail of the Tasmanian Tiger,* by Margaret Mittelbach and Michael Crewdson, teaches readers about all sorts of things including museums, wallabies, bugs, tigers, and the importance of carefully considering your travel companions.

Books that do not intend to teach usually intend to share an experience or explain a particular feeling or event. David Sedaris's riotous essays, such as *Me Talk Pretty One Day* and *Dress Your Family in Corduroy and Denim,* Homer Hickam's moving memoir of growing up, *Rocket Boys,* and Ann Patchett's *Truth and Beauty: A Friendship* all intend the reader to experience life as the author experienced it—to open a door into the author's mind and allow the reader a glimpse of what it meant to be in that real situation, moment, or space.

These concomitant effects—learning and experiencing—create in nonfiction a marked difference from the effect of fiction and can, for some readers, outweigh any other consideration when they are searching for a book.

Language

The language aspect of appeal addresses the kind of language used in the book. The question to consider with language is, Does the writing style matter? Is it lyrical, well constructed, sharp, clear, and beautifully described, or not?

Consider the differences in language used between a brilliant comic and a brilliant nature writer. Dave Barry writes hilarious essays that make readers laugh, but he does not sit down to write in a lyrical, high style. Certainly the words he selects matter—otherwise his stories would not be as funny. But he does not write in a style that makes one underline text or go back to savor the language. The reader relishes his jokes, certainly, but not the particular expression. Peter Matthiessen, on the other hand, uses beautiful and mythic writing in *The Snow Leopard.* Matthiessen is as concerned with the expression of the moment as he is with the moment itself. His style makes his use of language important in a way that Barry's use of language is not.

Clarity of language matters a great deal in nonfiction, as does the ability to describe events, action, theory, and motivations. Readers need a balance of beautifully described moments and clear explanations when they read, especially in works from which they want to learn. Master nonfiction writers such as Nathaniel Philbrick and David McCullough have a gift for describing the moment in evocative and beautiful ways at the same time they craft clear explanations of events and motivations. Science writers such as Simon Singh and Matt Ridley also have a huge talent for making the complex understandable and enthralling. This type of writing, the kind that infuses fact with lyrical majesty, is what many readers appreciate in nonfiction.

Some readers cannot read what they consider a badly written book; others are less concerned with the language and read for other elements that are more important to them. Readers' concerns about language also vary with the type of book they are reading. Some books need a raw, edgy language palate while others need an elegant and lyrical form of expression. The importance of language to the reader is idiosyncratic to the book and to the reader's mood and tastes.

Setting

We look at setting to find the extent to which the location of a book is important to the reading experience. In works where setting is integral to the story, readers are firmly placed in a location, and that location is richly detailed and important to the total experience of the book. In much of nonfiction, a fully described and detailed setting is vital. Almost all nonfiction takes place at some point in time and in some location, and readers need to feel that they are grounded in the setting to fully experience the book.

When considering nonfiction, ask if the setting is important to the story and if the location is brought to life. History, biography, memoir, travel, and true adventure all demand settings that are fully realized and well described. Working in tandem with detail and language, setting can often make a book work. In *Blue Latitudes: Boldly Going Where Captain Cook Has Gone Before*, Tony Horwitz goes to great pains to describe the setting of each part of Cook's explorations. Without his careful attention to the landscape of the journey, this brilliant work would have fallen flat. Similarly, in *Into Thin Air: A Personal Account of the Mt. Everest Disaster*, Jon Krakauer conjures the cold and ice so well that readers understand via the setting how the chain of tragic events unfolded. Reading a travel book that does not make one seem to be on location, wandering the streets, meeting the people, boarding the train, is a lesser experience than reading one in which location is realized fully.

Tone

Tone is a description of how it feels to read a book. Books can be light and funny, dark and moody, suspenseful, frightening, comforting, educational, inspiring, grim. More than any other aspect of appeal, tone is based on the mood of the reader. Some days a reader might want a comforting cozy read, and other times the same reader might want a suspenseful, dark tale. For example, a reader in the mood for a fast, raw read could find that Mark Bowden's *Black Hawk Down: A Story of Modern War* is just what he is after. Even if in a different mood he would find Rick Atkinson's longer, more reflective explanation of war, *An Army at Dawn: The War in Africa, 1942–1943*, to be greatly enjoyable, its tone does not match the reader's mood *now* and therefore would not be a good suggestion. Similarly, a reader who needs the comfort of light and funny escapist reading will find no solace in Adam Hochschild's amazing *King Leopold's Ghost: A Story of Greed, Terror, and Heroism in Colonial Africa*, even if she is interested in the topic, but she could very well find *A Year in Provence*, by Peter Mayle, to be just what she is looking for.

Tone is the aspect of appeal that readers are least willing to be flexible about. They may set aside the fact that a book is less detailed or slower paced than they would like if some other element is carrying them forward, such as the story line or the characters. But if a reader is in the mood for a cozy, comforting read, then a grim, brooding, true crime thriller is not going to please them, no matter how well it matches all the other appeal elements they enjoy.

⊹⇌ ⇌⊹

The four intertwined aspects of nonfiction should be considered as individual elements that work collectively to determine the experience of reading. None of these elements stays neatly in a box all its own. Subject and type work in unison. Appeal wanders all over a book. The appeal elements blend into one another, affect one another, and affect narrative nature as well.

How readers respond to each of these elements is part of what determines whether they enjoy a given title, but individual responses vary depending on many factors—reader's mood, life experience, reading history, importance of each element at a particular time, and skill of the author. Additionally, factors such as the social and political climate, the amount of publicity a book receives, its critical reception, the opinions of family and friends, and the reader's own point of view all affect the way a reader experiences a title. None of us reads the same way each time we pick up a book. We should be open to the fact that, although narrative nature, subject, type, and appeal capture aspects of what we enjoy, they cannot completely account for our enjoyment.

Readers' advisory work is an art, not a science. We can classify and control all we want. We can make up terms and agree to use them uniformly so we all speak the same language. We can collectively decide how fast a book has to read to be fast paced and how well described a landscape has to be before it becomes almost like another character. We can do all of that, but in the end we are really working with the most amorphous, slippery, mutable, and insubstantial of elements—an individual reader's reaction to a book, a reaction that is inevitably personal and chaotic and unwilling to be governed by anything we agree to at a conference, talk about online, or write in a book. You can use these four intertwined aspects of nonfiction as a framework and a guide, but your readers will always know best what they want and what matters to them. Don't let that scare you. It is as it should be and has to be. We do not offer readers' advisory service in a vacuum. We offer it in conversation with a reader. As you progress through the following chapters, you will see how these elements interact and how we are able to use them to identify, more and more easily, what readers seek and which titles might meet their needs.

To make this process easier, the table that follows summarizes the key points of the four intertwined aspects of nonfiction. Each term is defined and the aspect the term measures is explained so that you can see what interests readers about particular elements. Ways to articulate each term are also included to give an indication of the type of language readers' advisors use when talking about the element.

Term	What it is	What it measures	Ways to express it
Narrative Context	Extent to which story is present or important	Degree of narrative content	Reads like a novel, gripping account, fact based
Subject	What the book is about	Degree of interest	String theory, food, hockey, Arctic exploration
Type	Kind of book	Degree of pattern	Memoir, essay, biography, exploration, reporting
Pacing	How it feels to move through the story arc	Degree of perceived speed	Fast, leisurely, measured
Characterization	Character types and how readers are intended to respond to the characters	Degree of attachment/ interest	Quirky, introspective, set, faceted, historical figures, author as character, sympathetic, objective, reader identifies with
Story Line	Impact of story line on the feel of the book, plot, narrative levels	Degree of reaction and effort	Tells narrative story, teaches, creates a scholarly work, presents a satirical essay
Detail	Richness of the interior life of the book	Degree and quality of description or explication	In-depth description of battle movements; full explanation of the invention of Morse code; includes graphic elements, charts, maps, indexes, other aids
Learning/ Experiencing	What readers want from the reading experience	Character of the knowledge transfer	Sense of times and what it was like to . . . , how the jet stream works

Term	What it is	What it measures	Ways to express it
Language	Importance of writing and style	Quality of "art"	Lyrical, sharp, prosaic
Setting	Extent to which location is important to the reading experience	Degree of vividness	Evocative, lush, immersed, well described
Tone	Emotional reactions, as intended by author and experienced by readers	Character of emotion	Dark, bleak, suspenseful, comforting, light, illuminating

NOTES

1. Mark Bowden, *Black Hawk Down* (New York: Atlantic Monthly Press, 1999), 80.
2. Nathaniel Philbrick, *Sea of Glory: America's Voyage of Discovery, the U.S. Exploring Expedition, 1838–1842* (New York: Viking, 2003), 334.
3. Roger Penrose, *Road to Reality: A Complete Guide to the Laws of the Universe* (New York: Knopf, 2005), 196.

2

OFFERING THE SERVICE

Barriers to Nonfiction

Most practitioners of readers' advisory service know fiction and are comfortable dealing with it. They know the appeal characteristics Joyce Saricks has promoted and are at ease viewing a book from that perspective. For a readers' advisor first working with nonfiction, however, becoming familiar with the narrative continuum, the importance of subject, the type of book, and the expanded concepts of appeal can feel like learning a foreign language. Even when you learn the appeal terms and understand their definitions, know how the author uses the subject of a book, and can clearly see its type, it can be hard to articulate the lure of a book to a reader. Opening up nonfiction as a suggestible base of titles takes a bit of mental reorganization, self-discipline, and will. Nonfiction readers' advisory can be intimidating. Even aces at fiction readers' advisory—people who you would think are well versed in every aspect of the practice—tend to shy away from the Dewey side of the stacks. It takes effort to start to include nonfiction into readers' advisory work and to overcome our initial built-in reluctance to have to relearn something we thought we knew cold.

In spite of our best intentions, there are barriers to overcome in order to cross the Dewey divide and offer robust nonfiction readers' advisory service. These barriers include our own reading habits, how we think about nonfiction, what we know generally about all nonfiction topics, the breadth of nonfiction, the physical layout of the library, the collection development focus of our collections, the lack of easy-to-use readers' advisory tools, and our readers.

Ourselves

Many of us do not read as widely in nonfiction as we do in fiction, so we are not as comfortable with the books, the lines and connections between books and authors, the quality of the writing, or the huge range of subjects. We feel that, since we do not know what is in those books, we have no standing to suggest them. Nonfiction was never part of our training, and it feels odd. Additionally, nonfiction writers do not tend, as a whole (there are some notable exceptions), to be as prolific as fiction writers, especially genre fiction writers, so there is not a huge body of work to suggest once we do discover an author one of our readers enjoys. Years can go by between an author's first and second books, or between the second and third, making readers (and us) forget about that author during the lull. Also, the next book an author writes can sometimes be nothing like that first, beloved book. There is not an easily learned, small, well-defined list of core authors writing in nonfiction. Instead there is a large, amorphous list of key authors. The thought of committing to memory this great number of authors and great number of titles can be daunting.

On top of this, there are many more subjects in nonfiction than there are fiction genres, and that can feel overwhelming. This feeling is compounded by the fact that most of us do not know a great deal about all the subjects collectively. We may know a bit about the poets of World War I, but we know nothing about string theory; we may know a lot about baseball but nothing about art history. So we feel at sea with a topic, unsure and unwilling to venture forth with suggestions in an area we do not know, all the while forgetting that we felt the same way when we started with fiction and its genres. But perhaps most difficult of all, there do not seem to be as many match points as there are with fiction to get a series of suggestions started. Nonfiction books seem so specialized that we view their audience as more limited. A really good mystery can be enjoyed regardless of its setting by the vast majority of mystery readers. Can a really good book on rats truly be enjoyed by a broad group of patrons? Even though the answer is yes, can we really sell both ourselves and our readers on that notion?

Our Space

Many libraries have collections that are physically divided in a way that makes including nonfiction difficult. We have fiction upstairs and nonfiction downstairs or vice versa. We have the readers' advisory desk in fiction and the reference desk in nonfiction. We have staffs divided by territories, or we have a single floor and overworked staff members who are called on to add the amorphous world of nonfiction to their readers' advisory efforts. Aside from the inevitable turf wars (which are a function of manners and management), how do we get the readers from upstairs to downstairs or vice versa? And if we build displays that mix fiction with nonfiction on two levels, how is the staff going to know where to find a book that happens to be on hold? And how are we going to make time to offer a service when patron demand pulls us toward managing the computers and finding a lost magazine?

As with almost all problems we think up to stop ourselves from moving forward, there are fixes. A divided collection can be overcome by simply writing down titles for patrons to pick up on the other floor. If you have a separate readers' advisory desk, then the staffs of both the reference desk and the readers' advisory desk need to work together to come up with a way to channel patrons to the appropriate desk at the appropriate time, or even better, move around themselves! If your library, like many, has only one service desk, by all means let patrons know that you are there to answer reference questions and readers' advisory queries. Staff members working in the nonfiction area actually have it a bit easier because they can start with nonfiction and use online readers' advisory tools to make lists of fiction titles to be picked up and browsed on the other floor. Items on display can be checked out to a location-specific "display status" so everyone knows where they are no matter how mixed up the displays become.

Our Collections

The typical public library collection development focus tends to be toward popular fiction, leaving less and less money for nonfiction. And though bestseller nonfiction is bought in multiple copies in most libraries, lots of other wonderful nonfiction is either purchased in limited quantities or not purchased at all. That is always going to be a problem. In fact, in addition to the pressure of the fiction budget, the fact that lots of task-oriented nonfiction circulates so well (cookbooks, craft books, diet books, how-to books) puts pressure on the remaining and limited resources of the nonfiction budget. We may be accustomed to having a hundred or more copies of a fiction bestseller and certainly at least several copies of almost all fiction titles we might suggest to readers, but with nonfiction we simply do not have that luxury.

Additionally, titles may not be on the shelves to show readers or trigger connections to other books. This challenge is also present in fiction readers' advisory, but it is likely to be more of an issue for nonfiction. Complicating this is the lack of nonfiction titles in most of our readers' advisory tools. Although this is slowly changing, *Booklist Online* and *The Reader's Advisor Online* already have nonfiction content, and *NoveList* is soon coming out with a version that includes nonfiction. Time will tell if we ever reach a point with our readers' advisory tools where nonfiction is as richly treated as fiction.

Our Readers

Perhaps second only to our own issues, a huge barrier to nonfiction readers' advisory is the reader. We have trained our readers to think of us as a fiction resource. They know that we can share with them the next great read for books similar to Matthew Reilly's *Temple* or *Runaway: Stories,* by Alice Munro. They are less likely to realize that there is a nonfiction book similar to *The Alienist,* by Caleb Carr, or to trust us when we point out that they might also enjoy *The Devil in the White City,* by Erik Larson. But at least that suggestion includes a fiction title as a starting point. How do we convince readers to even try a nonfiction title that seems on its surface not to be appealing or to relate to something they already find familiar? Much of nonfiction tends to be longer than fiction. It does not, in general, get the publicity buzz that fiction gets. And, most of all, it is hard to unteach readers what we have collectively spent years teaching them—that the catalog can help them find the nonfiction books they need by subject and that those subject headings tell them everything they need to know about a book. We know there are many books that rise above their seemingly surface subjects, such as *Seabiscuit: An American Legend,* by Laura Hillenbrand, *Rats: Observations on the History and Habitat of the City's Most Unwanted Inhabitants,* by Robert Sullivan, and *Annals of the Former World,* by John McPhee—but it is often difficult to convince a reader who is not interested in horses, rats, or geology that a book is more than its collective subject headings.

It all leaves us wondering why we should do this. The answer is simple. All readers deserve help finding the next book to love regardless of what they like to read, and there is richness in the Dewey side of the stacks too great to ignore. Many readers who love nonfiction have too long been without our focused assistance, and many more readers who do not know the rewards awaiting them in those stacks have no way into the nonfiction world without us pointing it out.

The Habit of Nonfiction

So what do we do? We need to get into the habit of including nonfiction when we think about books, and we need to work consciously to overcome the barriers in the way of offering great nonfiction readers' advisory service. We need to practice describing nonfiction to readers and include nonfiction suggestions along with fiction—first as a matter of will and later as a matter of habit.

We need to start writing nonfiction annotations so the supporting work is there when it's time to make a booklist or build a display or find a suggestion for a reader. We need to get comfortable using new appeal terms and get used to how they work so that we can see that the match points in nonfiction are as similar and as easy as they are in fiction. We need to apply narrative structure in a way that in the past we have not had to consider—that it exists on a continuum that allows for reader response. We need to get into the habit of thinking across the Dewey divide when readers ask us for book suggestions, when building displays, when creating reading guides, and when choosing book discussion titles. Most important of all, we need to get into our nonfiction stacks, look around, learn the books, and start reading them. Before going further then, resolve now to make reading and thinking about nonfiction a part of how you conceive readers' advisory work. The titles in this book are treasures just waiting to be discovered. The world of nonfiction is simply too rich to be ignored and too wonderful to be overlooked.

Ways to Practice the Habit

Appendix A presents a plan to help you walk into your nonfiction stacks and start exploring books and creating your own subject guides. In chapter 13, on reading maps, there is an explanation of how to create the ultimate guide when working with nonfiction. But both of these activities take work and at least some basic knowledge of nonfiction. To kick-start your efforts with nonfiction, try the following:

Start reading nonfiction. There are many resources in this book to help you find titles to enjoy. Each chapter contains an annotated example of each type of writing, a listing of key authors, and a selected bibliography of titles to read and suggest. Additionally, appendix B offers a basic reading plan for each of the basic subject areas reviewed in this book.

As you read, keep some kind of record. Ideally you should annotate each title, but if you simply do not have the time, you should keep reading notes or, at a minimum, a running list of each title you read. A blank annotation form is provided in appendix C along with an explanation about the unique aspects of annotating nonfiction. Appendix D includes a form for recording reading notes.

Whenever you work with a reader and suggest a fiction title, ask yourself if there is a nonfiction equivalent or other nonfiction work that would expand on or complement the suggested fiction title. For example, if a reader wants a historical novel set in ancient Rome, you might think of the biographies on figures of the time, books on early Roman social customs, or even books on major buildings of the era. Even if you do not mention those books to the reader, or even if the reader is not interested when you do, you will be building the habit of making connections between fiction and nonfiction. You will be bridging the Dewey divide.

Practice articulating the four intertwined aspects of nonfiction (narrative context, subject, type, and appeal). Whenever you read a nonfiction book, ask yourself the following questions and use this matrix to mentally run through each nonfiction title you read. A copy of the matrix and a filled-out example are available in appendix E.

Where is the book on the narrative continuum?

> Highly narrative (reads like fiction)
>
> A mix (combines highly narrative moments with periods of fact-based prose)
>
> Highly fact based (has few or no narrative moments)

What is the subject of the book?

What type of book is it?

Articulate appeal:

> What is the pacing of the book?
>
> Describe the characters of the book.
>
> How does the story feel?
>
> What is the intent of the author?
>
> What is the focus of the story?
>
> Does the language matter?
>
> Is the setting important and well described?
>
> Are there details and, if so, of what?
>
> Are there sufficient charts and other graphic materials? Are they useful and clear?
>
> Does the book stress moments of learning, understanding, or experience?

Why would a reader enjoy this book (rank appeal)?

1.

2.

3.

Try talking about the four intertwined aspects of nonfiction with your friends, family, and coworkers. Practice until you no longer feel at sea and the language becomes second nature. Once you have gained a familiarity with thinking of nonfiction books in terms of their functional aspects, try working with different expressions of the four intertwined elements to see how they work in concert. By using the familiar childhood language game Mad Libs, you can see just how much reader responses depend on the way we talk about books and the importance of clearly and truthfully describing books to them. What follows is a game of readers' advisory Mad Libs. Practicing in this way helps increase your skill in juggling all four intertwined aspects of nonfiction. It is also a lot of fun.

To understand how the game is played, here is an example with fiction. See how the reader response changes in the following brief descriptions when the appeal terms are changed:

> In this *sweeping and slowly unfolding* novel, Jane Smith, known for creating *large casts of connecting* characters, crafts a *tragic love* story of war and its aftermath.

> In this *dark and brooding* novel, Jane Smith, known for creating *grim and introspective* characters, crafts a *horrific and bloody* story of war and its aftermath.

You can imagine that reader responses will vary depending on how appeal terms are used. If a readers' advisory librarian told a reader only that Jane Smith's newest book was about war and its aftermath, it would be up to the reader to imagine what that book would be. Some might imagine an action thriller; some might imagine a harrowing look at lost souls left in the devastating wake of a civil war; and others might conjure up ideas of a psychological suspense novel.

In nonfiction, the reader response changes not just on the basis of appeal but on all the intertwining aspects of nonfiction. It is these aspects that allow readers to know if they are in the mood to read a particular book and if the title is similar to other books they enjoy or avoid.

Here are some nonfiction examples. They are longer than fiction because they have to accommodate all four aspects of nonfiction: narrative, subject, type, and appeal:

> In this somber and lyrical memoir, biologist Jane Smith, known for her mix of personal story with details of history and politics, crafts a heartbreaking and stunning look at the world of gorilla poaching.

> In this provocative investigative report, journalist Jane Smith, known for her use of interviews and observation, crafts a troubling look at the world of low-wage workers.

> In this hilarious travelogue, chef Jane Smith, known for her historical vignettes on the origins of recipes, crafts a delicious look at the world of French cheese.

> In this dark and graphic personal account, pathologist Jane Smith, known for her gripping and fast-paced stories, crafts a frightening look at the world of baby snatchers.

Try coming up with your own versions of readers' advisory Mad Libs for nonfiction titles you have read. First, write one that is an accurate description of a book you know well and include all four aspects of nonfiction, and then try to change the reader response to the book with the words you select to describe each aspect.

Working with Patrons: The Many Ways of the Readers' Advisory Conversation

Once you are ready to begin working nonfiction suggestions into your readers' advisory work, how do you do it? As with fiction readers' advisory, you engage the reader in a conversation—a special conversation about books that ranges from fiction to nonfiction that depends on what the reader has read and enjoyed in the past.

These conversations are the most challenging part of readers' advisory work. Building displays and creating reading lists, doing your own reading, walking a book through the readers' advisory matrix, writing annotations, and playing readers' advisory Mad Libs—this is all work you do on your own. Through this work you create the foundation to help patrons, but once you have to face a reader one-on-one and talk about nonfiction (or fiction for that matter), all bets are off. It is just you and the reader and everything you are uncomfortable about. What if you look like an idiot? Will the reader ever trust you again? What if the reader asks you about an author or topic you have never heard of? What if you blank out? What if you confuse tone and story line? What if you still do not understand story line?

To step out onto the floor and offer any readers' advisory service is a daunting undertaking, but offering nonfiction readers' advisory service is even harder than advising about fiction, in part for all the reasons already outlined and in part simply because it is new and we have neither the tools nor the collective knowledge to feel firm on our feet.

Keep in mind as both a mantra and a comfort that a successful readers' advisory conversation is one that results in the patron leaving with the knowledge that the library staff welcomes questions about books and is willing and eager to help patrons find books to read. Success is not measured by how many books a reader checks out; it is measured by how comfortable the reader now is coming back to the library to have more conversations about books. You know that when you are working the reference desk and get a question, no one expects you to know the answer. *They expect you to know how to find the answer.* It is the same with readers' advisory. If you do not know any titles to suggest to a reader who just finished *Seabiscuit*, that's okay. But you do need to know how to find out what about *Seabiscuit* the reader enjoyed and how to find other titles, based on those points, to suggest next. If you think of the readers' advisory conversation as one between two readers—one in which you are sharing your love of books with a reader who loves them too—it all seems less scary and reminds you why you became a librarian to start with.

We interact with readers in a variety of ways. We offer various self-service aspects to readers' advisory such as displays, booklists, reading guides, spine stickers, signs, and our readers' advisory websites. We offer readers' advisory service when a patron approaches us at our desk and asks us for help. And we offer readers' advisory service when we approach the patrons in the stacks and offer assistance. While we do all of this, we need to make a conscious effort to include fiction and nonfiction together. Mixing the two is the best way to offer rich readers' advisory service and mine the resources of our collections. When you build a display, include fiction and nonfiction titles. When you create booklists or reading guides, include both fiction and nonfiction as appropriate, or at least include nonfiction as supplementary material. For example, any booklist on *The Da Vinci Code* should include not only other books with similar appeals in fiction but the host of nonfiction resources available on the topics raised in the novel, such as art, symbolism, and religious history. And when you talk to readers, talk about both fiction and nonfiction together. Readers like to read, and if you expand your range of title suggestions to include both fiction and nonfiction, they will be delighted in the wider range of choices.

So how do you do that? In *Readers' Advisory Service in the Public Library*, Joyce Saricks does an excellent job of outlining a basic readers' advisory conversation, and her book should be the first stop for readers unfamiliar with the practice. Here I discuss such conversations with the assumption that readers of this book already know the basics. When you hold a readers' advisory conversation that includes nonfiction, you do it differently depending on what prompted the conversation.

Starting from Fiction

Suppose you approach a patron in the stacks and offer one of the traditional opening gambits, such as, "Would you like some suggestions, or are you happy to browse the collection?" If the patron specifies interest in a fiction book, you have two choices. You can conduct the conversation as if nonfiction did not exist, or you can introduce nonfiction into the discussion. You know your readers better than anyone else, and you know when it is appropriate to include nonfiction and when it is not. But keep in mind, even the most die-hard fiction fans may be open to nonfiction when it is presented in an engaging and intriguing way.

Not only can nonfiction be a suggestion in and of itself, but nonfiction can also be a support to fiction reading, expanding the world of the book beyond the limits of its bound pages. For example, if a patron has just finished reading and really enjoyed *Devil's Bride,* by Stephanie Laurens, then ask her if she enjoys the Regency period in general. If the answer is yes, you can suggest not only the romances of Julia Quinn and Amanda Quick but also nonfiction such as Carolly Erickson's vivid portrait of the age, *Our Tempestuous Day: A History of Regency England,* or Saul David's compelling biography of Prinny, *Prince of Pleasure: The Prince of Wales and the Making of the Regency,* as books that expand on the period. Additionally, you could suggest *The Prince Regent's Style: Decorative Arts in England, 1800–1830,* by the Cooper Union Museum for the Arts of Decoration, and *John Nash: A Complete Catalogue,* by Michael Mansbridge, to supply a visual picture of the era. After all, a patron who just enjoyed reading about the details of dress and architecture present in *Devil's Bride* might want to see more details of the period.

I cannot think of a fiction book that does not have some parallel in non-fiction if we are creative enough to look for it. From Sarah Dunant's amazing historical novels, to the atmospheric and character-rich mysteries of Laurie R. King, to the detail-laden works of Bernard Cornwell, to the shopping-mad chick lit of Sophie Kinsella—all of them can be supported not only with read-alike fiction but with nonfiction counterparts and read-around nonfiction as well.

One of the best things about introducing nonfiction this way is that we do not have to worry about where the work falls on the narrative continuum. If it is offered as a support to expand the world of a novel, then the reader will feel free to dip into the title and take from it what she wants. Even if a patron does not read the entire book, she will know that you are there to help suggest a wider range of books and that the library she has been visiting for years has resources to enliven her fiction reading choices. And do not stop with books. I am a strong advocate of whole collection readers' advisory service (see chapter 13). It is essential that we all break free of the Dewey divide and offer readers not only books from our fiction and nonfiction collections but also audiobooks, music, movies, and any other applicable resources we own or have access to. Regency fans who have not yet seen the Colin Firth version of *Pride and Prejudice* or listened to the associated period music will only find their reading enriched when you include the widest range of choices in your suggestions.

Starting from fiction might be the easiest way to introduce nonfiction into your readers' advisory work. You are on more familiar ground this way, and you can ease books into your conversations as you think of them. You can also simply suggest that you and the reader check the catalog to see if there are any supporting nonfiction books that might be of interest as well. This way, you do not really have to think through the four intertwined elements of nonfiction when you are stuck for a suggestion, and you can use the resources of your library to their full effect. The catalog may not have subject tracings designed for in-depth readers' advisory work, but it is a great mental prompt, and it never hurts to show patrons the richness of your collection.

Starting from Nonfiction

Starting from nonfiction is a bit trickier because there are two ways conversations get started, and each has its own particular issues. One is when readers come to you (or you go to them), and their question is ambiguous. Many libraries do not have separate service desks for readers' advisory and reference work. Many of us encounter patrons at our one service desk and have to figure out what they want. We may not understand a nonfiction query as a readers' advisory request, especially if we do not make it a point of thinking that way. After all, "Can you help me find a book on George Washington?" is an ambiguous request when read through the lens of nonfiction readers' advisory service. And if we approach a patron in the nonfiction stacks and ask our favorite opening line, "Are you finding what you are looking for, or would you like some help?" the reply can be even more ambiguous: "I want to find out about the Declaration of Independence." Well, how are we to take that? Should we show them *World Book* or offer *American Scripture,* by Pauline Maier? Or both?

No matter where you are, in the stacks or at the reference desk, it is important to offer readers' advisory service. In fact, I advocate turning all reference questions into readers' advisory questions as well. While you have the patron's attention, you might as well sell your readers' advisory service too. Of course, if a patron simply wants to know where you keep the dictionary, there is no need to tell him about Simon Winchester's wonderful *The Professor and the Madman: A Tale of Murder, Insanity, and the Making of the "Oxford English Dictionary,"* but when a patron has asked when George Washington was elected, there is no reason not to ask if she is interested in reading more about George Washington and indicate that you have some really wonderful biographies and histories of the time, like Ellis's *His Excellency: George Washington.* If in the end the patron turns out to want only the date of the inaugural, she will let you know. But, just perhaps, she is interested in more.

Offering more help is always appreciated as long as it is done in a manner that allows the patron a way out of the conversation quickly. If a patron approaches the desk asking for a specific cookbook or a cookbook on a specific topic, it is easy to chat with them while you either give them a call number or walk them to the stacks. It would be easy at this time to ask if they enjoyed reading about food as well as using cookbooks. If the patron offers a response that seems open to further conversation, then you can use the information gained during the brief conversation to start suggesting titles.

Getting many different types of nonfiction into a patron's hands takes carrying on conversations like this between you and readers as well as creating displays and reading lists that include nonfiction. Some readers may think to look for the next Ruth Reichl or Mark Kurlansky or to ask for a book like *Kitchen Confidential,* but only if they know about them already. By displaying the widest range of reading possibilities and engaging in readers' advisory conversations, you have not only expanded your patrons' view of the library, you have shown them that the reference desk is a good place to get book suggestions as well as reliable information. You increase your circulation, you make use of your nonfiction collection, and you begin the process of offering nonfiction readers' advisory service in an easy and nonthreatening way.

The second way to start from nonfiction is more challenging and more like a regular fiction readers' advisory interaction—when a reader says to you that he just finished a particular nonfiction book and wants another book just like it. When this happens, and it will, it's time to conduct a readers' advisory conversation, keeping in mind the four intertwined aspects of narrative nonfiction: narrative context, subject, type, and appeal.

Ask the reader what the book he enjoyed was about and what he liked about it. Listen to what he tells you. Invariably he will tell you the part of the subject that matters to him and other clues about type, narrative nature, and appeal.

Ask him if he wants another book on that topic or if he wants a book that feels like the book he enjoyed, even if it is on a different subject altogether. Subject can be a ruling factor, and it is important to identify that up front before you move on. Right now the reader may just be at a point in his reading that he is fascinated by the subject beyond any other consideration. If so, you can help him find more books on the topic by using your catalog's subject access, but let him know that the books may not read the same as the book he liked. Tell him that, when he is done with the list you are getting for him, if he wants additional books that feel like the book he loved, you can suggest some.

If he says that he is looking for a book that feels like the book he loved, then it's time to consider the book's narrative nature, type, and appeal points as well. Ask the patron questions to find that out.

For the narrative nature, ask questions like these:

- Does the book need to tell a gripping story all the time, or is it okay with you if it is a mix of fact and story?
- Do you like books with lots of story elements, or do you like books that explain facts and pose theories?

To figure out what type the reader enjoys, ask questions such as these:

- Do you like books that report on a topic or books that are more about characters and personal stories?
- Do you enjoy books that include a lot of history, books that muse about issues, or books that explain or explore ideas and concepts?

For appeal, you can ask the same types of questions you would ask for a fiction book, but be sure to ask about experiencing/learning and added elements such as charts or photographs. For example, you can use questions such as these:

- Do you like fast-paced books or books that unfold more slowly?
- Do you like certain kinds of characters? Quirky and odd or heroic and brave?
- Is the setting or time period important?
- Do you like books with photographs, charts, or maps?
- Do you want to learn from this book, or be entertained, or both?

Armed with answers to such questions, you can start trying to find books for the reader. If you know some titles to suggest, that's great, but don't worry if nothing comes to mind. As you gain more experience and broaden your reading to include nonfiction, and as more tools become available, you will have a wider range of resources from which to draw titles.

Simply walking into the stacks and showing books to patrons help spark ideas that lead you from one book to the next. You can use the new book section of your library or the book display areas to help spark ideas as well, so choose a broad range of fiction and nonfiction titles for your displays whenever possible. But don't drag the poor patron pillar to post. It is always a good idea to either pull the books yourself if you have time, suggest a few authors the patron can go find himself, or give the patron a list of suggestions rather than drag him around the building.

Most important, just as with fiction, and particularly when you start out with nonfiction, do not be afraid to say that you need some time to find some suggestions and ask the reader to stop back by the desk on his way out or to leave an e-mail address so you can send a list of books. This gives you some time to think of suggestions and, if you are unfamiliar with the title mentioned, time to investigate.

If the book your reader loved is listed in one of your readers' advisory tools, there may be ready-made reading suggestions, but if not, that does not mean you do not have resources. Read the reviews of the book in whatever source you prefer, and see if you can get a sense of the title. If you have the book in your collection, pull it and see what you can discover. Often by skimming the book, reading the jacket copy, and seeing who is endorsing the work you can get a good sense of its type, narrative nature, and many of its appeal elements.

Talk to your colleagues—since we all know more collectively than we do alone—and use the resources we already have for readers' advisory such as Fiction_L, which is growing as a resource for nonfiction titles. Also, keep in mind that the suggestions you come up with do not just have to be all non-fiction. You can mix fiction with nonfiction just as you did when you started from a fiction query.

Once you have an idea of what the patron is looking for, it is time to suggest some books. Try to suggest a range of titles—at least three—and try to describe each in terms of their narrative nature, subject, type, and appeal. What should you say? As little as possible. You have about thirty seconds to sell the book before the patron is going to tune you out or wonder how to escape.

Focus on the narrative nature, pace, and tone since these three factors are most dependent on a reader's mood, and then on one or two other notable features of the book—the use of language, the odd characters, the intriguing story line, and so on.

Look at the following list of key points and see how brief you can be while still helping the reader. These are the key points of *The Devil's Teeth: A True Story of Obsession and Survival among America's Great White Sharks*, by Susan Casey:

> *The narrative is* gripping, merging fact and story well and falling in the medium-to-high range on the continuum.
>
> *The pace is* a good readable mix, flexing in and out of fast passages and more medium-paced sections.
>
> *The tone is* amusing, adventuresome, informative, and a bit creepy.
>
> *The special feature of this book is* wonderful descriptions of place and shark behavior, interesting characters, with some good illustrations, though maybe not enough for some readers.
>
> *What you need to know about the story:* In this memoir mixed with natural history and great science, Casey relates the story of two biologists studying great white sharks, the evolution of sharks, and the geology of the Farallon Islands, where they congregate.

To practice this, fill in the spaces below with a nonfiction book you know well. See how little you can say and still help patrons decide if the book is one they would be interested in.

The narrative is

The pace is

The tone is
The special feature of this book is
What you need to know about the story is

Here is how a nonfiction readers' advisory conversation could go if a reader loved *Devil's Teeth.*

Patron: Hi, I just finished *Devil's Teeth* and I really loved it. Can you help me find another book like it?

Librarian: I would be glad to. Can you tell me what it was about and what you liked most about it?

Patron: Oh, it's about sharks and I loved how funny it was and what I learned about the sharks and where they live. Did you know that they are older than trees?

Librarian: No, I did not know that. Are you looking for more shark books or books that are funny and teach you something, perhaps about other animals?

Patron: Funny is fine, but I want to learn something too—on any kind of animal.

Librarian: Okay, do you want a fast-paced book or one that is more leisurely? And do you like a certain type of character? Quirky, funny? Does the setting matter?

Patron: Oh, quirky is good. I like books that are not too slow and I don't care where it is set, as long as it is about an animal and tells me something about where they live.

Librarian: Let me get some choices for you. Can you stop back by on your way out or would you like me to e-mail you a list?

Patron: I would love it if you e-mailed me a list.

Now you know quite a lot. This patron is looking for a book that

- teaches him something about animals
- has characters, preferably quirky or funny
- has at least a medium pace
- has a well-described setting

Additionally, you can find out several things about *Devil's Teeth* by reading a review and skimming the book:

- It contains elements of a memoir and nature writing (type).
- It tells at least a somewhat constant story (narrative context).
- It has an adventuresome tone that is both suspenseful and creepy (tone aspect of appeal).
- It teaches a great deal about sharks and geology (learning/experiencing aspect of appeal).
- It has interesting science characters as well as some slightly odd characters (character aspect of appeal).
- It is written in an engaging way at a layperson's level (language and story line aspects of appeal).

And finally, you know how to interpret the four intertwined aspects of nonfiction for this reader:

Narrative. The reader knew he liked the story elements of the book but also that he enjoyed the factual information. This indicates that he does need a somewhat narrative reading experience but that it can be broken up with facts. Titles that fall somewhere in the medium-to-high range on the narrative continuum would be good choices.

Type. The type of book may not have been something the reader knew to talk about, but both memoirs and nature writing are strongly defined types in nonfiction and affect the way a book reads and feels. So even though he did not mention it, type is something to pay attention to when making suggestions based on this title.

Subject. The reader was clear on the subject elements; he wants a book about animals.

Appeal. The reader likes quirky characters and wants a book that has as part of its story line the intent to teach something about animals from a naturalistic or conservationist point of view. The tone of the book is also going to be important, as are the language, pace, and detail.

Based on what the reader likes and what you know about the book, you can make connections between his points of reading enjoyment and other titles. The following might make good suggestions:

Blue Meridian: The Search for the Great White Shark, by Peter Matthiessen. This classic work on great white sharks combines wonderful nature writing with a bit of memoir in the form of journals kept by the divers. Like *Devil's Teeth,* this book is connected to a documentary film, *Blue Water, White Death,* and shares a bit of the same ethos of science and exploration. The work certainly teaches the reader about sharks and has an exciting and fun tone.

Carnivorous Nights: On the Trail of the Tasmanian Tiger, by Margaret Mittelbach and Michael Crewdson. Although not about sharks, this book contains elements of memoir and nature writing as well as travel elements also present in *Devil's Teeth.* It has the same adventuresome tone and is also funny. It has quirky characters and teaches a great deal about the Tasmanian tiger and other animals.

Rats: Observations on the History and Habitat of the City's Most Unwanted Inhabitants, by Robert Sullivan. This fascinating account of rats shares with *Devil's Teeth* the focus on place and firsthand observations of an animal in its natural habitat. Sullivan provides plenty of narrative stories and a steady pace along with solid science and a large dose of creepy fun.

The Orchid Thief: A True Story of Beauty and Obsession, by Susan Orlean. Although not about animals, this book actually shares a great many of the elements the reader liked about *Devil's Teeth.* It is funny, it is firmly placed in a particular location, and that location informs the entire narrative. It also combines many of the same types present in *Devil's Teeth:* memoir, nature writing, and investigation with a strong, medium- to fast-paced story. It is full of odd and quirky characters and teaches the reader a great deal about orchids.

Jaws, by Peter Benchley. There are many thriller shark books the reader could select, but just for fun and to add range to the suggestions, *Jaws* is the classic work of shark fiction and might be something the reader would enjoy. After all, part of the appeal of *Devil's Teeth* is the creepy-fun-danger elements of sharks attacking their prey and checking out the scientists. This title could also be offered as a movie to give dimension to the list.

All of these suggestions make use of what the reader said he liked about *Devil's Teeth* and were shaped by the four-part approach to nonfiction titles, considering the narrative context, subject, type, and appeal. The librarian engaged the reader in conversation, offered to help, and used the full range of the collection in making suggestions. Ideally, of course, the reader would return to the library and share with the librarian his thoughts on the titles he chose to read, and thus a deeper and sustained reading conversation would develop. As you can see by this example, though there is more to nonfiction suggestions than with fiction, simply because of the nature of the works, it is neither a dissimilar process to fiction advising nor something too complex to undertake. You can do this, and you can have fun with it as well.

No matter where you start with nonfiction readers' advisory service, from a fiction base, from a reference question, or from an actual nonfiction readers' advisory query, the important thing is to start. Bridging the Dewey divide takes conscious effort. If you do not make nonfiction a habit in your work, it is all too easy to ignore it.

The more ways you incorporate nonfiction into your daily readers' advisory work, the easier it becomes to discuss nonfiction with readers. Here is a summary of suggestions for working with nonfiction titles:

Start building a list of sure-bet nonfiction titles, ones that you feel will hold wide appeal to a range of readers. Compile this list from your reading, audiobook catalogs, bestseller lists, award winners, and titles you glean from other sources. When you are at the desk and are asked for nonfiction readers' advisory suggestions, you will have something to turn to.

Pair fiction and nonfiction whenever you can. Start to see the paths through the Dewey divide. You can

- Mix displays: include fiction and nonfiction titles in every display you make.
- Include nonfiction titles in every booklist you make, either as title suggestions in their own right or as supporting reading.
- Include nonfiction on your readers' advisory website.
- Consider nonfiction choices when you select your next book discussion title.
- Include at least one nonfiction suggestion in with your fiction reading suggestions every time you assist a reader.

See reference questions as opportunities to include nonfiction suggestions.

Apply what you know about working with fiction to working with nonfiction. Remember that readers enjoy reading nonfiction for many of the same reasons they enjoy reading fiction, and build on that to offer nonfiction suggestions.

Practice! Walk books through the nonfiction matrix and play with readers' advisory Mad Libs until you feel fluent with the language of nonfiction.

I do not want to suggest that incorporating nonfiction into your readers' advisory work happens quickly. Readers' advisory librarians well know how long it takes to read enough books in a given fiction genre to become familiar with how the genre works, and there are many more subjects and types in nonfiction than there are genres in fiction. You should realize up front that nonfiction books cover a huge number of fields and that there is no way to get comfortable or knowledgeable enough with all of them right away. Nor do I want to suggest that all readers are going to appreciate the mix of fiction and nonfiction or that it will be an easy sell or even always a fruitful one. But it is important to include nonfiction in your advisory work and to create a robust and vital service that addresses the needs of all your readers.

3

FOOD AND COOKING

Judging by the number of cooking magazines and the popularity of Food TV, the nation is interested in all things culinary. From fancy gourmet grocery stores to the growing interest in farmer's markets, from celebrity chefs to destination restaurants, it seems all of us are showing more interest in a range of cooking and food-related subjects.

And why not? Reading about food is almost as fulfilling as consuming it. We begin reading food-related texts at the earliest of ages. Who hasn't read the cereal box while eating breakfast or selected Bazooka gum because of the comic strip inside? Food and reading seem to go together naturally. There are book clubs that have monthly dinners based on the food featured in the titles they are reading; there are cookbooks designed for those clubs; there is even a fiction subgenre of novels with recipes. And certainly librarians know that there is a never-ending stream of cookbooks published each year, with an accompanying holds queue of avid fans impatiently waiting their turn. It seems that two of life's sweetest pleasures, food and books, make an irresistible combination for many.

What Readers Enjoy in These Books

Chief among the reasons readers enjoy these books is the appeal element of learning/experiencing. There is a great deal to learn about and much to savor in culinary titles, be it the knowledge of how food is produced, how to make healthy choices for ourselves and the planet, the vicarious enjoyment found in reading about elaborate meals, or the skills to be gained from the experts who create them.

Culinary works are often strongly narrative, and with that comes other reading pleasures. The language in food books can be rich, lush, and evocative as well as raw and descriptive. Readers attracted to books for their language find much to enjoy among the pages of many titles. Details about food are another reason these books are so enjoyable. In the hands of a fine writer, both exotic and familiar food comes to life for readers who would never dream of paying hundreds of dollars for a glass of wine, have never considered how a pig becomes bacon, or have not had the opportunity to travel abroad and experience the sensory pleasures of a French farmer's market.

Character is another point of pleasure in these books. From competent and capable chefs who explain their love of cooking in a manner supportive of nervous home cooks to the high drama of prima donna personalities who rant and rave and scare the line staff to death, there is a huge range of characters scattered among the pages of culinary works.

The variety of approaches and topics is also a draw for readers. The history of food and its impact on society is a fascinating subject, as are the politics of food and the issues surrounding its production. These nuanced accounts take readers beyond the glossy covers of magazines or the slick production of cookbooks into the reality of food as big business with priorities of its own, the multilayered history of how ingredients contribute to culture, or how cooking can become a social prison. On the lighter side, many titles take food-related road trips that are sharply funny, and others invite readers into a comforting world of cozy reflection.

Given the wide range of approaches, it should be no surprise that tone is important in reader enjoyment as well. Just as food can be eaten for comfort, it can be read for comfort too. Food books of all kinds remind readers of their parents' or grandparents' recipes, of family meals and holiday gatherings, and they offer an escape into the multiple pleasures of reading and eating. Other titles use rigorous prose and insightful reporting to challenge readers to consider the consequences of their food choices in depth.

Types of Books

The books most people think of when they consider culinary titles are cookbooks, but there is more to the subject than good recipes for lentil soup. We consider five type classifications in this chapter:

- Essays
- History
- Biography and Memoir
- Reporting
- Narrative Cookbooks

Essays, history, biography, memoir, and reporting are all common type classifications in nonfiction. Narrative cookbooks, on the other hand, are unique to this subject area and are becoming more and more popular with readers. It might be the perfect mix for many—story and recipe blended together. The early works of James Beard combined recipes with narrative comments about the food, the setting in which the dish was invented, and serving suggestions. He may have been the first contemporary writer to publish such a work. Nigella Lawson's modern adaptation of the narrative cookbook blends offhand stories, short essays, and tidbits about food into beautiful publications. Other writers, such as Patricia Wells, interpret the narrative cookbook as travelogue and include recipes with discussions of the markets, people, and customs of a particular locale. Narrative cookbooks illustrate the differences between task-based and nontask-based titles. It is one thing to need a lentil soup recipe and quite another to want to read a story about that recipe as well.

Benchmark Books to Read and Suggest

The titles listed below are some of the best examples of each type of culinary work. Reading these five books will lead a readers' advisory librarian toward fluency in the types of books represented in this section. Understanding how a book represents its type and how readers respond to it helps readers' advisory librarians gain a deeper appreciation of the differences in type and the desires of readers. Thinking about how titles relate to each other helps readers' advisory librarians see the connections between nonfiction and the broader scope of literature in general. It is important when reading these books to focus not only on the enjoyment they bring but also on how they exhibit narrative context, subject, type, and appeal. Although readers' advisory librarians are constantly keeping lists of books they want to read, selecting a few well-considered choices from a core reading list is crucial to developing skills that align with the sympathies of readers.

Essays

Essays provide room to ramble, and authors are quick to pick up on that invitation and explore a wide range of topics. Food essays are frequently collections of magazine or newspaper columns and mix story and fact in a medium-to-high point on the narrative continuum. They are filled with descriptive passages and fine writing and often contain quirky and fascinating characters (who frequently turn out to be the author). This classification is the perfect place to begin a reading plan of your own or to start readers just beginning to explore the subject.

Home Cooking: A Writer in the Kitchen, by Laurie Colwin

Colwin was a novelist and contributor to *Gourmet* magazine, for which she wrote a series of columns called "Home Cooking." She is a beloved foodie who died tragically in 1992. The essays in this collection are part memoir, part instruction, and part rumination on a certain type of life. They tell of Colwin's early twenties in New York City: tiny apartments, napping children, and a young woman finding both her way in life and her voice. Sprinkled in, every now and then, are recipes that consist more of explanation than ingredients. Colwin writes about life, her modern female self-discovered life, while she writes about food. Her stories are personal and warm, friendly and inviting. Much of her appeal owes to the fact that she is nonthreatening and engaging. She deconstructs food into its most elemental parts and invites others to join her in the enjoyment. Also read her *More Home Cooking: A Writer Returns to the Kitchen.*

Read this book because it allows you to see the tone many readers want in food books—friendly, warm, and sympathetic—and because it helps illustrate the nature of the food essay in terms of both subject and style.

Suggest this book to readers who want something cozy, female oriented, funny, and comforting. It matches well with books such as *84, Charing Cross Road*, by Helene Hanff, and *Bread Alone*, a novel by Judith Ryan Hendricks. Colwin was also a novelist, so suggest any of her five novels (*Happy All the Time; Family Happiness; Goodbye without Leaving; Shine on Bright and Dangerous Object;* and *A Big Storm Knocked It Over*).

History

These titles look at culture and history through the prism of a particular food or culinary touchstone. They contain a wonderful blend of well-researched facts and rich story-filled accounts. Works in this classification hold broad appeal not just to foodies but to history fans of all sorts.

Salt: A World History, by Mark Kurlansky

Kurlansky is a man who thinks in complex and creative ways on a big-picture scale. The author of *Cod: A Biography of the Fish That Changed the World; The*

Basque History of the World; The Big Oyster: History on the Half Shell; and *1968: The Year That Rocked the World,* Kurlansky is known for his mix of history, culture, and food. He excels at mixing odd and disparate facts, colorful individuals, and multiple cultures and societies into fascinating histories that use a single item to explain much of our collective history. *Salt* is food history at its most interesting and expansive. Salt was the driving force for establishing the early trade routes and the reason for the founding of the city of Jericho. Salt has provoked wars and was a factor in both the American Revolution and the American Civil War. Salt has financed empires and led to their demise. Kurlansky explores salt from the historical and cultural aspects and from the creative and scientific as well. Salt is significant in many religious events and customs and drove such inventions as gas furnaces and drilling methods. Salt even supports the creation of other foods, from cheese to olives. Kurlansky includes illustrations and recipes in his wide-ranging, multidisciplinary exploration of this most basic and elemental ingredient.

Read this book because it illustrates the basic appeal of food history—the literate presentation of many historical threads intertwined with food and culture.

Suggest this book to readers who like details and well-described settings and enjoy learning about a wide range of subjects through their reading. It matches well with books such as *Zarafa: A Giraffe's True Story from Deep in Africa to the Heart of Paris,* by Michael Allin, and *Nathaniel's Nutmeg,* by Giles Milton.

Biography and Memoir

The recollections of those who have devoted their lives to food can be richly illuminating. Writers of culinary memoirs have often spent their lives writing about food and honed their descriptive skills crafting restaurant reviews and essays. Consequently, their memoirs are a delight to read—filled with lush language and heady description. Biographers, on the other hand, bring the required sense of distance and perspective to their subjects. Whatever the form, however, memoir and biography both are character-filled and story-rich experiences, making them great choices for readers who enjoy character and need at least a moderately narrative level of writing.

Tender at the Bone: Growing Up at the Table, by Ruth Reichl

Ruth Reichl is the editor of *Gourmet* magazine and former restaurant critic for both the *Los Angeles Times* and *New York Times.* Her stories are funny, open, and inviting but have a sharp edge. Reichl introduces readers to her mother, the Queen of Mold, who apparently had a stomach of iron and no regard at all for the concept that food can spoil. Following her mother is a cast of finely drawn characters who all interact with Reichl over food—from the maid who taught her to cook, to a French banker whose love of food rivaled Reichl's, to Marion Cunningham, who taught Reichl lessons about food and life. This memoir is as much about becoming who you want to be as is it is about cooking. Reichl followed *Tender at the Bone* with *Comfort Me with Apples* and *Garlic and Sapphires*.

Read this book because it shows how fine a memoir can be, introduces you to much of the early groundwork of food culture, and blends food and other forms of writing seamlessly.

Suggest this book to readers who enjoy good memoirs and good writing overall, those interested in family tales, or those who enjoy coming-of-age stories. Other books to suggest include *The Sixteen Pleasures,* a novel by Robert Hellenga, and *Eating My Words: An Appetite for Life,* by Mimi Sheraton.

Reporting

Books in this category range from the gossipy, insider look to the serious tone of narrative journalism. The books can be highly story based or fact filled and are written in styles ranging from the lyrical to the scientific. They appeal to readers who want to know what is going on, be it in Mario Batali's kitchen or in the slaughterhouse where their next steak is being prepared.

Heat: An Amateur's Adventures as Kitchen Slave, Line Cook, Pasta-Maker, and Apprentice to a Dante-Quoting Butcher in Tuscany, **by Bill Buford**

Bill Buford is a writer who was nervy enough to invite one of America's most famous chefs over for dinner—Mario Batali. Batali showed up with a lot of wine and pure pig lard and apparently took over the kitchen, placed slices of pig fat in everyone's mouth, and accepted Buford's request to apprentice in one of Batali's kitchens. And so starts an amazing story. Buford, like the rest of us, only thought he knew how to cut up carrots. He did not fully understand the importance of uniform size and shape when it comes to dicing, and he had no idea whatsoever how neurotic the world of high-stakes cooking can be. But he found out, produced a decent dice, and traveled to some great places to eat and learn. His story of Batali, restaurants, and cooking makes for delicious entertainment and offers a delightful insider/outsider look at the rigors of restaurant life.

Read this book because it is a great example of narrative reporting, illustrates the strong appeal of the type (insider perspectives, vivid details, and strong personalities), and thanks to the press coverage and power of Batali's name is a book readers know about and thus can be used as a touchstone for making other connections.

Suggest this book to readers who want to know what it is really like to work in a restaurant and what is going on with their food. *Kitchen Confidential: Adventures in the Culinary Underbelly,* by Anthony Bourdain, makes for great parallel reading. Readers who enjoy both interesting characters and gossip mixed with the unveiling of secrets will also enjoy *Cosmopolitan: A Bartender's Life,* by Toby Cecchini.

Narrative Cookbooks

Narrative cookbooks are part memoir, part food history, part essay, and part cookbook. Perhaps the purest form of food and writing, they hold wide appeal. All kinds of culinary readers, from those who enjoy skimming through recipes to those hungry to know more about the lives of chefs or the development of food, can find much to enjoy.

The Olive and the Caper, by Susanna Hoffman

Susanna Hoffman is an anthropologist and has written several cookbooks. This is her breakout effort and is a model narrative cookbook. The work begins with a brief illustrated history of Greece and an annotated table of contents. The first twenty-three pages cover the types and histories of the beverages of Greece—with nary a recipe in sight. Once the recipes begin, it is often hard to focus on them, for surrounding each are excerpts from Greek poetry, snippets of history, glimpses of Greek daily life, the importance of certain foods to the Greek people, and photos of people, markets, historical sites, and food. Interspersed between sections are special entries on such topics as Greek history, politics, historical figures, and the Olympics. Hoffman writes with a deep, apparent joy for her subject, infusing her cookbook with a sense of celebration and rich cultural awareness. All the recipes are put into historical and cultural context, and many include a litany of variations. Hoffman teaches about food in depth as she describes how to cook a dish and offers readers a wealth of information on the nature of the ingredients. This cookbook is full of wonderful and interesting recipes, but one could read it for the extra information alone.

Read this book because it perfectly illustrates the nature of a narrative cookbook and how different it is from a regular cookbook. It also reveals how multidimensional a narrative cookbook can be in terms of helping patrons find books to read on all aspects of a vacation destination, a country study, or for personal pleasure.

Suggest this book to readers who are interested in the culture of food, interested in Greece, or enjoy multifaceted explorations of a topic. Other books to suggest include *The Provence Cookbook,* by Patricia Wells, and *Mangoes and Curry Leaves: Culinary Travels through the Great Subcontinent,* by Jeffrey Alford and Naomi Duguid. Both contain many of the same elements as *The Olive and the Caper,* including looks into markets, people, culture, and food history.

Key Authors

This listing contains the top culinary writers, both past and present. Readers' advisory librarians should become familiar with these names and at least glance through a sampling of their work. Use this list to make suggestions, build displays, fill a sure-bet cart, or make booklists.

James Beard	Holly Hughes	Eric Schlosser
Anthony Bourdain	Mark Kurlansky	Laura Shapiro
Laurie Colwin	Frances Moore Lappé	Mimi Sheraton
Elizabeth David	Nigella Lawson	Jeffrey Steingarten
John T. Edge	Gina Mallet	John Thorne
M. F. K. Fisher	Ruth Reichl	Calvin Trillin
Betty Fussell	Alan Richman	Patricia Wells

Selected Bibliography of Culinary Writing to Read and Suggest

Essays

The Nasty Bits: Collected Varietal Cuts, Usable Trim, Scraps, and Bones and *A Cook's Tour: Global Adventures in Extreme Cuisines,* by Anthony Bourdain

Home Cooking: A Writer in the Kitchen and *More Home Cooking: A Writer Returns to the Kitchen,* by Laurie Colwin

An Omelette and a Glass of Wine (and her other work), by Elizabeth David

The Art of Eating, by M. F. K. Fisher (this is a collected volume of many of her works)

The Raw and the Cooked: Adventures of a Roving Gourmand, by Jim Harrison

Best Food Writing, edited by Holly Hughes (published annually)

Adventures on the Wine Route: A Wine Buyer's Tour of France, by Kermit Lynch

On Food and Cooking: The Science and Lore of the Kitchen and *Curious Cook: More Kitchen Science and Lore*, by Harold McGee

Endless Feasts: Sixty Years of Writing from "Gourmet" and *Remembrance of Things Paris: Sixty Years of Writing from "Gourmet,"* edited by Ruth Reichl

Fork It Over: The Intrepid Adventures of a Professional Eater, by Alan Richman

It Must've Been Something I Ate and *The Man Who Ate Everything*, by Jeffrey Steingarten

Simple Cooking, by John Thorne

American Fried; Alice, Let's Eat; and *Third Helpings* (and his other work), by Calvin Trillin

Stalking the Green Fairy, and Other Fantastic Adventures in Food and Drink, by James Villas and Jeremiah Tower

Are You Really Going to Eat That? Reflections of a Culinary Thrill Seeker, by Robb Walsh

History

American Appetite: The Coming of Age of a Cuisine, by Leslie Brenner

The True History of Chocolate, by Sophie D. Coe and Michael D. Coe

Curry: A Tale of Cooks and Conquerors, by Lizzie Collingham

Apple Pie: An American Story; Hamburgers and Fries; Donuts: An American Passion; and *Fried Chicken: An American Story*, by John T. Edge

Charlemagne's Tablecloth: A Piquant History of Feasting, by Nichola Fletcher

From Hardtack to Home Fries: An Uncommon History of American Cooks and Meals, by Barbara Haber

Hooked: Pirates, Poaching, and the Perfect Fish, by G. Bruce Knecht

The Big Oyster: History on the Half Shell; Cod: A Biography of the Fish That Changed the World; and *Salt: A World History*, by Mark Kurlansky

Finding Betty Crocker: The Secret Life of America's First Lady of Food, by Susan Marks

Stand Facing the Stove: The Story of the Women Who Gave America "The Joy of Cooking," by Anne Mendelson

Nathaniel's Nutmeg, by Giles Milton

Consuming Passions: A History of English Food Appetite, by Philippa Pullar

Vanilla: A Cultural History of the World's Favorite Flavor and Fragrance, by Patricia Rain

Sweets, by Tim Richardson

Chocolate: A Bittersweet Saga of Dark and Light, by Mort Rosenblum

Caviar: The Strange History and Uncertain Future of the World's Most Coveted Delicacy, by Inga Saffron

A Thousand Years Over a Hot Stove: A History of American Women Told through Food, Recipes, and Remembrances, by Laura Schenone

Something from the Oven: Reinventing Dinner in 1950s America and *Perfection Salad: Women and Cooking at the Turn of the Century,* by Laura Shapiro

A History of the World in Six Glasses, by Tom Standage

Eat My Words: Reading Women's Lives through the Cookbooks They Wrote, by Janet Theophano

Serious Pig: An American Cook in Search of His Roots, by John Thorne

Spice: The History of a Temptation, by Jack Turner

Much Depends on Dinner: The Extraordinary History and Mythology, Allure and Obsessions, Perils and Taboos of an Ordinary Meal, by Margaret Visser

Biography and Memoir

The Language of Baklava, by Diana Abu-Jaber

Kitchen Confidential: Adventures in the Culinary Underbelly, by Anthony Bourdain

Cosmopolitan: A Bartender's Life, by Toby Cecchini

The Perfectionist: Life and Death in Haute Cuisine, by Rudolph Chelminski

My Life in France, by Julia Child, with Alex Prud'Homme

Writing at the Kitchen Table: The Authorized Biography of Elizabeth David, by Artemis Cooper

Take Big Bites: Adventures Around the World and Across the Table, by Linda Ellerbee

Out of the Kitchen: Adventures of a Food Writer, by Jeannette Ferrary

My Kitchen Wars, by Betty Fussell

Insatiable: Tales from a Life of Delicious Excess, by Gael Greene

Cooking for Mr. Latte: A Food Lover's Courtship, with Recipes, by Amanda Hesser

Daughter of Heaven: A Memoir with Earthly Recipes, by Leslie Li

Candy and Me (A Love Story), by Hilary Liftin

Last Chance to Eat: The Fate of Taste in a Fast Food World, by Gina Mallet

Monsoon Diary: A Memoir with Recipes, by Shoban Narayan

The Apprentice: My Life in the Kitchen, by Jacques Pepin

Julie and Julia: 365 Days, 524 Recipes, 1 Tiny Apartment Kitchen, by Julie Powell

Poet of the Appetites: The Lives and Loves of M. F. K. Fisher, by Joan Reardon

Tender at the Bone: Growing Up at the Table; Comfort Me with Apples: More Adventures at the Table; and *Garlic and Sapphires: The Secret Life of a Critic in Disguise,* by Ruth Reichl

Untangling My Chopsticks: A Culinary Sojourn in Kyoto, by Victoria Abbott Riccardi

From Here, You Can't See Paris: Seasons of a French Village and Its Restaurant, by Michael S. Sanders

Tea and Pomegranates: A Memoir of Food, Family, and Kashmir, by Nazneen Sheikh

Eating My Words: An Appetite for Life, by Mimi Sheraton

Toast: The Story of a Boy's Hunger, by Nigel Slater

Two for the Road: Our Love Affair with American Food, by Jane Stern and Michael Stern

Stuffed: Adventures of a Restaurant Family, by Patricia Volk

Consuming Passions: A Food-Obsessed Life, by Michael Lee West

Reporting

Candyfreak: A Journey through the Chocolate Underbelly of America, by Steve Almond

Heat: An Amateur's Adventures as Kitchen Slave, Line Cook, Pasta-Maker, and Apprentice to a Dante-Quoting Butcher in Tuscany, by Bill Buford

Fat Land: How Americans Became the Fattest People in the World, by Greg Critser

Noble Rot: A Bordeaux Wine Revolution, by William Echikson

Dinner at the New Gene Cafe: How Genetic Engineering Is Changing What We Eat, How We Live, and the Global Politics of Food, by Bill Lambrecht

Diet for a Small Planet, by Frances Moore Lappé

Hope's Edge: The Next Diet for a Small Planet, by Frances Moore Lappé and Anna Lappé

Hungry Planet: What the World Eats, by Peter Menzel and Faith D'Aluisio

Food Politics: How the Food Industry Influences Nutrition and Health, by Marion Nestle

The Accidental Connoisseur: An Irreverent Journey through the Wine World, by Lawrence Osborne

The Omnivore's Dilemma: A Natural History of Four Meals, by Michael Pollan

The Making of a Chef: Mastering Heat at the Culinary Institute; The Reach of a Chef: Beyond the Kitchen; and *The Soul of a Chef: The Journey toward Perfection,* by Michael Ruhlman

Fast Food Nation: The Dark Side of the All-American Meal, by Eric Schlosser

Cookoff: Recipe Fever in America, by Amy Sutherland

A Very Good Year: The Journey of a California Wine from Vine to Table, by Mike Weiss

Narrative Cookbooks

Mangoes and Curry Leaves: Culinary Travels through the Great Subcontinent, by Jeffrey Alford and Naomi Duguid

Catalan Cuisine: Europe's Last Great Culinary Secret and *Flavors of the Riviera,* by Colman Andrews

Hallelujah! The Welcome Table: A Lifetime of Memories with Recipes, by Maya Angelou

James Beard's American Cookery, by James Beard

A Culinary Traveller in Tuscany: Exploring and Eating off the Beaten Track, by Beth Elon

Matzoh Ball Gumbo: Culinary Tales of the Jewish South, by Marcie Cohen Ferris

The Olive and the Caper, by Susanna Hoffman

Feast: Food to Celebrate Life, by Nigella Lawson

On Rue Tatin: Living and Cooking in a French Town, by Susan Herrmann Loomis

Arabesque: A Taste of Morocco, Turkey, and Lebanon, by Claudia Roden

Hidden Kitchens: Stories, Recipes, and More from NPR's the Kitchen Sisters, by Nikki Silva and Davia Nelson; see also the NPR podcasts of the Kitchen Sisters

Pot on the Fire: Further Confessions of a Renegade Cook, by John Thorne

The Paris Cookbook and *The Provence Cookbook,* by Patricia Wells

Resources and Awards

Perhaps the best way to get familiar with the subject is to leaf through the annual publication of *Best Food Writing.* This collection gathers the most notable works of a given year and can provide readers' advisory librarians an easy entry into the culinary world. Many of the writers included in this chapter got their starts, and in some cases continue, writing in magazines and newspapers; authors such as Laurie Colwin, Gina Mallet, Mimi Sheraton, and Ruth Reichl are all good examples. Readers' advisory librarians should become familiar with who is writing for such magazines as *Gourmet; Food and Wine; Saveur;* and *Bon Appetite.* These magazines also review culinary titles and should be skimmed for summary articles on food books and holiday book-giving sections regularly. Reviews often point out if a cookbook offers more than a simple compilation of recipes—which if you do not buy the cookbooks or are not in the habit of skimming through them when they arrive may be the only way you can find narrative cookbooks, the hardest of all the food books to find and to suggest.

In addition to familiarization with magazines, readers' advisory librarians should also watch Food TV, PBS, and the Style Network from time to time to see who is cooking and writing about food. Patrons almost always ask for works by the major personalities on cooking shows, and often these cooks publish both narrative cookbooks and other nonfiction titles.

There are also several awards for food writing that should be monitored yearly. Though fiction awards garner a great deal of attention, specialized nonfiction awards often pass unnoticed by our patrons.

JAMES BEARD FOUNDATION AWARD FOR WRITING ON FOOD

The James Beard awards are given in many categories, but the writing on food category is particularly important to monitor. In addition, there are Beard awards for writing in magazines and in newspapers. Scanning the winners can quickly catch a readers' advisory librarian up on who is who in the food writing world. See http://www.jamesbeard.org.

GLENFIDDICH FOOD AND DRINK AWARDS

The Glenfiddich awards are based in Britain and are highly regarded. The Glenfiddich website, http://uk.glenfiddich.com/events/date.html, offers more information on each category. Past winners include *Toast*, by Nigel Slater, and *Cod: A Biography of the Fish That Changed the World*, by Mark Kurlansky.

IACP AWARDS

The awards given by the International Association of Culinary Professions (formerly known as the Julia Child Cookbook Awards) have several categories worth investigation. Of particular interest is the literary food writing category and the reference/technical award. See http://www.iacp.com.

4

SCIENCE, MATHEMATICS, AND NATURE WRITING

Science is all around us. It is in the everyday things we do, as when we wonder if a half a cup is really the same as 4 ounces, when we pretend to our kids that we really remember how to do long division with decimal points, and when we look up at the sky and repeat "arc to Arcturus speed to Spica." Science and its sibling subjects hold sway in our everyday lives in ways we never suspected when we were studying in school. The answer to that age-old question—"Are we really going to use this in real life?"—is a resounding yes, but in ways that are hidden and more subtle than questions that began "If one train left Easttown and another train left Northtown. . . ." Indeed, in the everyday world, the sciences are embedded in our lives, and as readers we are drawn into the wonder of it all.

As librarians, we might at times feel a bit uneasy with the topic, because the huge array of subjects touching on some aspect of science makes identifying books to suggest somewhat overwhelming. Just a few of the subjects covered in this nonfiction area are astronomy, biology, chemistry, computer science, earth science, environmental science, genetics, mathematics, natural history, oceanography, physics, and zoology. Science awes in its grandeur and scope but, rest assured, you do not need to know the difference between organic and inorganic chemistry to suggest books to readers who do. But you do need an appreciation for the deep appeal of these books.

What Readers Enjoy in These Books

It is perhaps the need to learn as an adult, triggered by some life experience or moment of wonder, our never-ending curiosity, or the sheer delight of understanding the world around us more clearly that draws us to the world of science books and underscores one of their major appeals, that of learning/

experiencing. Science books appeal directly to readers who want to learn and discover through their reading, to those who appreciate sharp, intelligent writing and enjoy exploring the complex, figuring out puzzles, and making connections. Science book readers want things made clear, but not in a condescending way, and they are willing, in fact eager, to puzzle their way through a book toward the goal of mastering a subject. Competency, intelligence, and curiosity are common threads in all manner of science books.

There are many other reasons readers are fascinated by these books. Their narrative continuum is huge, ranging from fact-based hard sciences to highly narrative personal stories, and therefore all types of readers find a narrative fit within their pages. Science books are also usually written in an elegant, lucid, and vigorous manner that makes reading them a pure joy. Additionally, science does not have to be serious, and many readers enjoy the quirky nature of some science topics. Still other readers, maybe following the path of a lifelong interest, deeply enjoy the musing nature of many science topics. The invitation to stop and wonder along with an expert is beguiling. Readers who enjoy other aspects of appeal, such as character and detail, can also find much to please them in the pages of these books. Science books are full of details, from how stars are born to how zero became a number. They include characters, be they fascinating individuals or quirky groups, who are compelling and well drawn. Collectively, these books offer a wealth of rewards for the committed reader and the dabbler alike, inviting us all into the captivating web of things known and those just waiting for discovery.

Types of Books

We can break science books into five type classifications:

- Explanations
- Investigations
- Nature and Natural History
- Literary or Historical Slants
- Biography and Memoir

Type is vital in this subject area. Remember that, although subject leads a reader to a book, it is not what keeps the reader happily reading the book— *that* is a mix of all the other elements of nonfiction. So although it may be tempting in an area as diverse and wide ranging as science to look at books in terms of their narrow subjects, it is more useful to combine subject with the wider considerations of nonfiction. It helps both the readers' advisory librarian and the reader to discuss books based on narrative context, type, and appeal rather than just on subject. Though it is likely that a patron interested in a subject will enjoy many different types of books on that same subject, it is as likely that a patron who enjoys reading challenging investigations will enjoy that same type of investigation into quarks as into dinosaur extinctions, since it is often the type and appeal of a book readers enjoy as much as the subject. And, in practical terms, there are not enough nonfiction books on quarks (or many other micro subjects) to satisfy a reader for long. Thus, matching readers to type as well as to subject helps both the readers' advisory librarian and the patron by ensuring that, once the quark books run out, there are other books to suggest and enjoy.

Keep in mind that science material presented in visual and audio formats can be more accessible to some patrons. Films can visually explain or display a difficult construct, and audio formats can often be more easily understood since the narration eases readers into unfamiliar language and concepts.

Benchmark Books to Read and Suggest

Reading in the sciences is a lifelong pursuit of wonder and exploration, but readers' advisory librarians can get a taste for the range of science titles by reading these five books. Each is one of the best examples of its type, and collectively they offer the readers' advisory librarian a way to become familiar with the range of science writing. Annotations seek to explain the appeal of the book and why it should be read as a sample title, explain why a reader would enjoy it, and suggest other books that might be enjoyed for similar reasons. As you read these books, focus on the differences between them and the reasons you enjoyed each. Getting a firm understanding of the vast variation within the subject will help you suggest books to patrons.

Explanations

Explanations seek to explain science to the general reader. They have wide appeal, are written for the generalist, and typify popular science writing. Not only are these great books for readers interested in science topics, they are good books to suggest to readers who are simply looking for something different to read. The narrative continuum of these books falls within the medium range and provides a good blend of fact and narrative writing.

Big Bang: The Origin of the Universe, by Simon Singh

The central questions of cosmology are how did the universe start and how does it grow? Singh, renowned for making the complex clear, has applied his special brand of explanation to this central question. What is the Big Bang and how did/does it work? Starting with the roots of science, he explains the move from creation myths to the earliest theories about the sun, the earth, and the universe. This early chapter provides the framework for the larger model to come. It, like the rest of the book, is full of illustrations, pictures, charts, and a charming set of handwritten notes that summarize the key points covered thus far. Once Singh lays the groundwork, his narrative pace picks up and he begins to trace the modern development of the Big Bang model. He contrasts this model with the idea of a steady state and uses key scientific figures—their thoughts, theories, inventions, and efforts—as the map in which he lays out the explanation. It is a grand tour of science and clearly illustrates scientific theory in practice as readers track the debate, proofs, and experiments that led to the understanding and acceptance of the Big Bang theory.

Read this book because it is a perfect example of the scientific explanation type—clear yet rigorous, and written specifically to help lay readers understand key concepts.

Suggest this book to those interested in the Big Bang model or to readers wanting clear explanations of scientific theory in practice. It works well with Singh's other two books, *Fermat's Enigma: The Epic Quest to Solve the World's Greatest Mathematical Problem* and *The Code Book: The Science of Secrecy from Ancient Egypt to Quantum Cryptography,* because they take the same approach to explaining difficult concepts. Readers also might enjoy *A Short History of Nearly Everything,* by Bill Bryson, for more genial and witty explanations of science. For another personality-based tour of scientific theory, consider *Coming of Age in the Milky Way,* by Timothy Ferris.

Investigations

Whereas explanatory science books explain scientific theories for the layman, investigations argue and expand on theory at a more sophisticated level. The subject nature of the two types can be similar; the primary differences are in their intent and focus (story line aspects), narrative context, detail, language, and tone. Investigations take commitment and effort to read, for they often contain difficult concepts and some level of jargon, or they assume that the reader already understands basic scientific theory. They tend to fall low on the narrative continuum and are detail and fact laden. Fans of these books find pleasure in working through a text and gaining understanding, and they appreciate that the writing is typically elegant, illuminating, and fascinating.

The Road to Reality: A Complete Guide to the Laws of the Universe, by Roger Penrose

This massive book is a tour de force of the mathematical underpinnings of science and an eye-rolling, giddy delight for those readers ready to tackle its thousand-plus pages. Penrose covers three main threads—the laws of the universe and how it all works, the math that explains these laws, and the differences between two theories of physics (Einstein's general theory of relativity and quantum theory). To say Penrose's book is a challenge is an understatement. Just the chapter titles alone—"Riemann Surfaces and Complex Mappings," "Fourier Decomposition and Hyperfunctions," "Manifolds of n Dimensions"—need translation, and the multitude of formulas, equations, and graphs need something akin to the Rosetta stone to decipher. But that is the point. Working through the book is the mathematical equivalent of "Let's Do This," and it offers readers a great and rewarding challenge. Understanding just a bit of Penrose's work is illuminating, but reading it all and coming to grasp its beauty and order is forever enriching.

Read this book because it shows how difficult but grand scientific investigations can be and illustrates what readers are doing when they grapple with this type of work.

Suggest this book to readers who are up for the challenge and want to work through the fundamental concepts of physics. This is a singular title, but works such as *The Fabric of the Cosmos: Space, Time, and the Texture of Reality,* by Brian Greene, and *Warped Passages: Unraveling the Mysteries of the Universe's Hidden Dimensions,* by Lisa Randall, make fine parallel reading.

Nature and Natural History

Melding the exploration of the land with the study of its inhabitants and landscape, nature writing is an elegant and eloquent testament to place. These books are often very narrative and appeal to readers who read for language, character, detail, and, of course, setting and description. Some are intimately personal, straying almost into memoir, while others are closer to detailed log notes and wander across subjects to mix with history, travel, essay (both political and personal), and true adventure. Accordingly, readers' advisory librarians should consider works in those subject areas as well as the titles listed in this section when making suggestions.

Arctic Dreams: Imagination and Desire in a Northern Landscape, by Barry Lopez

This lyrical ode to the wide, icy North is both alluring and instructive. Lopez spent many years in the Arctic and knows its landscape, flora, and inhabitants well. His work is a meandering journey through those cold plains, touching on history, environment, and change. With a lovely and rhythmic pace, Lopez begins his book in 1823 with the whaler *Cumbrian,* out of Hull, England, and seductively and subtly extends his story onward through time, walrus, ice, and the polar seas. He braids these strings into a fabric containing still more threads on mirages, wolverines, Eskimos, and Erik the Red. His book is about everything, singular and collective, to do with the North and his own journey into its dark and light places.

Read this book because it perfectly illustrates many elements of this type—respect for the land, the use of large, overarching metaphors for the writer's place within a landscape, vivid descriptions, and a focus on science, ecology, and place.

Suggest this book to readers interested in nature writing, especially those who want a stronger focus on the land and its inhabitants than on the writer's experiences. Consider pairing it with *The Future of Ice: A Journey into Cold,* and *This Cold Heaven: Seven Seasons in Greenland,* by Gretel Ehrlich, or with the novel *Voyage of the* Narwhal, by Andrea Barrett.

Literary or Historical Slants

Perhaps occupying the place where the hesitant science reader feels most comfortable, these books are literature tinged with science and science melded with history—books that explore, in a more familiar way, less familiar subjects. They are easy to read, deeply engaging, and cover all sorts of topics from the history of a scientific idea to the tragic effects of natural disasters.

The Map That Changed the World: William Smith and the Birth of Modern Geology, by Simon Winchester

In 1793 a canal digger discovered something that would change the face of history. He saw striations in the dirt he was excavating and noticed that the fossils in one striation were always the same and that they were also always different from fossils in another striation. Geology was born. William Smith, the poor son of a blacksmith, set off across the length of Britain looking at striations and fossils. He spent twenty years investigating the land and in 1815 published his brilliant map of the geology of Britain. It was huge, 8 feet tall and 6 feet wide, and brightly hand tinted. It was also the start of his downfall. Ostracized by the elite of the Geological Society, who published a poor imitation of his map, badly in debt, and struggling with a wife going insane, Smith fell into ruin. It was only much later, when events had passed him by, that Smith was given his due as the founder of geology. Winchester tells this fascinating tale with a warm tone and lively pace, inviting readers to share both the wonders of Smith's era and his inventive and brilliant work.

Read this book because it captures the essence of scientific history—it is inviting, explanatory, and character rich.

Suggest this book to readers interested in how things get discovered and to those who enjoy strongly narrative works that are quickly paced, character centered, and rich in detail. Readers might also enjoy *The Seashell on the Mountaintop: A Story of Science, Sainthood, and the Humble Genius Who Discovered a New History of the Earth*, by Alan Cutler, *Stealing God's Thunder: Benjamin Franklin's Lightning Rod and the Invention of America*, by Philip Dray, and *Longitude: The True Story of a Lone Genius Who Solved the Greatest Scientific Problem of His Time*, by Dava Sobel.

Biography and Memoir

Biography and memoir are both singular types of nonfiction and common to almost every subject area. The books are character focused and generally fall into the medium-to-high narrative range. The stories of the men and women who explore scientific theories make for fascinating reading and blend two key appeal points of science books: character and learning/experiencing. Many of the works listed at the end of this chapter under the literary or historical slants type are blends of scientific biography and history. Readers' advisory librarians should therefore check both lists since, depending on the reader, titles from both types work well together.

A Primate's Memoir: A Neuroscientist's Unconventional Life among the Baboons, by Robert M. Sapolsky

Robert Sapolsky starts his book with the intriguing line, "I joined the baboon troop during my twenty-first year. I had never planned to become a savanna baboon when I grew up; instead, I had always assumed I would become a mountain gorilla." And so begins this charming and funny exploration of life as a field scientist studying stress and baboons. Sapolsky is passionate about his work, and his memoir is equally heartfelt as it flows from topic to topic. Though he devotes a great deal of time to the science of primates, he also addresses the people and landscape of Africa, the critical and often devastating balance in caring for and studying animals (including a section on Dian Fossey), and his riotous learning curve when first introduced to the realities of science conducted in the bush: bugs, supply issues, more bugs, and meals made from canned mackerel. This compelling memoir is written with a lovely blend of whimsy and scientific rigor and offers readers a view into a world they will not soon forget.

Read this book to get a sense of the blend of personal story and scientific exploration that is at the heart of science memoirs.

Suggest this book to readers who enjoy funny tales, great descriptions, and story and character but still appreciate reading about the details of the working life of scientists. Readers may also enjoy *Awakenings*, by Oliver Sacks, which has the same graceful writing and intimate view into another world of science inquiry. *Swimming with Giants: My Encounters with Whales, Dolphins, and Seals,* by Anne Collet, is another option, a charming memoir about a marine biologist and her work in the wild.

Key Authors

The world of science writing is always changing as new theories emerge and new science stars take the stage. There are classic names in the field that always make worthwhile suggestions, and there is a core group of scientists, shifting slightly based on research schedules and interests, that constitutes a list of contemporary writers one should know. The works by the authors listed here are reliable to suggest to readers, can be used in displays and booklists, and should be considered part of any core collection.

Diane Ackerman	Richard Dawkins	Stephen Jay Gould
Amir D. Aczel	Jared Diamond	Brian Greene
Walter Alvarez	Richard Ellis	John Gribbin
Natalie Angier	Timothy Ferris	Stephen W. Hawking
David Attenborough	Richard P. Feynman	Robin Marantz Henig
Rick Bass	Richard Fortey	Hannah Holmes
David Bodanis	James Gleick	Steven Johnson
Paul Davies	Jane Goodall	Michio Kaku

Robert P. Kirshner	Steven Pinker	Neil deGrasse Tyson
Edward J. Larson	Roy Porter	Peter Ward
Alan Lightman	David Quammen	Jonathan Weiner
Barry Lopez	Richard Rhodes	Terry Tempest Williams
Peter Matthiessen	Matt Ridley	Edward O. Wilson
Bill McKibben	Oliver Sacks	Simon Winchester
John McPhee	Carl Sagan	Carl Zimmer
Sy Montgomery	Simon Singh	
Sherwin B. Nuland	Dava Sobel	

Selected Bibliography of Science Writing to Read and Suggest

Explanations

God's Equation: Einstein, Relativity, and the Expanding Universe, by Amir D. Aczel

T. rex and the Crater of Doom, by Walter Alvarez

Woman: An Intimate Geography (and her other work), by Natalie Angier

Life in the Undergrowth; The Private Life of Plants; The Life of Mammals; and *The Life of Birds,* by David Attenborough

Reading the Rocks: The Autobiography of the Earth, by Marcia Bjornerud

Electric Universe: The Shocking True Story of Electricity and *E = mc²: A Biography of the World's Most Famous Equation,* by David Bodanis

A Short History of Nearly Everything, by Bill Bryson

Out of Eden: An Odyssey of Ecological Invasion, by Alan Burdick

Coincidences, Chaos, and All That Math Jazz: Making Light of Weighty Ideas, by Edward B. Burger and Michael Starbird

Postcards from the Brain Museum: The Improbable Search for Meaning in the Matter of Famous Minds, by Brian Burrell

Songbird Journeys: Four Seasons in the Lives of Migratory Birds, by Miyoko Chu

The Hole in the Universe: How Scientists Peered over the Edge of Emptiness and Found Everything, by K. C. Cole

Teleportation: The Impossible Leap, by David Darling

The Fifth Miracle: The Search for the Origin and Meaning of Life (and his other work), by Paul Davies

Universe on a T-shirt: The Quest for the Theory of Everything, by Dan Falk

The Whole Shebang: A State-of-the-Universe(s) Report and *Coming of Age in the Milky Way* (and his other work), by Timothy Ferris

How to Dunk a Doughnut: The Science of Everyday Life, by Len Fisher

The Weather Makers: How Man Is Changing the Climate and What It Means for Life on Earth, by Tim Flannery

Earth: An Intimate History and *Trilobite: Eyewitness to Evolution* (and his other work), by Richard Fortey

The Coming Plague: Newly Emerging Diseases in a World Out of Balance, by Laurie Garrett

The First Human: The Race to Discover Our Earliest Ancestors, by Ann Gibbons

Chaos: Making a New Science (and his other work), by James Gleick

The Prophet and the Astronomer: A Scientific Journey to the End of Time and *The Dancing Universe: From Creation Myths to the Big Bang*, by Marcelo Gleiser

I Have Landed: The End of a Beginning in Natural History (and his other work), by Stephen Jay Gould

Animals in Translation: Using the Mysteries of Autism to Decode Animal Behavior, by Temple Grandin and Catherine Johnson

The Great Beyond: Higher Dimensions, Parallel Universes and the Extraordinary Search for a Theory of Everything, by Paul Halpern

A Brief History of Time and *The Universe in a Nutshell*, by Stephen W. Hawking

Einstein's Mirror and *The New Quantum Universe*, by Tony Hey and Patrick Walters

Suburban Safari: A Year on the Lawn and *The Secret Life of Dust: From the Cosmos to the Kitchen Counter, the Big Consequences of Little Things*, by Hannah Holmes

Mind Wide Open: Your Brain and the Neuroscience of Everyday Life and *Emergence: The Connected Lives of Ants, Brains, Cities, and Software*, by Steven Johnson

Lucy's Legacy: Sex and Intelligence in Human Evolution, by Alison Jolly

The Physics of Superheroes, by James Kakalios

Chances Are . . . : Adventures in Probability, by Michael Kaplan and Ellen Kaplan

Journey beyond Selene: Remarkable Expeditions Past Our Moon and to the Ends of the Solar System, by Jeffrey Kluger

Field Notes from a Catastrophe, by Elizabeth Kolbert

The Future of Ideas: The Fate of the Commons in a Connected World, by Lawrence Lessig

Programming the Universe: A Quantum Computer Scientist Takes On the Cosmos, by Seth Lloyd

Frozen Earth: The Once and Future Story of Ice Ages, by Doug MacDougall

Beating Back the Devil: On the Front Lines with the Disease Detectives of the Epidemic Intelligence Service, by Maryn McKenna

Enough: Staying Human in an Engineered Age (and his other work), by Bill McKibben

How We Die: Reflections on Life's Final Chapter (and his other work, including *How We Live*), by Sherwin B. Nuland

The Truth about Hormones, by Vivienne Parry

When the Rivers Run Dry: Water—The Defining Crisis of the Twenty-first Century, by Fred Pearce

The Demon in the Freezer and *The Hot Zone: A Terrifying True Story*, by Richard Preston

Monster of God: The Man-Eating Predator in the Jungles of History and the Mind and *The Song of the Dodo: Island Biogeography in an Age of Extinction* (and his other work), by David Quammen

Stiff: The Curious Lives of Human Cadavers and *Spook: Science Tackles the Afterlife*, by Mary Roach

An Anthropologist on Mars: Seven Paradoxical Tales and *The Man Who Mistook His Wife for a Hat, and Other Clinical Tales* (and his other work), by Oliver Sacks

Cosmos, by Carl Sagan

The Rock from Mars: A Detective Story on Two Planets, by Kathy Sawyer

Decoding the Universe: How the New Science of Information Is Explaining Everything in the Cosmos, from Our Brains to Black Holes, by Charles Seife

Big Bang: The Origin of the Universe and *The Code Book: The Science of Secrecy from Ancient Egypt to Quantum Cryptography*, by Simon Singh

Opening Skinner's Box: Great Psychological Experiments of the Twentieth Century, by Lauren Slater

Letters to a Young Mathematician, by Ian Stewart

Origins: Fourteen Billion Years of Cosmic Evolution, by Neil deGrasse Tyson and Donald Goldsmith

The Ape and the Sushi Master: Cultural Reflections of a Primatologist and *Our Inner Ape*, by Frans de Waal

Before the Dawn: Recovering the Lost History of Our Ancestors, by Nicholas Wade

Snowball Earth: The Story of the Great Global Catastrophe That Spawned Life as We Know It, by Gabrielle Walker

DNA: The Secret of Life, by James D. Watson

Darwin: The Indelible Stamp, edited by James D. Watson; also consider *From So Simple a Beginning: Darwin's Four Great Books*, edited by Edward O. Wilson

The Whale and the Supercomputer: On the Northern Front of Climate Change, by Charles Wohlforth

Parasite Rex: Inside the Bizarre World of Nature's Most Dangerous Creatures, by Carl Zimmer

Investigations

Endless Forms Most Beautiful: The New Science of Evo Devo, by Sean B. Carroll

The Ancestor's Tale: A Pilgrimage to the Dawn of Evolution (and his other work), by Richard Dawkins

Aquagenesis: The Origin and Evolution of Life in the Seas (and his other work), by Richard Ellis

Six Easy Pieces: Essentials of Physics Explained by Its Most Brilliant Teacher, by Richard P. Feynman (start here, and then move on to his other work)

The Elegant Universe: Superstrings, Hidden Dimensions, and the Quest for the Ultimate Theory and *The Fabric of the Cosmos: Space, Time, and the Texture of Reality*, by Brian Greene

Deep Simplicity: Bringing Order to Chaos and Complexity (and his other work), by John Gribbin

Parallel Worlds: A Journey through Creation, Higher Dimensions, and the Future of the Cosmos and *Hyperspace: A Scientific Odyssey through Parallel Universes, Time Warps, and the 10th Dimension*, by Michio Kaku

The Plausibility of Life: Resolving Darwin's Dilemma, by Marc W. Kirschner and John C. Gerhart

The Extravagant Universe: Exploding Stars, Dark Energy, and the Accelerating Cosmos, by Robert P. Kirshner

Life on a Young Planet: The First Three Billion Years of Evolution on Earth, by Andrew H. Knoll

Power, Sex, Suicide: Mitochondria and the Meaning of Life, by Nick Lane

Microcosmos: Four Billion Years of Evolution from Our Microbial Ancestors, by Lynn Margulis

The Road to Reality: A Complete Guide to the Laws of the Universe (and his other work), by Roger Penrose

The Language Instinct: How the Mind Creates Language and *The Blank Slate: The Modern Denial of Human Nature* (and his other work), by Steven Pinker

Warped Passages: Unraveling the Mysteries of the Universe's Hidden Dimensions, by Lisa Randall

The Red Queen: Sex and the Evolution of Human Nature; Genome: The Autobiography of a Species in 23 Chapters; and *Nature via Nurture: Genes, Experience, and What Makes Us Human*, by Matt Ridley

Into the Cool: Energy Flow, Thermodynamics, and Life, by Eric D. Schneider and Dorion Sagan

Does God Play Dice? The New Mathematics of Chaos, by Ian Stewart

The Cosmic Landscape: String Theory and the Illusion of Intelligent Design, by Leonard Susskind

The Future of Life; On Human Nature; and *Consilience: The Unity of Knowledge* (and his other work), by Edward O. Wilson

At the Water's Edge: Fish with Fingers, Whales with Legs, and How Life Came Ashore but Then Went Back to Sea, by Carl Zimmer

Nature and Natural History

Desert Solitaire: A Season in the Wilderness, by Edward Abbey

Cultivating Delight: A Natural History of My Garden, by Diane Ackerman

Land of Little Rain, by Mary Hunter Austin

The Ninemile Wolves (and his other work), by Rick Bass

The Outermost House: A Year of Life on the Great Beach of Cape Cod, by Henry Beston

Robbing the Bees: A Biography of Honey—The Sweet Liquid Gold That Seduced the World, by Holley Bishop

In the Shadows of the Morning: Essays on Wild Lands, Wild Waters, and a Few Untamed People, by Philip Caputo

Silent Spring, by Rachel L. Carson

The Devil's Teeth: A True Story of Survival and Obsession among America's Great White Sharks, by Susan Casey

The Secret Knowledge of Water: Discovering the Essence of the American Desert (and his other work), by Craig Childs

Silent Snow: The Slow Poisoning of the Arctic, by Marla Cone

The Voyage of the Beagle, by Charles Darwin

Pilgrim at Tinker Creek, by Annie Dillard

My Story as Told by Water: Confessions, Druidic Rants, Reflections, Bird-Watchings, Fish-Stalkings, Visions, Songs and Prayers Refracting Light, from Living Rivers, in the Age of the Industrial Dark, by David James Duncan

The Future of Ice: A Journey into Cold and *This Cold Heaven: Seven Seasons in Greenland*, by Gretel Ehrlich

Sweetness and Light: The Mysterious History of the Honeybee, by Hattie Ellis

Throwim Way Leg: Tree-Kangaroos, Possums, and Penis Gourds, by Tim Flannery

Gorillas in the Mist, by Dian Fossey

The Swamp: The Everglades, Florida, and the Politics of Paradise, by Michael Grunwald

In the Company of Light, by John Hay

PrairyErth: An Epic History of the Tallgrass Prairie Country, by William Least Heat-Moon

Bird Songs of the Mesozoic: A Day Hiker's Guide to the Nearby Wild, by David Brendan Hopes

Waiting for Aphrodite: Journeys into the Time before Bones, by Sue Hubbell

Kangaroo Dreaming: An Australian Wildlife Odyssey, by Edward Kanze

Out There: In the Wild in a Wired Age, by Ted Kerasote

Local Wonders: Seasons in the Bohemian Alps, by Ted Kooser

The Singing Life of Birds: The Art and Science of Listening to Birdsong, by Donald Kroodsma

Big Muddy Blues: True Tales and Twisted Politics along Lewis and Clark's Missouri River, by Bill Lambrecht

Stinging Trees and Wait-a-Whiles: Confessions of a Rainforest Biologist, by William Laurance

A Sand County Almanac, by Aldo Leopold

Arctic Dreams: Imagination and Desire in a Northern Landscape (and his other work), by Barry Lopez

The Snow Leopard and *End of the Earth: Voyages to Antarctica* (and his other work), by Peter Matthiessen (see the travel chapter as well)

Annals of the Former World and *The Pine Barrens,* by John McPhee (and his other nature writing; McPhee is diverse and writes on several nonfiction subjects)

The Anthropology of Turquoise: Reflections on Desert, Sea, Stone, and Sky, by Ellen Meloy

Carnivorous Nights: On the Trail of the Tasmanian Tiger, by Margaret Mittelbach and Michael Crewdson

Journey of the Pink Dolphins: An Amazon Quest, by Sy Montgomery

Never Cry Wolf and *High Latitudes: An Arctic Journey* (and his other work), by Farley Mowat; also suggest *Farley: The Life of Farley Mowat,* by James King

John Muir: Nature Writings (and his other work), by John Muir

The Island Within, by Richard Nelson

The Orchid Thief: A True Story of Beauty and Obsession, by Susan Orlean

Exploration of the Colorado River and Its Canyons, by John Wesley Powell

Where Bigfoot Walks: Crossing the Dark Divide, by Robert Michael Pyle

Lost Mountain: A Year in the Vanishing Wilderness, by Erik Reece

Voyage of the Turtle: In Pursuit of the Earth's Last Dinosaur, by Carl Safina

The Cockroach Papers: A Compendium of History and Lore, by Richard Schweid

Rats: Observations on the History and Habitat of the City's Most Unwanted Inhabitants, by Robert Sullivan

On the Wing: To the Edge of the Earth with the Peregrine Falcon, by Alan Tennant

Walden, or Life in the Woods, by Henry David Thoreau

The Abstract Wild, by Jack Turner

*The Eighth Continent: Life, Death, and Discovery in the Lost World of
    Madagascar*, by Peter Tyson

The Golden Spruce: A True Story of Myth, Madness, and Greed, by John Vaillant

Return to Wild America: A Yearlong Search for the Continent's Natural Soul, by
    Scott Weidensaul

Red: Passion and Patience in the Desert (and her other work), by Terry
    Tempest Williams

Literary or Historical Slants

A Natural History of the Senses (and her other work), by Diane Ackerman

The Riddle of the Compass: The Invention That Changed the World and *Fermat's
    Last Theorem: Unlocking the Secret of an Ancient Mathematical Problem*, by
    Amir D. Aczel

Madame Bovary's Ovaries: A Darwinian Look at Literature, by David P. Barash
    and Nanelle R. Barash

The Great Influenza: The Epic Story of the Deadliest Plague in History, by John
    M. Barry

The Oracle: The Lost Secrets and Hidden Messages of Ancient Delphi, by William
    J. Broad

Under a Flaming Sky: The Great Hinckley Firestorm of 1894, by Daniel James
    Brown

Terrible Lizard: The First Dinosaur Hunters and the Birth of a New Science
    and *Space Race: The Epic Battle between America and the Soviet Union for
    Dominion of Space*, by Deborah Cadbury

Close to Shore: A True Story of Terror in an Age of Innocence, by Michael
    Capuzzo

*The Fly in the Cathedral: How a Group of Cambridge Scientists Won the
    International Race to Split the Atom*, by Brian Cathcart

A Man on the Moon, by Andrew Chaikin

*Kepler's Witch: An Astronomer's Discovery of Cosmic Order amid Religious War,
    Political Intrigue, and the Heresy Trial of His Mother*, by James Connor

*The Seashell on the Mountaintop: A Story of Science, Sainthood, and the Humble
    Genius Who Discovered a New History of the Earth*, by Alan Cutler

One River: Explorations and Discoveries in the Amazon Rain Forest (and his other work), by Wade Davis

The Living Great Lakes: Searching for the Heart of the Inland Seas, by Jerry Dennis

Yellow Fever: A Deadly Disease Poised to Kill Again, by James L. Dickerson

Reef Madness: Charles Darwin, Alexander Agassiz, and the Meaning of Coral, by David Dobbs

Plundering Paradise: The Hand of Man on the Galapagos Islands, by Michael D'Orso

Stealing God's Thunder: Benjamin Franklin's Lightning Rod and the Invention of America, by Philip Dray

The Devil and the Disappearing Sea: A True Story about the Aral Sea Catastrophe, by Rob Ferguson

Mauve: How One Man Invented a Color That Changed the World, by Simon Garfield

On Being Born and Other Difficulties (and his other work), by F. Gonzalez-Crussi

Reason for Hope: A Spiritual Journey and *In the Shadow of Man,* by Jane Goodall

The Red Hourglass, by Gordon Grice

The Invention of Clouds: How an Amateur Meteorologist Forged the Language of the Skies, by Richard Hamblyn

Five Quarts: A Personal and Natural History of Blood and *Sleep Demons: An Insomniac's Memoir,* by Bill Hayes

Pandora's Baby: How the First Test Tube Baby Sparked the Reproductive Revolution, by Robin Marantz Henig

13 Dreams Freud Never Had: The New Mind Science, by J. Allan Hobson

End of Science: Facing the Limits of Knowledge in the Twilight of the Scientific Age, by John Horgan

Broadsides from the Other Orders: A Book of Bugs, by Sue Hubbell

Defining the Wind: The Beaufort Scale, and How a 19th-Century Admiral Turned Science into Poetry, by Scott Huler

A World on Fire: A Heretic, an Aristocrat, and the Race to Discover Oxygen, by Joe Jackson

Quest for the African Dinosaurs: Ancient Roots of the Modern World, by Louis Jacobs

Aspirin: The Remarkable Story of a Wonder Drug, by Diarmuid Jeffreys

Mind Wide Open: Your Brain and the Neuroscience of Everyday Life, by Steven Johnson

The Nothing That Is: A Natural History of Zero and *The Art of the Infinite: The Pleasures of Mathematics*, by Robert Kaplan

The Great Mortality: An Intimate History of the Black Death, the Most Devastating Plague of All Time, by John Kelly

Splendid Solution: Jonas Salk and the Conquest of Polio, by Jeffrey Kluger

Hope Diamond: The Legendary History of a Cursed Gem, by Richard Kurin

Evolution: The Remarkable History of a Scientific Theory and *Summer for the Gods: The Scopes Trial and America's Continuing Debate over Science and Religion* (and his other work), by Edward J. Larson

Isaac's Storm: A Man, a Time, and the Deadliest Hurricane in History, by Erik Larson

The Mold in Dr. Florey's Coat: The Story of Penicillin and the Modern Age of Medical Miracles, by Eric Lax

Napoleon's Buttons: 17 Molecules That Changed History, by Penny Le Couteur and Jay Burreson

Descent: The Heroic Discovery of the Abyss, by Brad Matsen

Every Second Counts: The Race to Transplant the First Human Heart, by Donald McRae

Empire of the Stars: Obsession, Friendship, and Betrayal in the Quest for Black Holes, by Arthur I. Miller

Riding Rockets: The Outrageous Tales of a Space Shuttle Astronaut, by Mike Mullane

The Lost Dinosaurs of Egypt: The Astonishing and Unlikely True Story of One of the Twentieth Century's Greatest Paleontological Discoveries, by William Nothdurft

Secrets of the Savanna: Twenty-three Years in the African Wilderness Unraveling the Mysteries of Elephants and People and *Cry of the Kalahari*, by Mark James Owens and Cordelia Dykes Owens

The Grand Contraption: The World as Myth, Number, and Chance, by David Park

Driving Mr. Albert: A Trip across America with Einstein's Brain, by Michael Paterniti

The Evolution of Useful Things: How Everyday Artifacts—from Forks and Pins to Paper Clips and Zippers—Came to Be as They Are (and his other work), by Henry Petroski

The Botany of Desire: A Plant's-Eye View of the World, by Michael Pollan

Flesh in the Age of Reason: The Modern Foundations of Body and Soul (and his other work), by Roy Porter

Before the Fallout: From Marie Curie to Hiroshima, by Diana Preston

First Light: The Search for the Edge of the Universe, by Richard Preston

Walking Zero: Discovering Cosmic Space and Time along the Prime Meridian (and his other work), by Chet Raymo

The Man Who Found Time: James Hutton and the Discovery of Earth's Antiquity, by Jack Repcheck

Why Birds Sing: A Journey through the Mystery of Bird Song, by David Rothenberg

Monkeyluv, and Other Essays on Our Lives as Animals, by Robert M. Sapolsky

The Genome War: How Craig Venter Tried to Capture the Code of Life and Save the World, by James Shreeve

Fermat's Enigma: The Epic Quest to Solve the World's Greatest Mathematical Problem, by Simon Singh

Longitude: The True Story of a Lone Genius Who Solved the Greatest Scientific Problem of His Time, by Dava Sobel

The Noonday Demon: An Atlas of Depression, by Andrew Solomon

On the Wing: To the Edge of the Earth with the Peregrine Falcon, by Alan Tennant

Everything and More: A Compact History of Infinity, by David Foster Wallace

Gorgon: Paleontology, Obsession, and the Greatest Catastrophe in Earth's History, by Peter Ward

The Double Helix: A Personal Account of the Discovery of the Structure of DNA, by James D. Watson

His Brother's Keeper: A Story from the Edge of Medicine and *The Beak of the Finch: A Story of Evolution in Our Time* (and his other work), by Jonathan Weiner

The Map That Changed the World: William Smith and the Birth of Modern Geology, by Simon Winchester

What Einstein Told His Cook: Kitchen Science Explained and *What Einstein Told His Cook 2: The Sequel—Further Adventures in Kitchen Science,* by Robert L. Wolke

Soul Made Flesh: The Discovery of the Brain—and How It Changed the World, by Carl Zimmer

Biography and Memoir

American Prometheus: The Triumph and Tragedy of J. Robert Oppenheimer, by
  Kai Bird and Martin J. Sherwin

Curious Minds: How a Child Becomes a Scientist, edited by John Brockman

Swimming with Giants: My Encounters with Whales, Dolphins, and Seals, by
  Anne Collet

Hot Lights, Cold Steel: Life, Death and Sleepless Nights in a Surgeon's First Years,
  by Michael J. Collins

Obsessive Genius: The Inner World of Marie Curie, by Barbara Goldsmith

Incompleteness: The Proof and Paradox of Kurt Gödel, by Rebecca Goldstein

*The Demon under the Microscope: From Battlefield Hospitals to Nazi Labs, One
  Doctor's Heroic Search for the World's First Miracle Drug,* by Thomas Hager

A Life of Discovery: Michael Faraday, Giant of the Scientific Revolution, by James
  Hamilton

First Man: The Life of Neil A. Armstrong, by James R. Hansen

*Audubon's Elephant: America's Greatest Naturalist and the Making of "The Birds
  of America,"* by Duff Hart-Davis

Rocket Boys and *The Coalwood Way,* by Homer Hickam

An Unquiet Mind: A Memoir of Moods and Madness, by Kay Redfield Jamison

*Miss Leavitt's Stars: The Untold Story of the Woman Who Discovered How to
  Measure the Universe,* by George Johnson

Rosalind Franklin: The Dark Lady of DNA, by Brenda Maddox

*A Beautiful Mind: The Life of Mathematical Genius and Nobel Laureate John
  Nash,* by Sylvia Nasar

Tigers in Red Weather: A Quest to See the Last Wild Tigers, by Ruth Padel

*The Reluctant Mr. Darwin: An Intimate Portrait of Charles Darwin and the
  Making of His Theory of Evolution,* by David Quammen

Ecology of a Cracker Childhood, by Janisse Ray

John James Audubon: The Making of an American and *The Making of the Atomic
  Bomb,* by Richard Rhodes

Francis Crick: Discoverer of the Genetic Code, by Matt Ridley

King of Infinite Space: Donald Coxeter, the Man Who Saved Geometry,
  by Siobhan Roberts

The Humboldt Current: Nineteenth-Century Exploration and the Roots of American Environmentalism, by Aaron Sachs

A Primate's Memoir: A Neuroscientist's Unconventional Life among the Baboons, by Robert M. Sapolsky

On Call: A Doctor's Days and Nights in Residency, by Emily R. Transue

The Right Stuff, by Tom Wolfe

Resources and Awards

To get a sense of who is writing what, a scientific survey is called for. Luckily, readers' advisory librarians have ready-made lab results in the form of the *Best American Science Writing* series and the *Best American Science and Nature Writing* series. These anthologies include essays and articles collected from the best selection of writing during the year and illustrate the breath of topics and the varying types of approaches used in science writing. Other good resources are magazines such as *Scientific American; Natural History; Science News; Audubon;* and *Discover.* All have articles on popular science topics and often have reviews of major science books. In addition, PBS has accessible programs on scientific topics that are narrated or hosted by major science authors and podcasts such as *NPR: Hmmm . . . Krulwich on Science* and *NOVA scienceNOW.* These offer clear explanations and introductions to key subject areas.

Although science books are generally widely reviewed, it is often hard for a readers' advisory librarian who is not an expert in the various fields to know when one book is better than another. To help ensure that one is aware of the best writing, readers' advisory librarians should monitor the major science awards.

ROYAL SOCIETY PRIZES FOR SCIENCE BOOKS

The Royal Society Prizes, from the United Kingdom, focus on readable and accessible science books, which makes them an ideal resource for readers' advisory librarians. See http://www.sciencebookprizes.com/home_welcome .htm.

NATIONAL ACADEMIES COMMUNICATION AWARDS

The National Academies, which consist of the National Academy of Science, the National Academy of Engineering, the Institute of Medicine, and the

National Research Council, present a National Academies Communication Award each year to the author of an adult book who has demonstrated excellence in writing in an area of science. See http://www.keckfutures.org and click on Communication Award Winners.

NOTABLE BOOK LIST

The American Library Association's Notable Books Council sometimes includes general science books on its listing of the most notable books for adults. Since part of the mandate of the council is to select books that make a specialized topic accessible to the general reader, any science book that is listed is one that should have wide appeal. See http://www.ala.org/ala/rusa/rusaprotools/rusanotable/notablebooks.htm.

NOBA AWARD

The National Outdoor Book Award (NOBA) is a good place to look for nature titles. Awards are given in nine categories, one of which is outdoor literature. See http://www.isu.edu/outdoor/bookpol.htm.

There are a host of other science awards that are worth noting, including those given by these organizations:

American Institute of Physics, http://www.aip.org/aip/writing/index.html

History of Science Society, http://www.hssonline.org/society/awards/

Los Angeles Times Science and Technology Awards, http://www.latimes.com/extras/bookprizes/winners_byaward.html#science

National Association of Science Writers, http://www.nasw.org

5

MEMOIRS

Memoir is a particular, and lovely, form of nonfiction. It is a slice of life, remembered and recounted as much for the author as for the reader. The recollections can be quiet or significant, small daily battles or huge triumphs, but the point is to share a personal journey and in so doing widen out the story, like ripples on a pond, to make the individual universal.

Memory is a dicey thing, and what writers choose to remember or sequester from consciousness shapes the stories they have to tell. Many memoirs focus on childhood, an endlessly soupy place to try to gain perspective. Still others are coming-of-age stories or those of growing older. Memoirs can take many forms and are particularly slippery when it comes to content. Some skate close to fiction, using pace and story to craft memory, while others read like essays or captivating reporting and have a rhythm and pattern all their own.

Memoir is often the best way to share an experience, so writers employ variations of the form to relate all types of stories. This is why almost every other subject chapter in this book has a section related to memoir. Be they involved in food or science, or caught up in a crime, trip, or adventure, everyone has a story to tell. For example, in this book I list *Julie and Julia: 365 Days, 524 Recipes, 1 Tiny Apartment Kitchen* in the chapter on food and Robert M. Sapolsky's wonderful *A Primate's Memoir: A Neuroscientist's Unconventional Life among the Baboons* with the science books. But there are also amazing and luminous memoirs that do not relate directly enough to a subject to be included in any specific subject chapter. These memoirs, and a general consideration of the type, are included here.

What Readers Enjoy in These Books

Memoir is so personal on the part of the writer that it is little wonder it is personal to the reader as well. There are many pleasures in the pages of these books. Fans read based on interest, fancy, and word of mouth. They read to learn, observe, and identify with characters, and they read for endless other ineffable reasons that are individual to them at a particular time in their lives.

Some readers are fascinated by characters and enjoy reading character-centered accounts. As with other subjects, character study holds particular sway with readers since the characters are real and not imaginative creations. This is particularly notable in memoir. Reporters and some biographers do get to spend a great deal of time with their subjects, but nothing can substitute for living a life alongside your brother, mother, or lover and then writing about them. And, of course, nothing matches writing about yourself. The immediacy and intimacy the author brings to character description is often the major appeal of this type of nonfiction.

Other readers enjoy the gossipy connection they feel when reading memoirs. The personal becomes universal to readers, who can share the author's feelings and experiences of growing up in a family of crooks, seeing a beloved family member die, or struggling to make a home for an adopted child. Readers are able to experience lives they both know and could never dream of, through the lens of someone who understands just what that particular experience is like. Similar to the most engaging fiction, memoirs allow readers to escape into another's life with the added voyeuristic pleasure of knowing that life actually exists.

Another appeal of memoir is the opportunity readers have to experience an event similar to one they have suffered themselves, but from the distance of another's life and perspective. This experiential reading can be comforting and cathartic and helps explain the reason there are so many different memoir groupings—adoption accounts, medical stories, recovery memoirs, and immigrant experiences, just to name a few. Authors, it seems, as well as readers need the release of reexperiencing and controlling the story. The comfort one can take in witnessing a similar event in a different way cannot be understated. This consolation is directly related to the appeal of learning/experiencing.

Finally, readers enjoy memoirs for the appeal elements of language, setting, detail, and tone that are so prevalent in this type of nonfiction. Often readers can find descriptions of people, places, and events that are rendered in exquisitely crafted prose, laugh-out-loud funny romps, or darkly mournful elegies. Readers who enjoy detail can find an endless array of descriptions of careers, marriages, scams, parties, fights, and other fascinating accounts of real-life experiences. They can find memoirs to match any mood they may be in, from safe and cozy to violent and wicked. Whatever the draw, readers enjoy these books tremendously, and readers' advisory librarians should understand and become familiar with the type. Since the best examples of memoir are enlivened with amazing writing, fascinating subject matter, and enlightening detail, it should not be at all hard to find something to enjoy.

One last note. The occurrence of some memoirs turning out to be more fictional than factual raises a question that could well be applied to many other nonfiction subjects, travel and true adventure chief among them. Just how much can be made up before nonfiction becomes fiction? Many works of nonfiction use the tools of narrative to tell a story that is true or that is expected to be true. Yet those very devices lend themselves to the fictionalization of nonfiction. Just as nonfiction exhibits a continuum of narrative states, from the highly creative to the more factual, the precision of any given piece of nonfiction appears somewhere on a factual versus embellished continuum as well. Some writers believe strongly in reporting what happened as it happened, while others see little harm in creating one character based on a collection of real people or placing a Paris flower seller on a street corner rather than inside the store where the author actually encountered her. The debate will continue whenever the veracity of a blockbuster book is called into question, but readers' advisory librarians simply serve readers, and the readers decide what degree of accuracy is important to them.

Types of Books

Memoirs are a distinctive and individual style of writing that stand alone as a type without a need for further subclassification. But to aid the readers' advisory librarian in working with such a rich but broad collection, I include four annotated title examples and three grouping of memoirs based on their subjects in this chapter. These are meant to illustrate ways readers' advisory librarians can work with memoir by linking subject, title, and appeal.

Benchmark Books to Read and Suggest

Memoir is not a subject area from which it is hard to find something to suggest. Rather, readers' advisory librarians may have the opposite problem— finding it difficult to narrow the field of choices. It helps in such situations to use one popular or notable title as a touchstone and then branch off from there. The four books listed below can serve as touchstones for four popular memoir areas (childhood and coming of age, different cultural points of view, recovery, loss of a loved one) and assist librarians trying to contextualize the vast world of memoir. They represent a wide range of writing styles, treat diverse subjects, and illustrate how the different nonfiction elements (narrative, subject, type, and appeal) shape a reading experience.

Angela's Ashes: A Memoir, by Frank McCourt

Memoirs of childhood are commonplace, but a memoir as luminous and generous as McCourt's is rare. Without a whiff of self-pity and with an effortless grace, McCourt tracks his life: the courtship of his Irish immigrant parents in New York City during the Depression to their move back to Ireland, his childhood in the Limerick slums, his Catholic education, and his ultimate escape from it all. He spares the reader nothing. His life was miserable. He was achingly poor, abused, neglected, and surrounded by death. In a tiny, rat-infested flat, he and his family barely got by. His father rarely worked and drank what small wages he earned. His mother was depressed and too often helpless. McCourt lost two brothers and a sister, his first girl, and countless others. In sheer brilliant writing, he melds the relentless dark of his life with humor and forgiveness and creates a story that holds readers enthralled.

Read this book because it is simply one of the best memoirs yet written and allows you to see how engrossing a story-based memoir can be. It also illustrates the highest expressions of many appeal elements; it is richly observed, employs a rhythmic and subtle use of language, is full of detail, and has a strong sense of place and time.

Suggest this book to readers who like strong narratives rich in language and location. Because the qualities of memoir are so author specific, sometimes the best suggestion is simply more of the same. McCourt has written two other memoirs—*'Tis* (a sequel to *Angela's Ashes*) and *Teacher Man,* which make natural connections for readers. His brother, Malachy McCourt, has written two memoirs of his own: *A Monk Swimming* recounts his childhood and therefore may be of interest to *Angela's Ashes* fans, and *Singing My Him Song* is more a personal reflection of his adult life. Fiction titles to consider include *The Colony of Unrequited Dreams,* by Wayne Johnston, *A Goat's Song,* by Dermot Healy, and *The Woman Who Walked into Doors* and *A Star Called Henry,* by Roddy Doyle.

Reading "Lolita" in Tehran: A Memoir in Books, by Azar Nafisi

Employing a wonderfully readable mix of memoir, literary theory, and social and cultural history, Nafisi's story is both heartening and enraging. After resigning her job as a university professor in Tehran because of the repressive rules of the regime, she founded what once would have been called a literary salon. But this was not a tea, cake, and mannered social gathering. Nafisi and her seven female students met in secret, read photocopied pages of banned books (works of Fitzgerald, Austen, and James), and discussed their lives as women and readers in an Islamic republic. While the Iran-Iraq war ground on, lives were being judged by morality squads, and rhetoric about the Great Satan was ratcheted up by both the United States and Iran, Nafisi tried to hold on to herself and help her students do the same.

Read this book because it is a beautiful example of the reflection aspect of memoir and blends several types of works and subjects together, thus illustrating the multilayered reasons readers are drawn to certain titles.

Suggest this book to those interested in literature, history, and women's studies. The book is elegantly written, rich in perspective, and a treasure of learning/experiencing. It matches particularly well in terms of subject, narrative, and perspective with *Persepolis: The Story of a Childhood,* by Marjane Satrapi, and readers may also find that *The Kite Runner,* a novel by Khaled Hosseini, makes good pairing in terms of exploring a culture at war via its characters. Finally, for readers caught up in both the art and the female perspective, *A Room of One's Own,* by Virginia Woolf, might work as well.

Dry, by Augusten Burroughs

The author of the horrifying but zanily funny *Running with Scissors* and the self-referential confessional memoir *Possible Side Effects* also wrote a skewered tale that riffs off the conventions of recovery memoirs. *Dry* finds Burroughs safely employed at an ad agency but drinking madly, using expensive cologne on his tongue in an attempt to mask the stench of his indulgence, and embarrassing both coworkers and clients. Thus, his stint at a Minnesota detox center is required. Here readers get to experience Burroughs's wit and sharply observant eye in perhaps their best setting—for there is certainly plenty to mock and much to stupefy in group therapy sessions and admittance papers. Soon enough, Burroughs is back in Manhattan living the sober life, but he finds the straight and narrow a difficult path when he becomes involved with crack addicts and his best friend becomes ill with AIDS.

Read this book because it illustrates the zany, caustic, "me"-motivated memoir perfectly and because Burroughs is one of its best practitioners.

Suggest this book to readers looking for the edgy, pop, and witty side of memoirs and to those interested in recovery stories. Readers wanting more recovery works might like *A Drinking Life: A Memoir,* by Pete Hamill, and

Drinking: A Love Story, by Caroline Knapp. For readers after more of the zany and funny aspects of Burroughs, suggest *We Thought You Would Be Prettier: True Tales of the Dorkiest Girl Alive,* by Laurie Notaro, and *Dress Your Family in Corduroy and Denim,* by David Sedaris.

A Heartbreaking Work of Staggering Genius, by Dave Eggers

Dave Eggers helped define the hip-literate mode of experimental writing that has influenced much of what is published today. In his memoir, he both practiced the experimental style and proved that brilliance can compensate for the glib and self-aware. Questioning the very heart of what memoir is, memory, and suggesting early on that the book has its internal flaws, Eggers nevertheless has created a memoir masterpiece. When he was twenty-two, Eggers lost both his mother and father to different types of cancer and became the de facto guardian of his eight-year-old brother. His story of raising Toph, coping with grief, and forming an internal identity is engaging, funny, tender, and beautifully wrought.

Read this book because it defined a moment when memoir (and much of literature) changed and because it typifies the coming-of-age story so well.

Suggest this book to those interested in great and inventive storytelling and in works of self-definition. Readers may also enjoy *The Discomfort Zone: A Personal History,* by Jonathan Franzen, and *The Tender Bar,* by J. R. Moehringer.

Three Examples of Various Subject Groupings

Female Memoirs of Place: Iran

Journey from the Land of No: A Girlhood Caught in Revolutionary Iran, by Roya Hakakian

Even after All This Time: A Story of Love, Revolution, and Leaving Iran, by Afschineh Latifi

Lipstick Jihad: A Memoir of Growing Up Iranian in America and American in Iran, by Azadeh Moaveni

Reading "Lolita" in Tehran: A Memoir in Books, by Azar Nafisi

Persepolis: The Story of a Childhood and *Persepolis 2: The Story of a Return,* by Marjane Satrapi

The appeal here for many readers is the female perspective of a society where women are subject to laws and dictates so different from those of

Western culture. For readers either from Iran or who are the children or grand-children of Iranian immigrants, the appeal is firmly based in location: what is the land of their ancestry really like? Each memoir also has its own particular appeal beyond that of culture or country. *Lipstick Jihad* is particularly percep-tive when recounting the struggle to reconcile two cultures and forge a sense of identity; *Persepolis* is a brilliant example of the graphic form of storytelling; and *Journey from the Land of No* recounts prejudice and the strength it takes to overcome its effects. Together these books create a nuanced portrait of being female and offer a perspective on place that gives readers interested in the topic a myriad collection of viewpoints.

Writers on Death

The Year of Magical Thinking, by Joan Didion

The Best Day the Worst Day: Life with Jane Kenyon, by Donald Hall

Name All the Animals: A Memoir, by Alison Smith

Mourning literature has a strong tradition in American letters, and when accomplished authors suffer loss, they raise the bar on accounts of bereave-ment. The appeal for many readers is the articulation of their own feelings of grief in ways they could not have expressed as eloquently or as clearly. For readers who are still struggling to deal with the grief and loss of a loved one, the comfort of having a second voice express emotion is important. Other readers enjoy the lyrical writing, the observant eye, and the cathartic journey. All three of these memoirs are written in amazingly beautiful language as they detail the destruction death has on the living soul, with wide degrees of difference. Alison Smith brings to the story the viewpoint of a younger sister losing her older brother. Joan Didion's memoir of the loss of her husband of close to forty years is lyrical and expressive. Poet Donald Hall's account of the loss of his poet-wife Jane Kenyon is unsparing, generous, and wrenching. Readers' advisory librarians could also suggest *Without,* the book of poetry Donald Hall wrote about his wife's death. Readers in need of either comfort or articulation will find that these three books offer solace and support, and readers simply in search of amazing writing and heartfelt emotion will find both.

Memoirs of Parents

Another Bullshit Night in Suck City: A Memoir, by Nick Flynn

Them: A Memoir of Parents, by Francine du Plessix Gray

The Glass Castle: A Memoir, by Jeannette Walls

Oh the Glory of It All, by Sean Wilsey

Many authors seem to be driven to write about their parents, as this list of just some parental memoirs illustrates. Everyone carries baggage from childhood, but writers have the skill and platform to vent in public about the abuses of their past. The appeal of these books includes the voyeuristic fascination one receives from witnessing another's life, the comfort of knowing your own parents were not so bad after all, or the strangely helpful reassurance of knowing that you are not alone in suffering a horrible childhood. The writing in all four books is stellar, two brilliantly constructed and two raw, stylish, and realistic. The details range from overwhelmingly sad or frightening to oddly affirming. Jeannette Walls and Francine du Plessix Gray both write beautifully rendered memoirs about parents who were neglectful and far from nice, but whom they loved—a love that shows through in their compelling stories. Nick Flynn's memoir of his father is stark and experimental and resonates with the questions of perspective, while Sean Wilsey's tale of his horrible trio of parents (mother, father, and stepmother) is witty, harsh, and unflinching. Taken together, readers get a tour of different perspectives on family and family types, which may bring with it the wisdom of Tolstoy: all unhappy families are indeed different in their own ways.

Key Authors

Memoir is a funny subsection of the nonfiction world. In addition to being spread out across different subject areas and not really lending itself to further classification, there are few writers who actually write only memoir or write more than one memoir—perhaps because the slices of their lives they do share are so forthright and honest that they do not feel compelled to write another, perhaps because there is only the one story to tell, or perhaps because they move on to other forms of literature. Whatever the case, there are only a handful of authors writing multiple memoirs. This list includes both the few major memoirists who have written more than one story and those single-book authors whose work is so highly regarded that even one title is sufficient to remain vital years from now.

This list of authors should be used in conjunction with the longer bibliography below to aid in building and weeding collections and when making suggestions to readers. The area of memoir is one that is constantly being bombarded with new publications, and it is important that libraries keep and collect the key authors in the field. This list can aid in that endeavor and provide patrons with a larger landscape of reading experiences. It can also serve to build the comfort level of readers' advisory librarians dealing with this vast subject area.

Isabel Allende	Annie Dillard	James McBride
Maya Angelou	Dave Eggers	Frank McCourt
Russell Baker	Nick Flynn	Malachy McCourt
Judy Blunt	Alexandra Fuller	Nuala O'Faolain
Rick Bragg	Henry Louis Gates Jr.	Janisse Ray
Augusten Burroughs	Katharine Graham	Helene Stapinski
Frank Conroy	Mary Karr	Jeannette Walls
Jill Ker Conway	Haven Kimmel	Tobias Wolff
Joan Didion	Jennifer Lauck	Richard Wright

Selected Bibliography of Memoirs to Read and Suggest

The Language of Baklava: A Memoir, by Diana Abu-Jaber

A Border Passage: From Cairo to America—A Woman's Journey, by Leila Ahmed

The $64 Tomato: How One Man Nearly Lost His Sanity, Spent a Fortune, and Endured an Existential Crisis in the Quest for the Perfect Garden, by William Alexander

My Invented Country: A Memoir and *Paula,* by Isabel Allende

Two or Three Things I Know for Sure, by Dorothy Allison

Let Me Finish, by Roger Angell

I Know Why the Caged Bird Sings (and her other work), by Maya Angelou

A Woman in Berlin: Eight Weeks in the Conquered City—A Diary, by Anonymous

Limbo: A Memoir, by A. Manette Ansay

The Afterlife: A Memoir, by Donald Antrim

The Story of a Life: A Memoir, by Aharon Appelfeld

American Chica: Two Worlds, One Childhood, by Marie Arana

Epileptic, by David B.

Growing Up, by Russell Baker

The Prisoner's Wife: A Memoir, by Asha Bandele

Chameleon Days: An American Boyhood in Ethiopia, by Tim Bascom

Colter: The True Story of the Best Dog I Ever Had, by Rick Bass

Fun Home: A Family Tragicomic, by Alison Bechdel

The Life and Times of the Last Kid Picked, by David Benjamin

The Wild Parrots of Telegraph Hill: A Love Story . . . with Wings, by Mark Bittner

Breaking Clean, by Judy Blunt

Golden Boy: Memories of a Hong Kong Childhood, by Martin Booth

The Mystery Guest, by Gregoire Bouillier, translated by Lorin Stein

All Over but the Shoutin' and *Ava's Man,* by Rick Bragg

This Wild Darkness: The Story of My Death, by Harold Brodkey

A Piece of Cake: A Memoir, by Cupcake Brown

The Life and Times of the Thunderbolt Kid, by Bill Bryson

A Special Education: One Family's Journey through the Maze of Learning Disabilities, by Dana Buchman

Possible Side Effects; Running with Scissors; and *Dry,* by Augusten Burroughs

The King's English: Adventures of an Independent Bookseller, by Betsy Burton

The Yellow-Lighted Bookshop, by Lewis Buzbee

A Strong West Wind: A Memoir, by Gail Caldwell

I'll Know It When I See It: A Daughter's Search for Home in Ireland, by Alice Carey

An American Requiem: God, My Father, and the War That Came between Us, by James Carroll

Colors of the Mountain, by Da Chen

Educating Esmé: Diary of a Teacher's First Year, by Esmé Raji Codell

The Family on Beartown Road: A Memoir of Love and Courage, by Elizabeth Cohen

Sweet and Low: A Family Story, by Rich Cohen

Stop-Time: A Memoir, by Frank Conroy

The Road from Coorain and *True North,* by Jill Ker Conway

Swimming to Antarctica: Tales of a Long-Distance Swimmer and *Grayson,* by Lynne Cox

They Poured Fire on Us from the Sky: The True Story of Three Lost Boys from Sudan, by Alphonsion Deng, Benson Deng, and Benjamin Ajak, with Judy A. Bernstein

The Year of Magical Thinking, by Joan Didion

An American Childhood, by Annie Dillard

An Open Book: Chapters from a Reader's Life, by Michael Dirda

The Boy Who Fell Out of the Sky: A True Story, by Ken Dornstein

Broken Cord, by Michael Dorris

Narrative of the Life of Frederick Douglass, an American Slave: Written by Himself, by Frederick Douglass

Funny in Farsi: A Memoir of Growing Up Iranian in America, by Firoozeh Dumas

But Enough about Me: A Jersey Girl's Unlikely Adventures among the Absurdly Famous, by Jancee Dunn

A Heartbreaking Work of Staggering Genius, by Dave Eggers

Waiting for Snow in Havana: Confessions of a Cuban Boy, by Carlos Eire

I Was a Child of Holocaust Survivors, by Bernice Eisenstein

My Dark Places, by James Ellroy

Girlbomb: A Halfway Homeless Memoir, by Janice Erlbaum

Naked in the Promised Land: A Memoir, by Lillian Faderman

Crossing the Line: A Year in the Land of Apartheid, by William Finnegan

Finding Fish, by Antwone Q. Fisher

Mysteries of My Father, by Thomas Fleming

Another Bullshit Night in Suck City: A Memoir, by Nick Flynn

The Rice Room: Growing Up Chinese-American from Number Two Son to Rock 'n' Roll, by Ben Fong-Torres

The Diary of a Young Girl, by Anne Frank

The Autobiography of Benjamin Franklin, by Benjamin Franklin

The Discomfort Zone: A Personal History, by Jonathan Franzen

A Million Little Pieces and *My Friend Leonard*, by James Frey

The Cap: The Price of a Life, by Roman Frister

Don't Let's Go to the Dogs Tonight: An African Childhood, by Alexandra Fuller

How I Came into My Inheritance, and Other True Stories, by Dorothy Gallagher

Colored People, by Henry Louis Gates Jr.

Bleachy-Haired Honky Bitch: Tales from a Bad Neighborhood and *Confessions of a Recovering Slut, and Other Love Stories*, by Hollis Gillespie

About My Sisters (and her other work), by Debra Ginsberg

Prisoners: A Muslim and a Jew across the Middle East Divide, by Jeffrey Goldberg

Fierce Attachments: A Memoir, by Vivian Gornick

Stick Figure, by Lori Gottlieb

Personal History, by Katharine Graham

Them: A Memoir of Parents, by Francine du Plessix Gray

There Is No Me without You: One Woman's Odyssey to Rescue Africa's Children, by Melissa Fay Greene

Marley and Me: Life and Love with the World's Worst Dog, by John Grogan

Dancing with Cuba: A Memoir of the Revolution, by Alma Guillermoprieto

Journey from the Land of No: A Girlhood Caught in Revolutionary Iran, by Roya Hakakian

The Best Day the Worst Day: Life with Jane Kenyon, by Donald Hall

A Drinking Life: A Memoir, by Pete Hamill

A Romantic Education, by Patricia Hampl

84, Charing Cross Road (and her other work), by Helene Hanff

Tabloid Love: Looking for Mr. Right in All the Wrong Places, by Bridget Harrison

The Kiss (and her other work), by Kathryn Harrison

One Small Boat: The Story of a Little Girl, Lost Then Found, by Kathy Harrison

I Have Heard You Calling in the Night, by Thomas Healy

Now and Then: From Coney Island to Here, by Joseph Heller

All Creatures Great and Small (and his other work), by James Herriot

Half the Way Home: A Memoir of Father and Son, by Adam Hochschild

The White Masai, by Corinne Hofmann

Rescuing Patty Hearst: Memories from a Decade Gone Mad, by Virginia Holman

Things I Didn't Know: A Memoir, by Robert Hughes

Dust Tracks on a Road: An Autobiography, by Zora Neale Hurston

Left to Tell: Discovering God amidst the Rwandan Holocaust, by Immaculee Ilibagiza

The Know-It-All: One Man's Humble Quest to Become the Smartest Person in the World, by A. J. Jacobs

Secret Girl, by Molly Bruce Jacobs

Climbing the Mango Trees: A Memoir of a Childhood in India, by Madhur Jaffrey

Too Late to Die Young: Nearly True Tales from a Life, by Harriet McBryde Johnson

Casting with a Fragile Thread: A Story of Sisters and Africa, by Wendy Kann

The Liars' Club, by Mary Karr

We Are on Our Own, by Miriam Katin

A Walker in the City, by Alfred Kazin

I Am Not Myself These Days: A Memoir, by Josh Kilmer-Purcell

A Girl Named Zippy: Growing Up Small in Mooreland Indiana and *She Got Up Off the Couch, and Other Heroic Acts from Mooreland, Indiana*, by Haven Kimmel

My Brother, by Jamaica Kincaid

The Secret Life of a Schoolgirl, by Rosemary Kingsland

The Woman Warrior: Memoirs of a Girlhood among Ghosts, by Maxine Hong Kingston

Fargo Rock City: A Heavy Metal Odyssey in Rural North Dakota, by Chuck Klosterman

Drinking: A Love Story and *The Merry Recluse: A Life in Essays*, by Caroline Knapp

Cockeyed: A Memoir, by Ryan Knighton

Touchstones: Letters between Two Women, 1953–1964, by Patricia Lamb and Kathryn Hohlwein

Goat: A Memoir, by Brad Land

The Tulip and the Pope: A Nun's Story, by Deborah Larsen

Even after All This Time: A Story of Love, Revolution, and Leaving Iran, by Afschineh Latifi

Blackbird: A Childhood Lost and Found (and her other work), by Jennifer Lauck

Symptoms of Withdrawal: A Memoir of Snapshots and Redemption, by Christopher Kennedy Lawford

An Innocent, a Broad, by Ann Leary

If You Lived Here, I'd Know Your Name: News from Small-Town Alaska, by Heather Lende

Burning Fence: A Western Memoir of Fatherhood, by Craig Lesley

Not Buying It: My Year without Shopping, by Judith Levine

Walking with the Wind: A Memoir of the Movement, by John Lewis

Four Tenths of an Acre: Reflections on a Gardening Life, by Laurie Lisle

Fathers, Sons, and Brothers: The Men in My Family, by Bret Lott

Teta, Mother, and Me: Three Generations of Arab Women, by Jean Said Makdisi

Cancer Vixen, by Marisa Acocella Marchetto

The Color of Water: A Black Man's Tribute to His White Mother, by James McBride

Memories of a Catholic Girlhood, by Mary McCarthy

Angela's Ashes: A Memoir; Teacher Man; and *'Tis,* by Frank McCourt

A Monk Swimming: A Memoir and *Singing My Him Song,* by Malachy McCourt

Where We Have Hope: A Memoir of Zimbabwe, by Andrew Meldrum

The Lost: A Search for Six of Six Million, by Daniel Mendelsohn

Notes from the Hyena's Belly: An Ethiopian Boyhood, by Nega Mezlekia

The Story of My Father, by Sue Miller

The Tiger in the Attic: Memories of the Kindertransport and Growing Up English, by Edith Milton

Lipstick Jihad: A Memoir of Growing Up Iranian in America and American in Iran, by Azadeh Moaveni

The Tender Bar: A Memoir, by J. R. Moehringer

The Good Good Pig: The Extraordinary Life of Christopher Hogwood, by Sy Montgomery

Fat Girl: A True Story, by Judith Moore

My Battle of Algiers: A Memoir, by Ted Morgan

Don't Wake Me at Doyles: A Memoir, by Maura Murphy

Speak, Memory, by Vladimir Nabokov

Reading "Lolita" in Tehran: A Memoir in Books, by Azar Nafisi

Geronimo's Bones: A Memoir of My Brother and Me, by Nasdijj

The Unwanted: A Memoir of Childhood, by Kien Nguyen

Ice Bound: A Doctor's Incredible Battle for Survival at the South Pole, by Jerri Nielsen, with Maryanne Vollers

Dreambirds: The Strange History of the Ostrich in Fashion, Food and Fortune, by Rob Nixon

In the Unlikely Event of a Water Landing: A Geography of Grief, by Christopher Noël

Boy with Loaded Gun: A Memoir, by Lewis Nordan

Underwater to Get Out of the Rain: A Love Affair with the Sea, by Trevor Norton

Lost in America: A Journey with My Father, by Sherwin B. Nuland

Are You Somebody? The Accidental Memoir of a Dublin Woman and *Almost There,* by Nuala O'Faolain

The Book of Kehls, by Christine Kehl O'Hagan

Running in the Family, by Michael Ondaatje

Mostly True: A Memoir of Family, Food, and Baseball, by Molly O'Neill

Truth and Beauty: A Friendship, by Ann Patchett; then read *Autobiography of a Face,* by Lucy Grealy

Revenge of the Paste Eaters: Memoirs of a Misfit, by Cheryl Peck

Money: A Memoir: Women, Emotions, and Cash, by Liz Perle

Population: 485: Meeting Your Neighbors One Siren at a Time, by Michael Perry

A Whole New Life: An Illness and a Healing, by Reynolds Price

Songs of the Gorilla Nation: My Journey through Autism, by Dawn Prince-Hughes

The One That Got Away: A Memoir, by Howell Raines

Ecology of a Cracker Childhood, by Janisse Ray

The First and Final Nightmare of Sonia Reich: A Son's Memoir, by Howard Reich

The Face of a Naked Lady: An Omaha Family Mystery, by Michael Rips

Baghdad Burning: Girl Blog from Iraq, by Riverbend

Encyclopedia of an Ordinary Life, by Amy Krouse Rosenthal

An Ordinary Man: An Autobiography, by Paul Rusesabagina, with Tom Zoellner

Big Russ and Me: Father and Son: Lessons of Life, by Tim Russert; and consider his collection *Wisdom of Our Fathers: Lessons and Letters from Daughters and Sons*

Shooting Water: A Memoir of Second Chances, Family, and Filmmaking, by Devyani Saltzman

Song for My Fathers: A New Orleans Story in Black and White, by Tom Sancton

When I Was Puerto Rican: A Memoir, by Esmeralda Santiago

Persepolis: The Story of a Childhood and *Persepolis 2: The Story of a Return,* by Marjane Satrapi

The Commitment: Love, Sex, Marriage, and My Family, by Dan Savage

Jesus Land: A Memoir, by Julia Scheeres

Lucky: A Memoir, by Alice Sebold

Two Lives, by Vikram Seth

Lying: A Metaphorical Memoir, by Lauren Slater

Name All the Animals: A Memoir, by Alison Smith

You Must Set Forth at Dawn: A Memoir and *Aké: The Years of Childhood,* by Wole Soyinka

Five-Finger Discount: A Crooked Family History, by Helene Stapinski

The Autobiography of Alice B. Toklas, by Gertrude Stein

Darkness Visible: A Memoir of Madness, by William Styron

I Am a Pencil: A Teacher, His Kids, and Their World of Stories, by Sam Swope

Enslaved by Ducks: How One Man Went from Head of the Household to Bottom of the Pecking Order, by Bob Tarte

The Hiding Place, by Corrie Ten Boom

Down These Mean Streets, by Piri Thomas

Tomorrow to Be Brave: A Memoir of the Only Woman Ever to Serve in the French Foreign Legion, by Susan Travers

Falling through the Earth: A Memoir, by Danielle Trussoni

Love in the Driest Season: A Family Memoir, by Neely Tucker

Take the Cannoli: Stories from the New World, by Sarah Vowell

The Glass Castle: A Memoir, by Jeannette Walls

Flying over 96th Street: Memoir of an East Harlem White Boy, by Thomas L. Webber

My Lives: An Autobiography, by Edmund White

Brothers and Keepers: A Memoir, by John Edgar Wideman

Night, by Elie Wiesel

Oh the Glory of It All, by Sean Wilsey

Breakfast with Tiffany: An Uncle's Memoir, by Edwin John Wintle

This Boy's Life: A Memoir, by Tobias Wolff

Moments of Being, by Virginia Woolf

Black Boy, by Richard Wright

The Autobiography of Malcolm X, by Malcolm X

Confessions of a Tax Collector: One Man's Tour of Duty inside the IRS, by Richard Yancey

Resources and Awards

Memoirs are a nonfiction type that gets a lot of attention in both the professional and general press, so it is not too difficult to keep up with popular titles. If you are not a memoir reader yourself, though, this can be a difficult type to discuss with readers, since mood, style, and subject hold such strong sway in terms of appeal. Readers' advisory librarians have several sources to help them learn more about memoirs, including two anthologies and a host of prestigious awards. *When Memory Speaks,* by Jill Ker Conway, *Inventing the Truth: The Art and Craft of Memoir,* by William Zinsser, and *Modern American Memoirs,* edited by Annie Dillard and Cort Conley, each offer a way of looking at memoir and a range of examples of the type. These works can quickly give a sense of the broad range of forms being employed to write memoir and a gloss of some classic works.

Great memoir writing is recognized through a range of awards. Memoirs are perennially included on the short lists of title considerations and often win these awards outright. Though it is just a good habit for readers' advisory librarians to monitor awards, for memoir in particular this is a useful way to help winnow out the crowded field and to enrich one's own mental list of titles to read and suggest.

BOOK SENSE PICKS AND BOOK SENSE BOOK OF THE YEAR

The choices on the Book Sense Picks list and the Book of the Year are selected by booksellers as titles that hold high appeal to a wide range of readers. They are a great resource to monitor. See http://www.booksense.com/index.jsp.

NATIONAL BOOK AWARDS

The National Book Awards are the preeminent literary awards given in the United States. If a memoir is short-listed or wins this award, then it should be considered a key title. See http://www.nationalbook.org/nba.html.

NATIONAL BOOK CRITICS CIRCLE AWARDS

The National Book Critics Circle is an organization of book reviewers. Theirs is a wonderful award to monitor because it is decided by people whose job it is to read and evaluate all types of literature. A twenty-four-member board of directors select and vote on the winning titles each year. See http://www.bookcritics.org.

NEW YORK PUBLIC LIBRARY'S BOOKS TO REMEMBER

The staff of the New York Public Library select titles they think are worth remembering for years to come. Their lists often include memoirs that should automatically become titles we all pay attention to in terms of collection building and suggesting to readers. See http://www.nypl.org/branch/books/booklists.cfm.

NOTABLE BOOKS LIST

Memoirs often appear on the Notable Books List created by the American Library Association's Reference and User Services Association and the Collection Development and Evaluation Section. The books on this list are particularly useful in readers' advisory work, since each is selected for its readability and high appeal. The winning titles are chosen by librarians with a strong background in collection development, reference, or readers' advisory work. See http://www.ala.org/ala/rusa/rusaprotools/rusanotable/notable books.htm.

PULITZER PRIZE

The Pulitzers are given for biography and autobiography. Although the prize is awarded to biography more frequently, it is still an award worth monitoring. See http://www.pulitzer.org.

6

SPORTS

Sport is a national obsession fostered when we are young by T-ball clubs and soccer teams. Children grow up both watching and participating in many different sports, and often the books they enjoy most as kids center around the games they play. It is no wonder then that as they grow up many readers see sports books as great entertainment. Patrons often ask specifically for sports books, and they are frequently on the bestseller lists. Since readers know about and want these books, readers' advisory librarians should be aware of the best in the field.

Sports books range from those specifically about a game, player, or event to those that use sport as a metaphor for a broader look at the world. Some of the best writers of our times have written about sport, fascinated by its meaning, ethos, and personalities. In the range of titles available, readers' advisory librarians can find works that are fast paced and sport specific as well as titles that merge sports into history and biography and illuminate a specific time. With such a wide range of titles available, this subject offers a rich pool of suggestions for rabid sports fans and general-interest readers alike.

What Readers Enjoy in These Books

Many readers enjoy these books for the vicarious participation in sport they provide, the opportunity to learn more about the game they love, and the chance to read about the players they admire. Other readers enjoy the use of sports themes to open a wider world and explore the times, settings, and characters of past eras. Still others enjoy the lyrical reflection on nature and our place within it.

The major appeals of this subject area are story, character, setting, description, and detail. Sports figures run the gamut from the heroic, stoic, and strong to the cheating, lost, or simply lucky. Strong biographical elements underline many sports titles, filling the work with larger-than-life characters that even readers who don't particularly care for sports can enjoy. Other titles focus attention on social commentary and still others on history. This melding of themes appeals to many readers who enjoy seeing sports set into a wider context. Readers who enjoy detail are pleased with elements such as practice schedules, superstitious routines, the creation of bats and other equipment, and details on venues, fans, and curses.

Types of Books

Although the world of sport is vast, sports books can be divided into four large type classifications:

- Essays and Musings
- Biography and Memoir
- Reporting
- Time and Place: History, Location, and Players

Readers' advisory librarians should be aware of the differences between these types and keep them and appeal elements in mind when making suggestions. Readers usually ask for books based on specific sports, but if you listen to how they describe the books they are looking for, they reveal what type of book they want along with the appeal elements they enjoy.

As is true with science books, it is best for readers' advisory librarians to focus on the narrative context, appeal, and type of book rather than the subject when making suggestions to readers. One book on baseball can be very different from another, with the approach of the writer and type of book varying considerably. Readers who expect an elegantly written history of the sport, times, and society may be unsatisfied if handed a fast-paced, riotous exposé of the game's shortcomings. That being said, however, there are times when only a book on football will suffice. For those situations, see the sport-specific titles section below for assistance.

Benchmark Books to Read and Suggest

There is nothing like the thrill of reading about a sport we love, finding more about a favorite player, or participating vicariously in an epic sporting event.

It is important to become familiar with the various types of books in this subject area and the pleasures each holds for the reader. Doing so makes our suggestions more meaningful and allows us to engage in better conversations with our patrons. The books below are some of the best, or most iconic, writing in the subject classification. Use them to augment a personal reading program, to see how different types of books can be used to build reading suggestions, and to explore the range of pleasures to be found in the sporting world.

Essays and Musings

This section contains works that approach sports from the widest of aspects. Essays are the vehicle writers use to integrate sports with a way of life. They give writers the structure to be specific and the freedom to meander around, so these titles range from direct, almost journalistic writing to the sublime ruminations of the color of fish scales, the heft behind a punch, or the gait of a thoroughbred.

Still Life with Brook Trout, by John Gierach

With a warm, rambling, and chummy tone, Gierach invites readers to share his latest fishing season. It is a season full of road trips, hidden streams, and great fish; of friendships, bad knees, and keen observations. Combining the best aspects of both essays and musings, Gierach moves smoothly from one scene to the next, with little real point but with great enjoyment—which he generously explains to the reader. He shares stories of using a dog as a method to practice playing a fish on a line, accounts of actually fishing for gleaming trout, descriptions of the weather, and his fight with the water board that wants to turn his valley into a reservoir. It is all wonderful, languid, reflective, and sure to please those who understand his appreciation of a fish, a line, and the right kind of day.

Read this book because it provides a foundation to understand one side of the sport writing world—the reflective and meandering story rather than the fast, play-by-play account.

Suggest this book to readers interested in the environment, fishing, and the camaraderie of sport and to those who enjoy fine and observant writing. It works well with *The Habit of Rivers,* by Ted Leeson, *The Longest Silence: A Life in Fishing,* by Thomas McGuane, and *Confessions of a Fly Fishing Addict,* by Nick Lyons. Readers might also find *A River Runs Through It, and Other Stories,* by Norman Maclean, a suitable companion to Gierach.

Biography and Memoir

Ranging from the serious investigation of a player to the meditative memoir of a life, this section of sports books holds wide appeal to readers for the connections they make to their favorite athletes, the insight on their motivations, and the stories of their lives off the court, field, or venue. The writing in this classification ranges from the sturdy to the luminous, and character is most often the primary appeal point in these books.

Clemente: The Passion and Grace of Baseball's Last Hero, **by David Maraniss**

With a deft hand, balancing the well-deserved admiration Clemente inspires and the observant, critical approach great biography demands, Maraniss explores the life of one of the game's epic figures. Clemente was a brilliant player—justly joining in the pantheon of baseball's heroes—but he was also a man with an ambition larger than the game. In a society still judging ability by skin color, he was a leading figure for Latino aspirations. In a culture too given to self-indulgence, he believed in giving back and helping others—a belief that ultimately led to his tragic death. Maraniss crafts a vivid, multifaceted account of Clemente. His book is full of baseball, including great descriptions of World Series games, as well as a good sense of the politics and culture of both baseball and the nation. All of it is told with a wonderful blend of reporting and storytelling. But most of all, this book is about a man—his abilities, heart, flaws, and motivations—and Maraniss captures Clemente's life in this perfect blend of biography, social history, and sport.

Read this book because it illustrates the blend of sports and biography and typifies what many readers expect in these books—plenty of sports action but still a good grasp of the player's life and times.

Suggest this book to anyone interested in baseball or epic sports figures or who enjoys a mix of story and reporting. Team it with works such as *Joe DiMaggio: The Hero's Life,* by Richard Ben Cramer, *Luckiest Man: The Life and Death of Lou Gehrig,* by Jonathan Eig, *Sandy Koufax: A Lefty's Legacy,* by Jane Leavy, *The Big Bam: The Life and Times of Babe Ruth,* by Leigh Montville, or *King of the World: Muhammad Ali and the Rise of an American Hero,* by David Remnick.

Reporting

Titles in this classification provide fans with an insider's perspective that has great allure. Much of sports writing is reporting—the gathering of fact, the observation of a season, the interview of a player, and the reaction of fans. Sports reporting appeals to readers because it places fans into the games they love and allows them to see what goes on behind the scenes and after the season ends. Additional appeal points include the clarity of writing; the strong focus on character, setting, and action; and the innumerable details of sport.

Next Man Up: A Year behind the Lines in Today's NFL, by John Feinstein

Given an all-access pass to the world of the National Football League, Feinstein follows the Baltimore Ravens for a season. Starting at the end of a letdown year, when they missed going to the play-offs, he takes readers through the first firings of postseason evaluation and on to the new draft picks and the events of the next year. The book covers many games but also reports on the game itself, how it is structured, planned, and enacted. It is a book about the coaches, owners, and athletes—who plays, who leads, who follows, and who controls what happens both on the field and at headquarters. Feinstein shows just how brutal the game can be. Everyone involved knows that there is always that moment when a player gets hurt, a coach fails, or personalities clash. In those moments the next man up has his chance, be he player, scout, or offensive coordinator; and new replaces old, healthy replaces injured, and one idea wins out over another. With his trademark blend of insider cool and perceptive skill, Feinstein tracks the Ravens through all of this, conveying the excitement and everydayness of the sport perfectly.

Read this book because Feinstein is perhaps the best writer to learn from when it comes to sports reporting. His work is perceptive and explanatory, covers a huge range of sports, and includes many of the elements readers look for: great inside stories, a mix of game reporting and character insight, and a fast pace married to a direct and involving story line.

Suggest this book to readers who love football or like to read about the details and inside stories of any sport. Readers might also find *Three Nights in August,* by Buzz Bissinger, *Every Week a Season: A Journey inside Big-Time College Football,* by Brian Curtis, and *The Blind Side: Evolution of a Game,* by Michael Lewis, to be works that provide similar reading pleasure.

Time and Place: History, Location, and Players

The groundbreaking *Boys of Summer,* by Roger Kahn, inaugurated this classification with its mix of memoir, sport, history, and, most of all, sense of place and time. Sports books that illuminate more than just the game make for sublime reading and hold wide appeal for a large group of readers with their strongly story-based structure and involving characters. In these books sport is often a metaphor for life, an entry into a particular era, or a cultural touchstone for a larger issue.

Seabiscuit: An American Legend, by Laura Hillenbrand

The tale is simple enough: a horse nobody thought could win, a down-on-his-luck rider, an owner who was not welcome in the elite Eastern racing world, and a trainer with a magic touch. In Hillenbrand's hands, however, the story of Seabiscuit is an enchanting and compelling legend made real. Seabiscuit became the Horse of the Year, the awkward and knobby-kneed creature who beat the legendary War Admiral one-on-one in a showdown long coming and bitterly sought. Red Pollard, the jockey, is revealed as a character of heroic if quiet nature, a man who bonded with his horse so well that the two were able to save each other. Hillenbrand covers the races, training, and personalities (including Seabiscuit's brilliant trainer, Tom Smith, and his enthusiastic owner, Charles Howard), but she also captures the era of the 1930s and '40s with a painterly hand, pulling readers so deep into the times that they too can look out on Seabiscuit's races and experience them as did his legions of fans.

Read this book because it is a classic work of strongly narrative nonfiction and holds within its pages many of the elements readers look for in highly narrative works: compelling story, rich and three-dimensional characters, a great sense of pacing, and lots of detail and description.

Suggest this book to readers who like their sports writing to be heartwarming, strongly character based, and story rich. It is also a great book to suggest to all kinds of readers, even if they do not particularly enjoy sports books, for the characters and story transcend the subject of horseracing. The book spawned a bit of an industry on Seabiscuit, some of which makes for good additional reading for those not yet ready to leave Seabiscuit's world. Try *Seabiscuit: The Saga of a Great Champion,* by B. K. Beckwith, for pictures, or the movie version of the book starring Jeff Bridges, Tobey Maguire, and William H. Macy. *Funny Cide: How a Horse, a Trainer, a Jockey, and a Bunch of High School Buddies Took on the Sheiks and Blue Bloods . . . and Won,* by Sally Jenkins, though not matching Hillenbrand in tone or history, does have a similar, if modern-day, discounted-horse story. For books that share the mix of history, character, detail, and riveting story, try *Undaunted Courage: Meriwether Lewis, Thomas Jefferson, and the Opening of the American West,* by Stephen Ambrose, or *The Devil in the White City: Murder, Magic, and Madness at the Fair That Changed America,* by Erik Larson.

Sport-Specific Titles

Sport is a rich and diverse area, but it also has very specific subject subdivisions. Even though it is best to work with readers to make suggestions based on the type of book and appeal factors rather than by just the subject, it is often hard to pry a reader away from a specific sport. And it should be kept in mind that our job is to match readers to books they want to read. If a patron is determined to read a book about football, then suggesting a title on fishing, no matter how great and appealing it may be, will create the impression that we are not listening. Though it is important that books be looked at beyond their subject matter, sometimes it is best, to borrow a term from football, to punt. Suggesting sport-specific titles can be difficult because readers' advisory librarians will rapidly run out of books to suggest. But before we can expect readers to trust us and take our suggestion about reading a book on fishing when they came for a book on football, we may need to pave the way with good suggestions on football—or whatever their favored sport happens to be. Here then is a listing of titles to use in a pinch. Note: Not all sports writing covers each type equally (or at all), so books are listed only for types where good suitable examples are available.

Football

Biography and Memoir: *When Pride Still Mattered: A Life of Vince Lombardi,* by David Maraniss

Reporting: *Next Man Up: A Year behind the Lines in Today's NFL,* by John Feinstein

Time and Place: *Friday Night Lights: A Town, a Team, and a Dream,* by H. G. Bissinger

Baseball

Essays and Musings: *Twilight of the Long-Ball Gods: Dispatches from the Disappearing Heart of Baseball,* by John Schulian

Biography and Memoir: *Luckiest Man: The Life and Death of Lou Gehrig,* by Jonathan Eig

Reporting: *The Summer Game,* by Roger Angell

Time and Place: *The Boys of Summer,* by Roger Kahn

Basketball

Biography and Memoir: *Life on the Run*, by Bill Bradley

Reporting: *The Miracle of St. Anthony: A Season with Coach Bob Hurley and Basketball's Most Improbable Dynasty*, by Adrian Wojnarowski

Time and Place: *The Breaks of the Game*, by David Halberstam

Fishing

Essays and Musings: *Still Life with Brook Trout*, by John Gierach

Biography and Memoir: *The Hungry Ocean: A Swordboat Captain's Journey*, by Linda Greenlaw

Reporting: *Sowbelly: The Obsessive Quest for the World Record Largemouth Bass*, by Monte Burke

Hunting

Biography and Memoir: *Deep Enough for Ivorybills*, by James Kilgo

Reporting: *A Hunter's Road: A Journey with Gun and Dog across the American Uplands*, by Jim Fergus

Boxing

Essays and Musings: *The Sweet Science*, by A. J. Liebling

Biography and Memoir: *King of the World: Muhammad Ali and the Rise of an American Hero*, by David Remnick

Reporting: *The Gloves: A Boxing Chronicle*, by Robert Anasi

Hockey

Reporting: *Blades of Glory: The True Story of a Young Team Bred to Win*, by John Rosengren

Time and Place: *The Game*, by Ken Dryden

Soccer

Biography and Memoir: *The Miracle of Castel di Sangro: A Tale of Passion and Folly in the Heart of Italy*, by Joe McGinniss

Horseracing

Essays and Musings: *The Big Horse*, by Joe McGinniss

Biography and Memoir: *Laughing in the Hills*, by Bill Barich

Reporting: *The Race for the Triple Crown: Horses, High Stakes, and Eternal Hope*, by Joe Drape

Time and Place: *Seabiscuit: An American Legend*, by Laura Hillenbrand

Cycling

Biography and Memoir: *It's Not about the Bike: My Journey Back to Life*, by Lance Armstrong

Tennis

Biography and Memoir: *Days of Grace: A Memoir*, by Arthur Ashe

Time and Place: *Levels of the Game*, by John McPhee

Golf

Biography and Memoir: *Who's Your Caddy? Looping for the Great, Near Great, and Reprobates of Golf*, by Rick Reilly

Reporting: *The Greatest Game Ever Played: Harry Vardon, Francis Ouimet, and the Birth of Modern Golf*, by Mark Frost

Motor Racing

Biography and Memoir: *Bugatti Queen: In Search of a French Racing Legend*, by Miranda Seymour

Reporting: *Sunday Money: Speed! Lust! Madness! Death! A Hot Lap around America with NASCAR*, by Jeff MacGregor

Key Authors

The authors listed below are the major writers in the field and can be relied on to craft well-written and immensely readable works. This list can be used to make suggestions, to build displays, as a core reading list, and as a sure-bet resource.

Dave Ames	Linda Greenlaw	James Prosek
Roger Angell	Roderick L. Haig-Brown	John Schulian
Bill Barich	David Halberstam	Gary Smith
Allen Barra	Laura Hillenbrand	Red Smith
H. G. "Buzz" Bissinger	Roger Kahn	Tom Stanton
Frank Deford	Mark Kriegel	William G. Tapply
John Eisenberg	Ted Leeson	Rick Telander
John Feinstein	Nick Lyons	L. Jon Wertheim
Jim Fergus	David Maraniss	
John Gierach	Thomas McGuane	

Selected Bibliography of Sports Writing to Read and Suggest

Readers' advisory librarians should keep in mind that not all sports titles are written the same way and that a reader who enjoys one aspect of a sporting book may find titles in other subject categories to make good matches as well. Lyrical musings on fishing pair well with many of the nature titles listed in the science chapter of this book. Sailing books tend to be about disasters and thus have much in common with true adventure titles (chapter 9). Baseball is strong on historical slants that evoke time and place and thus works well with history titles like those in chapter 10. Finally, many sports biographies do what the best biographies are supposed to do—illuminate the subject and his or her times in ways that expand on the mere biographical detail—and therefore readers may find other works to enjoy in any of the biography sub-sections in this book.

Essays and Musings

Fly-Fishin' Fool: The Adventures, Misadventures, and Outright Idiocies of a Compulsive Angler, by James R. Babb

Crazy for Rivers, by Bill Barich

A Fly Fisherman's Blue Ridge, by Christopher Camuto

The Best of Frank Deford: I'm Just Getting Started, by Frank Deford

The Fish's Eye: Essays about Angling and the Outdoors, by Ian Frazier

Still Life with Brook Trout (and his other work), by John Gierach

The Seasons of a Fisherman and *To Know a River: A Haig-Brown Reader,* by Roderick L. Haig-Brown

The Habit of Rivers and *Jerusalem Creek: Journeys into Driftless Country,* by Ted Leeson

The Sweet Science, by A. J. Liebling

Spring Creek and *Confessions of a Fly Fishing Addict* (and his other work), by Nick Lyons

The Big Horse, by Joe McGinniss

An Outside Chance: Classic and New Essays on Sport and *The Longest Silence: A Life in Fishing,* by Thomas McGuane

Brook Trout and the Writing Life, by Craig Nova

In Service to the Horse: Chronicles of a Labor of Love, by Susan Nusser

On Boxing, by Joyce Carol Oates

A Hunter's Heart: Honest Essays on Blood Sport, edited by David Petersen

All Those Mornings . . . at the "Post," by Shirley Povich

Cut Time: An Education at the Fights, by Carlo Rotella

The Caddie Was a Reindeer, and Other Tales of Extreme Recreation, by Steve Rushin

Twilight of the Long-Ball Gods: Dispatches from the Disappearing Heart of Baseball, by John Schulian

An Honest Angler: The Best of Sparse Grey Hackle, edited by Patricia Miller Sherwood

Now I Can Die in Peace: How ESPN's Sports Guy Found Salvation, with a Little Help from Nomar, Pedro, Shawshank, and the 2004 Red Sox, by Bill Simmons

A Year at the Races: Reflections on Horses, Humans, Love, Money, and Luck, by Jane Smiley

Beyond the Game: The Collected Sportswriting of Gary Smith, by Gary Smith

The Best American Sports Writing, edited by Glenn Stout (published annually)

Blood Horses: Notes of a Sportswriter's Son, by John Jeremiah Sullivan

Gone Fishin': Ruminations on Fly Fishing, by William G. Tapply

Traver on Fishing (and his other work), by Robert Traver

Upland Stream: Notes on the Fishing Passion, by W. D. Wetherell

Biography and Memoir

Wrecking Crew: The Really Bad News Griffith Park Pirates, by John Albert

A Good Life Wasted, or Twenty Years as a Fishing Guide, by Dave Ames

It's Not about the Bike: My Journey Back to Life, by Lance Armstrong

Days of Grace: A Memoir, by Arthur Ashe

Let Me Tell You a Story: A Lifetime in the Game, by Red Auerbach and John Feinstein

They Don't Play Hockey in Heaven: A Dream, a Team, and My Comeback Season, by Ken Baker

Laughing in the Hills, by Bill Barich

The Last Coach: A Life of Paul "Bear" Bryant, by Allen Barra

Ball Four, by Jim Bouton

Life on the Run, by Bill Bradley

The Long Season, by Jim Brosnan

Sir Walter: Walter Hagen and the Invention of Professional Golf, by Tom Clavin

Play by Play: Baseball, Radio, and Life in the Last Chance League, by Neal Conan

My Losing Season, by Pat Conroy

Swimming to Antarctica: Tales of a Long-Distance Swimmer, by Lynne Cox

Lance Armstrong's War: One Man's Battle against Fate, Fame, Love, Death, Scandal, and a Few Other Rivals on the Road to the Tour de France, by Daniel Coyle

Joe DiMaggio: The Hero's Life and *What Do You Think of Ted Williams Now? A Remembrance,* by Richard Ben Cramer

Babe: The Legend Comes to Life and *Stengel: His Life and Times,* by Robert Creamer

Papa Bear: The Life and Legacy of George Halas, by Jeff Davis

Ben Hogan: An American Life and *Final Rounds: A Father, a Son, the Golf Journey of a Lifetime,* by James Dodson

Full Throttle: The Life and Fast Times of Curtis Turner, by Robert Edelstein

Luckiest Man: The Life and Death of Lou Gehrig, by Jonathan Eig

Native Dancer: The Grey Ghost: Hero of a Golden Age, by John Eisenberg

Citation: In a Class by Himself, by Phil Georgeff

Wait till Next Year: A Memoir, by Doris Kearns Goodwin

Why My Wife Thinks I'm an Idiot: The Life and Times of a Sportscaster Dad, by Mike Greenberg

The Hungry Ocean: A Swordboat Captain's Journey (and her other work), by Linda Greenlaw

Glory Road: My Story of the 1966 NCAA Basketball Championship and How One Team Triumphed against the Odds, by Don Haskins, with Dan Wetzel

Fever Pitch, by Nick Hornby

Wink: The Incredible Life and Epic Journey of Jimmy Winkfield, by Ed Hotaling

A Jerk on One End: Reflections of a Mediocre Fisherman, by Robert Hughes

Fishing on the Edge: The Mike Iaconelli Story, by Mike Iaconelli, with Andrew Kamenetzky and Brian Kamenetzky

A False Spring and *A Nice Tuesday,* by Pat Jordan

A Flame of Pure Fire: Jack Dempsey and the Roaring '20s, by Roger Kahn

Deep Enough for Ivorybills and *Colors of Africa,* by James Kilgo

She's Got Next: A Story of Getting In, Staying Open, and Taking a Shot, by Melissa King

Instant Replay: The Green Bay Diary of Jerry Kramer, by Jerry Kramer

Namath: A Biography, by Mark Kriegel

Sandy Koufax: A Lefty's Legacy, by Jane Leavy

America's Game: The Epic Story of How Pro Football Captured a Nation, by Michael MacCambridge

Pride of October: What It Was to Be Young and a Yankee, by Bill Madden

When Pride Still Mattered: A Life of Vince Lombardi and *Clemente: The Passion and Grace of Baseball's Last Hero,* by David Maraniss

Breakfast at Trout's Place: The Seasons of an Alaskan Flyfisher, by Ken Marsh

Season of Life: A Football Star, a Boy, a Journey to Manhood, by Jeffrey Marx

The Miracle of Castel di Sangro: A Tale of Passion and Folly in the Heart of Italy, by Joe McGinniss

Bat Boy: My True Life Adventures Coming of Age with the New York Yankees, by Matthew McGough

Bright Country: A Fisherman's Return to Trout, Wild Water, and Himself; On the Spine of Time: A Fly Fisher's Journey among Mountain Streams, Trout, and

People; and *The Earth Is Enough: Growing Up in a World of Fly Fishing, Trout, and Old Men* (and his other work), by Harry Middleton

Ted Williams: The Biography of an American Hero; At the Altar of Speed: The Fast Life and Tragic Death of Dale Earnhardt; and *The Big Bam: The Life and Times of Babe Ruth,* by Leigh Montville

Big Red of Meadow Stable: Secretariat, the Making of a Champion, by William Nack

Praying for Gil Hodges: A Memoir of the 1955 World Series and One Family's Love of the Brooklyn Dodgers, by Thomas Oliphant

Fly-Fishing the 41st: Around the World on the 41st Parallel (and his other work), by James Prosek

Who's Your Caddy? Looping for the Great, Near Great, and Reprobates of Golf, by Rick Reilly

King of the World: Muhammad Ali and the Rise of an American Hero, by David Remnick

Don't Look Back: Satchel Paige in the Shadows of Baseball, by Mark Ribowsky

Road Swing: One Fan's Journey into the Soul of America's Sports, by Steve Rushin

The Slam: Bobby Jones and the Price of Glory (and his other work), by Curt Sampson

Bugatti Queen: In Search of a French Racing Legend, by Miranda Seymour

Horse of a Different Color: A Tale of Breeding Geniuses, Dominant Females, and the Fastest Derby Winner since Secretariat, by Jim Squires

The Road to Cooperstown: A Father, Two Sons, and the Journey of a Lifetime, by Tom Stanton

Cobb: A Biography, by Al Stump

Blood Horses: Notes of a Sportswriter's Son, by John Jeremiah Sullivan

Unforgivable Blackness: The Rise and Fall of Jack Johnson, by Geoffrey C. Ward

Foul! The Connie Hawkins Story, by Dave Wolf

Reporting

The Long Ball: The Summer of '75—Spaceman, Catfish, Charlie Hustle, and the Greatest World Series Ever Played, by Tom Adelman

The Gloves: A Boxing Chronicle, by Robert Anasi

The Summer Game (and his other work), by Roger Angell

Wild Ride: The Rise and Fall of Calumet Farm Inc., America's Premier Racing Dynasty, by Anne Hagedorn Auerbach

A Fine Place to Daydream: Racehorses, Romance, and the Irish, by Bill Barich

Three Nights in August, by Buzz Bissinger

In These Girls, Hope Is a Muscle, by Madeleine Blais

About Three Bricks Shy . . . and the Load Filled Up: The Story of the Greatest Football Team Ever, by Roy Blount Jr.

Juicing the Game: Drugs, Power, and the Fight for the Soul of Major League Baseball, by Howard Bryant

Sowbelly: The Obsessive Quest for the World Record Largemouth Bass, by Monte Burke

The Home Run Horse: Inside America's Billion-Dollar Racehorse Industry and the High-Stakes Dreams That Fuel It, by Glenye Cain

Blue Blood: Duke–Carolina: Inside the Most Storied Rivalry in College Hoops, by Art Chansky

The Game They Played, by Stanley Cohen

Counting Coup: A True Story of Basketball and Honor on the Little Big Horn, by Larry Colton

Game Misconduct: Alan Eagleson and the Corruption of Hockey, by Russ Conway

Every Week a Season: A Journey inside Big-Time College Football, by Brian Curtis

The Race for the Triple Crown: Horses, High Stakes, and Eternal Hope, by Joe Drape

Little League, Big Dreams: The Hope, the Hype and the Glory of the Greatest World Series Ever Played and *The Last Nine Innings: Inside the Real Game Fans Never See,* by Charles Euchner

Game of Shadows: Barry Bonds, BALCO, and the Steroids Scandal That Rocked Professional Sports, by Mark Fainaru-Wada and Lance Williams

Next Man Up: A Year behind the Lines in Today's NFL; Last Dance: Behind the Scenes at the Final Four; Caddy for Life: The Bruce Edwards Story; A Good Walk Spoiled: Days and Nights on the PGA Tour; A Season on the Brink; and *The Majors: In Pursuit of Golf's Holy Grail* (and his other work), by John Feinstein

A Hunter's Road: A Journey with Gun and Dog across the American Uplands and *The Sporting Road: Travels across America in an Airstream Trailer—with Fly Rod, Shotgun, and a Yellow Lab Named Sweetzer,* by Jim Fergus

The Last Shot: City Streets, Basketball Dreams, by Darcy Frey

The Greatest Game Ever Played: Harry Vardon, Francis Ouimet, and the Birth of Modern Golf, by Mark Frost

The Education of a Coach and *The Amateurs: The Story of Four Young Men and Their Quest for an Olympic Gold Medal,* by David Halberstam

The Black Lights: Inside the World of Professional Boxing, by Thomas Hauser

Funny Cide: How a Horse, a Trainer, a Jockey, and a Bunch of High School Buddies Took on the Sheiks and Blue Bloods . . . and Won, by Sally Jenkins

Slouching toward Fargo: A Two-Year Saga of Sinners and St. Paul Saints at the Bottom of the Bush Leagues with Bill Murray, Darryl Strawberry, Dakota Sadie and Me, by Neal Karlen

Bloodties: Nature, Culture, and the Hunt, by Ted Kerasote

Ghosts of Manila: The Fateful Blood Feud between Muhammad Ali and Joe Frazier, by Mark Kram

Negro League Baseball: The Rise and Ruin of a Black Institution, by Neil Lanctot

Death and the Sun: A Matador's Season in the Heart of Spain, by Edward Lewine

Moneyball: The Art of Winning an Unfair Game and *The Blind Side: Evolution of a Game,* by Michael Lewis

Sunday Money: Speed! Lust! Madness! Death! A Hot Lap around America with NASCAR, by Jeff MacGregor

The Hardest Game: McIlvanney on Boxing, by Hugh McIlvanney

The Wildest Ride: A History of NASCAR (or, How a Bunch of Good Ol' Boys Built a Billion-Dollar Industry Out of Wrecking Cars), by Joe Menzer

Why Not Us? The 86-Year Journey of the Boston Red Sox Fans from Unparalleled Suffering to the Promised Land of the 2004 World Series, by Leigh Montville

The Jump: Sebastian Telfair and the High-Stakes Business of High School Ball, by Ian O'Connor

Faithful: Two Diehard Boston Red Sox Fans Chronicle the Historic 2004 Season, by Stewart O'Nan and Stephen King

Blacktop Cowboys: Riders on the Run for Rodeo Gold, by Ty Phillips

Paper Lion: Confessions of a Last-String Quarterback (and his other work), by George Plimpton

Buttercups and Strong Boys, by William Plummer

Loose Balls, by Terry Pluto

$40 Million Slaves: The Rise, Fall, and Redemption of the Black Athlete, by
William C. Rhoden

*A Necessary Spectacle: Billie Jean King, Bobby Riggs, and the Tennis Match That
Leveled the Game,* by Selena Roberts

Blades of Glory: The True Story of a Young Team Bred to Win, by John Rosengren

The Numbers Game: Baseball's Lifelong Fascination with Statistics, by Alan Schwarz

Red Smith on Baseball: The Game's Greatest Writer on the Game's Greatest Years
(and his other work), by Red Smith

*Beyond the Shadow of the Senators: The Untold Story of the Homestead Grays and
the Integration of Baseball,* by Brad Snyder

*The Wicked Game: Arnold Palmer, Jack Nicklaus, Tiger Woods, and the Story of
Modern Golf,* by Howard Sounes

Rammer Jammer Yellow Hammer: A Journey into the Heart of Fan Mania, by
Warren St. John

Where Dreams Die Hard: A Small American Town and Its Six-Man Football Team,
by Carlton Stowers

Heaven Is a Playground, by Rick Telander

Fantasyland: A Season on Baseball's Lunatic Fringe, by Sam Walker

Heartsblood: Hunting, Spirituality, and Wildness in America, by Ted Williams

Cubs Nation: 162 Games. 162 Stories. 1 Addiction, by Gene Wojciechowski

*The Miracle of St. Anthony: A Season with Coach Bob Hurley and Basketball's
Most Improbable Dynasty,* by Adrian Wojnarowski

Big Game, Small World: A Basketball Adventure, by Alexander Wolff

Time and Place: History, Location, and Players

Eight Men Out: The Black Sox and the 1919 World Series, by Eliot Asinof

Ice Time: A Tale of Fathers, Sons, and Hometown Heroes, by Jay Atkinson

The City Game: Basketball from the Garden to the Playgrounds, by Pete Axthelm

Friday Night Lights: A Town, a Team, and a Dream, by H. G. Bissinger

*To Hate Like This Is to Be Happy Forever: A Thoroughly Obsessive, Intermittently
Uplifting, and Occasionally Unbiased Account of the Duke–North Carolina
Basketball Rivalry,* by Will Blythe

The Boys of Winter: The Untold Story of a Coach, a Dream, and the 1980 U.S. Olympic Hockey Team, by Wayne Coffey

The Last Best League: One Summer, One Season, One Dream, by Jim Collins

The Old Ball Game: How John McGraw, Christy Mathewson, and the New York Giants Created Modern Baseball, by Frank Deford

The Game, by Ken Dryden

The Great Match Race, by John Eisenberg

Race of the Century: The Heroic True Story of the 1908 New York to Paris Auto Race, by Julie M. Fenster

The Breaks of the Game; The Teammates; Summer of '49; and *October 1964* (and his other work), by David Halberstam

Green Hills of Africa, by Ernest Hemingway

Seabiscuit: An American Legend, by Laura Hillenbrand

The Boys of Summer (and his other work), by Roger Kahn

Ladies and Gentlemen, the Bronx Is Burning: 1977, Baseball, Politics, and the Battle for the Soul of a City, by Jonathan Mahler

Beyond Glory: Joe Louis vs. Max Schmeling, and a World on the Brink, by David Margolick

Autumn Glory: Baseball's First World Series, by Louis P. Masur

Levels of the Game and *A Sense of Where You Are: Bill Bradley at Princeton,* by John McPhee; see also Bill Bradley's *Life on the Run*

Man o' War: A Legend Like Lightning, by Dorothy Ours

Beautiful Jim Key: The Lost History of a Horse and a Man Who Changed the World, by Mim Eichler Rivas

Cinderella Man: James Braddock, Max Baer, and the Greatest Upset in Boxing History, by Jeremy Schaap

The Last Good Season: Brooklyn, the Dodgers, and Their Final Pennant Race Together, by Michael Shapiro

The Ticket Out: Darryl Strawberry and the Boys of Crenshaw, by Michael Sokolove

Hank Aaron and the Home Run That Changed America and *The Final Season: Fathers, Sons, and One Last Season in a Classic American Ballpark,* by Tom Stanton

The Rivalry: Bill Russell, Wilt Chamberlain, and the Golden Age of Basketball, by John Taylor

Transition Game, by L. Jon Wertheim

Resources and Awards

This is one subject area where it is hard not to know at least a little about what is going on. Sport is a dominant topic in our culture, and sports figures are often in the news. Still, there are few of us who do not need at least some level of help keeping up with the range of topics and who is writing what. The best way to get a sense of the subject is to page through *ESPN: The Magazine; Sports Illustrated; Field and Stream; Sporting News;* and *Gray's Sporting Journal.* There is also a yearly selection of the best writing on sports published each year in *The Best American Sports Writing.* Though much of the writing in these resources is by columnists, some of whom have yet to write a book, scanning these titles helps readers' advisory librarians become familiar with the styles, topics, and types of writing in the field. In addition, not only do many of these writers go on to publish books, but our readers know who they are and often consider their style when evaluating titles.

To see an overview of what has been written in the past, try *The Best American Sports Writing of the Century,* by David Halberstam, and *Sports Illustrated: Fifty Years of Great Writing,* by the editors of *Sports Illustrated.*

There are few well-known sports book awards; there are, however, places where sport-specific titles are featured. In addition to the awards listed below, sports titles, especially reporting, biography, and history, are sometimes short-listed or win major book awards such as the Pulitzer Prize.

WILLIAM HILL SPORTS BOOK OF THE YEAR AWARD

The William Hill award is a British sports award and offers close to $30,000 in prize money. Often American books win (with interestingly different covers and titles), but the majority of winning titles have a decidedly British or European bent, and sometimes the winning titles are not readily available or reviewed in America. Cricket books may not interest many American sports fans at the moment, but with the growing globalization of television via satellite and pay-per-view, one never knows what will take off. See http://www .williamhillmedia.com/sportsbook_index.asp.

SOCIETY OF AMERICAN BASEBALL RESEARCH (SABR)

The Society of American Baseball Research (SABR) has several baseball book awards. They are mostly for scholarly approaches to the subject, but occasionally a more narrative take is either nominated or wins. It is a good resource to at least keep in mind for history readers. See http://www.sabr.org.

CASEY AWARD

The CASEY Award is for the most outstanding baseball book of the year. The winners are not always nonfiction, but the short list almost always contains a few nonfiction books worth noting. The award is sponsored by *Spitball, the Literary Baseball Magazine*. See http://www.angelfire.com/oh5/spitball/award.html.

BOOK SENSE PICKS AND BOOK SENSE BOOK OF THE YEAR

The choices for the Book Sense Picks list and the Book of the Year are selected by booksellers as titles that hold high appeal to a wide range of readers. They are a great resource to monitor. The picks are listed monthly, and any big sports titles are likely to show up. See http://www.booksense.com/index.jsp.

NOTABLE BOOKS COUNCIL

The American Library Association's Notable Book Council, a committee of the CODES section of RUSA, selects the most notable fiction, nonfiction, and poetry for adults each year. The books are uniformly well written, highly narrative in nature, and offer a wide range of appeal points for readers. Major sports books are included from time to time, making the list one to watch. See http://www.ala.org/ala/rusa/rusaprotools/rusanotable/notablebooks.htm.

ALEX AWARDS

The ALEX Awards are sponsored by the American Library Association's Young Adult Library Services Association. Each year a committee of librarians selects the top ten adult books for young adults. The members of the committee try to select books that hold appeal for a young adult audience, which means, among other things, that the works of nonfiction are highly narrative and readable. The list mixes fiction and nonfiction, but the nonfiction choices are always worth looking over. The site lists the winners from 1998 onward. See http://www.ala.org/ala/yalsa/booklistsawards/alexawards/alexawards.htm.

7

TRUE CRIME

True crime accounts are everywhere. They are the bread and butter of many cable TV newscasts, feature on the front page of newspapers ranging from the *New York Times* to the *National Enquirer,* and even appear in fictional TV shows enticingly advertised to viewers as "ripped from the headlines!"

Conventional wisdom would have it that anything so prevalent and popular would soon be reflected in the book industry, but actually the authors were ahead of the curve. True crime accounts have been popular in many different guises for some time. As many who studied nineteenth-century British literature in college know, Dickens had an observant eye for crime and wove true crime reporting and commentary into his fiction. And he was not alone. Sir Arthur Conan Doyle famously used a real-life thief as inspiration for his master criminal, Professor Moriarty. Today genre fiction, from mystery to horror to thrillers, reflects aspects of true crime in its story lines. True crime writers have in turn borrowed tools from the fiction writer's arsenal, and narrative elements are commonly incorporated into the gripping, tension-filled tales readers enjoy.

What Readers Enjoy in These Books

Many fans enjoy true crime books for the same appeal reasons they enjoy thrillers, horror, police procedurals, and other similar fiction. The appeal factors for these genres, in particular, pacing, story line, and tone, all translate directly to true crime, as does the sense of justice and the vicarious thrill of fear.

As would be expected, character plays a large role in true crime accounts. Readers like learning about the lives of criminals, their victims, and the individuals seeking to bring justice to both. As with all human interest stories, characters range from the dark and sinister to the valiant and dedicated. Readers who are interested in characters and their motivations have a large landscape in which to explore. Strangely enough, the writer is often a quasi character in these books, both via the format of memoir or personal account and as someone who directly knows the killer or the victims. The classic case is Ann Rule, who worked alongside Ted Bundy for a time and wrote *The Stranger beside Me.*

True crime books tend to be highly detailed, and readers enjoy learning about many different aspects of criminal investigations. Details of the crime (often described in gory minutiae), methods of murder, motivations and psychological aspects, police profiling, forensic science, investigative techniques, legal procedures, and much more are all used to bring the crime to life. The pacing of the story can also determine the reader's enjoyment, with some relishing high tension and gripping narratives and others enjoying a more measured or leisurely pace.

Finally, readers enjoy the vicarious pleasure that comes from tracking down a killer and ultimately understanding and outwitting the criminal mind. They like learning how the crime was planned and executed. They enjoy reading how cunning the criminal was and how smart the investigators are. One of the strongest appeals of true crime is readers' need to understand why someone would do something as horrible as the crimes discussed in these books and to experience the cathartic closure that comes with reaching the end of their story.

Types of Books

True crime, for all the many horrific events that happen each year, is a fairly small world in terms of the types of books published. There are four different classifications in this chapter:

- Historical and Literary Accounts
- Reporting
- Heists and Capers
- Biography, Memoir, and Personal Accounts

Reader demand tends to push for a quickly produced account of a crime making headlines and then allows for the fuller reporting of that crime later on. It should be of little surprise, then, that many true crime books are reporting titles. Readers also clamor for books by those involved in the story, such as family members, police, forensic experts, and profilers, so there is also a steady stream of personal stories. Contrarily, there are relatively few historical and literary accounts or caper and heist books published in a given year, so when one is published, readers' advisory and collection development librarians should take note.

The four types included below approach crime from a range of viewpoints, and the levels of gore, photos, and details vary widely. In each type summary I give a generalization about the levels of detailed descriptions of the crime, but this is simply a generalization. There can be very graphic and less graphic books in all types. Readers' advisory librarians should take care not to suggest an analytical study to a reader looking for high tension, suspense, and bloody detail or a book full of horrifying violence to a reader who is looking for something of a more literary and historical character. In the entire nonfiction world, the standard readers' advisory practice of knowing your reader's mood and tastes is no more relevant than in true crime.

Benchmark Books to Read and Suggest

The titles annotated below are some of the best examples of each type of true crime. Additional suggested readings are included to add a sense of scope to the annotation and give readers' advisory librarians a few other titles to suggest.

Figuring out how a book represents its subject area and how readers respond to each area allows readers' advisory librarians to build a wide-ranging appreciation for the genre. One of the skills readers' advisory librarians need to cultivate is the ability to see connections and patterns among titles, subject areas, types, and fiction genre titles. These connections are particularly helpful in nonfiction readers' advisory because the appeal points we traditionally use for fiction are complicated by the subjects of nonfiction.

For readers' advisory librarians, seeing as many connections as possible between titles and subject areas helps place all nonfiction, including true crime, within a larger context of nonfiction and fiction generally. Reading these books helps both underscore those connections and spark further connective thinking. It is important when reading these books to focus not solely on the crime and the level of description or even the type of book but on how each typifies the classification and how each brings enjoyment to the reader.

Historical and Literary Accounts

Historical accounts tend to be more literary and are often written by historians who just happen to get interested in a crime topic. Because their writing focus is not simply true crime but instead covers a huge array of subjects, their approach to crime is more holistic and includes a consideration of the society of the time. These authors bring a great body of research to their work. Because the crime happened long ago, they have the luxury of perspective and know the long-term consequences of the crime, which adds nuance to their work. The details of period and place are a strong appeal factor for readers. Historians and literary writers also tend to be good storytellers. These books range from medium to highly narrative and blend enough fact to satisfy readers looking for history with a sufficiently gripping story to please readers who want a story. These titles are generally more literary and nuanced and focus on style and writing rather than brutal detail.

The Devil in the White City: Murder, Magic, and Madness at the Fair That Changed America, **by Erik Larson**

In 1893 Chicago hosted the World's Fair and a serial killer of terrible imagination. This is a story of two men, the architect leading the building efforts of the fair, Daniel H. Burnham, and the killer, H. H. Holmes. In a narrative that is as gripping and well paced as any suspense thriller, Larson, in roughly alternating chapters, tracks the stories of each man and the world they live in and poses questions about the future they help to create. Burnham had a huge task, designing a setting fit for the fair. Overcoming great odds and employing a vision far grander than expected, he built the amazing "White City" and was, in large part, responsible for the success of the fair. Larson provides readers details about the buildings and the process of creating the setting for the fair as well as descriptions of the fair and its attendees. Readers get to rub shoulders with the likes of Susan B. Anthony and Thomas Edison. Larson also describes the horrible crimes. Holmes built a hotel with a crematorium and gas chamber close to the fair site and lured his victims inside. It is thought that he killed close to two hundred people. Blending the promise of the future, which is the embodiment of the World's Fair, with the dark side of progress that seemed to lurk hidden in the fair's wake, Larson has written what will become a classic literary and historical true crime title.

Read this book because, like *The Perfect Storm* and *Seabiscuit*, it is one of the books that builds the foundations of a highly narrative and story-centered nonfiction canon.

Suggest this book to readers who enjoy gripping stories, sharp writing, and history. Pair it with books such as John Berendt's *Midnight in the Garden of Good and Evil* for readers who are looking for additional literary crime books with a strong sense of place, or with the social history novel *The Alienist*, by Caleb Carr, for a literary and fictionalized account of another devious serial killer. Readers willing to wander farther afield might also enjoy *Wainewright the Poisoner*, by Andrew Motion.

Reporting

Crime reporting makes up the majority of the true crime books published. These books are often written by reporters who have followed the case and are skilled in researching the details of the crime, the criminal, the victims, and all the others associated with the story. Since journalists get most of their facts and information from the police, many reporting types of true crime have that prosecutorial perspective and can read like a good fiction police procedural. The reporter, however, often knows more in retrospect than the police did at the time and can therefore create a narrative full of suspense and tension and present multiple points of view. Many of these books are written by true crime experts who follow cases and write quick-to-market paperback accounts. Reporting books tend to be full of details, are fact based, and include writing that ranges from spare and solid to the more descriptive and gory, but they do not attempt strong elaborations of the wider culture or times.

Green River, Running Red: The Real Story of the Green River Killer— America's Deadliest Serial Murderer, by Ann Rule

Ann Rule is perhaps the best-known true crime writer working today. She spent more than twenty years researching this story, and apparently the killer, Gary Ridgeway, spent time following her career as well, attending many of her book signings. This creepy fact underscores Ridgeway's remarkable ability to blend in, even while he was actively seeking victims, murdering them, and hiding their bodies. His first victim was found in 1982, and police believe he was responsible for the deaths of as many as fifty people. This killing spree stumped police and led to the formation of the Green River Task Force, a group of investigators who considered thousands of possible suspects. It was only in 2001, when a new DNA process enabled investigators to match evidence in better ways, that the case broke. With her trademark blending of story and reporting, Rule relates the life of the killer, his victims, and the investigators. She also tells her own story related to this crime. She lived near the area where most of the victims were abducted, had unprecedented access to Dave Reichert, the sheriff of King County, reported the story for a Seattle newspaper, and spent years working on the idea of a book. Her efforts make for compelling crime reporting.

Read this book because it typifies the best aspects of true crime; it has a gripping story line, reports the details of the investigation, follows the motivations of the killer, and recounts the lives of the victims. Rule has a steady hand, unlike some of her more sensational colleagues, and her work makes for the perfect introduction to true crime reading.

Suggest this book to readers who like to follow the investigation more than dwell in the grisly details and who enjoy a blend of perspectives when reading about true crime. For more on the story, readers might follow up with *Chasing the Devil: My Twenty-Year Quest to Capture the Green River Killer,* by David Reichert. In addition to the rest of Ann Rule's work, readers who like her mix of reporting and detail may enjoy *A Death in Texas: A Story of Race, Murder, and a Small Town's Struggle for Redemption,* by Dina Temple-Raston, and *Bitter Blood: A True Story of Southern Family Pride, Madness, and Multiple Murder,* by Jerry Bledsoe. Readers looking for fiction as a companion to true crime might consider the novels of Patricia Cornwell and Kathy Reichs.

Heists and Capers

These books are defined by story line, tone, and approach. The type focuses on theft, forgery, or similar crimes. The tone is typically lighter than any other true crime type, the tension is less frantic, and the details are less gory. These books are more about derring-do than dark and deadly murder and therefore make good reading suggestions for the squeamish.

Ballad of the Whiskey Robber: A True Story of Bank Heists, Ice Hockey, Transylvanian Pelt Smuggling, Moonlighting Detectives, and Broken Hearts, by Julian Rubinstein

In this uproarious escapade through the crumbling communist block of Eastern Europe, Attila Ambrus acts as a modern-day Robin Hood, a rakish figure several steps ahead of a bumbling police force, a headline-grabbing common prince, and a really bad hockey player. His crimes are legion—he managed to steal millions from assorted banks—but then so is his life. He slipped into Hungry from Transylvania as the cold war ended. There he talked himself onto a hockey team and used it as cover while stealing his loot, enthralling women, and planning his next heist. It was a wild ride, one Rubinstein covers with a belly laugh, appreciating the actions of a motley mix of characters. But he also has a fine eye for the setting and times and captures Eastern Europe on the verge of becoming some odd mix of strange energy and new capitalism. The result is a fun and perceptive book that melds sports, cultural history, and true crime into an entertaining treat.

Read this book because it is fun and shows the tone many readers want in a heist and caper tale.

Suggest this book to readers who are looking for something unique, enjoy funny stories told well, or are interested in quirky characters. It is an unusual book, but readers looking for something similar may enjoy *A Fool's Gold: A Story of Ancient Spanish Treasure, Two Pounds of Pot, and the Young Lawyer Almost Left Holding the Bag,* by Bill Merritt, and *Final Confession: The Unsolved Crimes of Phil Cresta,* by Brian P. Wallace and Bill Crowley.

Biography, Memoir, and Personal Accounts

This type includes books by lawyers, police, specialists, and others who have a professional, or accidental, role in criminal justice. These books bring an insider's perspective to the procedures of a crime and its aftermath, and they vary widely. There can be detailed, story-focused accounts that read like a script for a TV crime show, musing and lyrical memoirs, or analytical and less narrative accounts of the scientific side of crime.

Blue Blood, by Edward Conlon

In his beautifully written memoir, Edward Conlon tells readers what it is like to be a cop—from rookie on patrol to detective on a case—in vividly rough and honest ways. His insider look at the profession makes for compelling reading, and his history of the New York Police Department is fascinating. Conlon comes from a family of police officers, and his understanding and affection for the force resonate on every page. After graduating from Harvard, Conlon joined the ranks and worked his way up the line. His story is richly descriptive of what it is like to walk the beat, respond to calls, and work with partners who become family. He describes the city he loves and protects in vibrant and sprawling detail and talks about cases with a great mix of step-by-step action and insider explanation. His account touches on some of the most stressful, horrible, and heroic actions of the force, Amadou Diallo, Abner Louima, and September 11, 2001, but it is mostly about the daily life of a dedicated cop.

Read this book to get a sense of the inside life of police officers and to understand the allure of the professional account.

Suggest this book to readers interested in police life and to anyone who enjoys fine writing and great stories. Consider as well *The Restless Sleep: Inside New York City's Cold Case Squad*, by Stacy Horn; though a work of excellent reporting and not a professional account, it nevertheless has enough insider details and perspective to hold appeal to readers who enjoyed Conlon. *A Cop's Life: True Stories from the Heart behind the Badge* and *True Blue: Police Stories by Those Who Have Lived Them*, by Randy Sutton, are both excellent collections of stories from the blue line and share both the immediacy and reflection of Conlon's work. For a different take altogether, *Kitchen Confidential: Adventures in the Culinary Underbelly*, by Anthony Bourdain, is a frank and honest look at a different secret world—this time the raunchy realm of restaurant life.

Key Authors

There are many true crime key authors, and their styles range from the thoughtful to the sensational. This can be a frustrating subject for readers' advisory librarians who either do not read in the area or do not read as widely as their patrons. The comfort of having a list of names to work from cannot be overstated when faced with a patron who has read all of Ann Rule and is looking for other suggestions. The authors listed below are the major writers in the field and can be relied on to produce titles holding wide appeal to several different types of readers. Use this list to make suggestions, build displays, and aid in weeding (which can be hard in the true crime area since titles are so reactive to the media surrounding the event but can then become core titles in the field). As is true with most subject areas, keep in mind that the quantity of books is not what determines if a writer is a key author, but rather the impact of their work on the field and the reaction of readers to their books.

John Berendt	Lowell Cauffiel	Kurt Eichenwald
Jerry Bledsoe	Ted Conover	T. J. English
Charles Bowden	Miles Corwin	Diane Fanning
Vincent Bugliosi	Roger L. Depue	Mark Fuhrman
Truman Capote	John Douglas	Rick Geary
Kathryn Casey	Dominick Dunne	John Glatt

Robert Graysmith
Jonathan Harr
Joe Jackson
Aphrodite Jones
Erik Larson
Gary M. Lavergne
Dick Lehr
Peter Maas

Joe McGinniss
Corey Mitchell
James Neff
Jack Olsen
Nicholas Pileggi
Ann Rule
Harold Schechter
Lawrence Schiller

Stephen Singular
Carlton Smith
Carlton Stowers
Thomas Thompson
Joseph Wambaugh
Peter Watson

Selected Bibliography of True Crime Books to Read and Suggest

Historical and Literary

London 1849: A Victorian Murder Story, by Michael Alpert

Midnight in the Garden of Good and Evil, by John Berendt

Arc of Justice: A Saga of Race, Civil Rights, and Murder in the Jazz Age, by Kevin Boyle

A Sentimental Murder: Love and Madness in the Eighteenth Century, by John Brewer

Public Enemies: America's Greatest Crime Wave and the Birth of the FBI, 1933–34, by Bryan Burrough

In Cold Blood, by Truman Capote

The Adversary: A True Story of Monstrous Deception, by Emmanuel Carrere

The Last Posse: A Jailbreak, a Manhunt, and the End of Hang-'Em-High Justice, by Gale E. Christianson

The Murder of Helen Jewett, by Patricia Cline Cohen

Tough Jews: Fathers, Sons, and Gangster Dreams, by Rich Cohen

Portrait of a Killer: Jack the Ripper—Case Closed, by Patricia Cornwell

The Doctor, the Murder, the Mystery: The True Story of the Dr. John Branion Murder Case, by Barbara D'Amato

Cosa Nostra: A History of the Sicilian Mafia, by John Dickie

Greentown: Murder and Mystery in Greenwich, America's Wealthiest Community, by Timothy Dumas

The Bobbed Haired Bandit: A True Story of Crime and Celebrity in 1920s New York, by Stephen Duncombe and Andrew Mattson

The Elements of Murder: A History of Poison, by John Emsley

Swift Justice: Murder and Vengeance in a California Town, by Harry Farrell

Author Unknown: On the Trail of Anonymous, by Donald W. Foster

Treasury of Victorian Murder: The Case of Madeleine Smith (and his other work), by Rick Geary

Under the Bridge, by Rebecca Godfrey

Crash Out: The True Tale of a Hell's Kitchen Kid and the Bloodiest Escape in Sing Sing History, by David Goewey

The Island of Lost Maps: A True Story of Cartographic Crime, by Miles Harvey

Leavenworth Train: A Fugitive's Search for Justice in the Vanishing West, by Joe Jackson

A Death in Belmont, by Sebastian Junger

Dynamite Fiend: The Chilling Tale of a Confederate Spy, Con Artist, and Mass Murderer, by Ann Larabee

The Devil in the White City: Murder, Magic, and Madness at the Fair That Changed America and *Thunderstruck*, by Erik Larson

The Napoleon of Crime: The Life and Times of Adam Worth, Master Thief, by Ben Macintyre

The Executioner's Song, by Norman Mailer (Many libraries catalog this as fiction, and Mailer himself called it a "true-life novel." It is included here because it was one of the very early attempts at blending fiction and nonfiction and helped start the development of new journalism and creative nonfiction.)

The Informant: The FBI, the Ku Klux Klan, and the Murder of Viola Liuzzo, by Gary May

Arsenic under the Elms: Murder in Victorian New Haven, by Virginia A. McConnell

The Story of Chicago May, by Nuala O'Faolain

And the Dead Shall Rise: The Murder of Mary Phagan and the Lynching of Leo Frank, by Steve Oney

Death at the Priory: Love, Sex, and Murder in Victorian England, by James Ruddick

Facing the Wind: A True Story of Tragedy and Reconciliation, by Julie Salamon

Honor Killing: How the Infamous "Massie Affair" Transformed Hawai'i, by David E. Stannard

The Beautiful Cigar Girl: Mary Rogers, Edgar Allan Poe, and the Invention of Murder, by Daniel Stashower

Manhunt: The 12-Day Chase for Lincoln's Killer, by James L. Swanson

The Vendetta, by Alston Purvis, with Alex Tresinowski

Moonlight: Abraham Lincoln and the Almanac Trial, by John Evangelist Walsh

The Italian Boy: A Tale of Murder and Body Snatching in 1830s London, by Sarah Wise

The Poet and the Murderer, by Simon Worrall

Reporting

Death Sentence: The True Story of Velma Barfield's Life, Crimes and Execution and *Bitter Blood: A True Story of Southern Family Pride, Madness, and Multiple Murder* (and his other work), by Jerry Bledsoe

Courtroom 302: A Year behind the Scenes in an American Criminal Courthouse, by Steve Bogira

Down by the River: Drugs, Money, Murder, and Family (and his other work), by Charles Bowden

Killing Pablo: The Hunt for the World's Greatest Outlaw, by Mark Bowden

I Heard You Paint Houses: Frank "The Irishman" Sheeran and the Inside Story of the Mafia, the Teamsters, and the Final Ride of Jimmy Hoffa, by Charles Brandt

Helter Skelter: The True Story of the Manson Murders and *And the Sea Will Tell,* by Vincent Bugliosi

Dangerous Waters: Modern Piracy and Terror on the High Seas, by John Burnett

The Night Stalker: The True Story of America's Most Feared Serial Killer, by Philip Carlo

She Wanted It All: A True Story of Sex, Murder, and a Texas Millionaire, by Kathryn Casey

Forever and Five Days (and his other work), by Lowell Cauffiel

Takedown: The Fall of the Last Mafia Empire, by Douglas Century and Rick Cowan

Body Brokers: Inside America's Underground Trade in Human Remains, by Annie Cheney

Crime Beat: A Decade of Covering Cops and Killers, by Michael Connelly

Newjack: Guarding Sing Sing (and his other work), by Ted Conover

Homicide Special: On the Streets with the LAPD's Elite Detective Unit and *The Killing Season,* by Miles Corwin

A Rip in Heaven: A Memoir of Murder and Its Aftermath, by Jeanine Cummins

Ungodly: The Passions, Torments, and Murder of Atheist Madalyn Murray O'Hair, by Ted Dracos

The Shark Net, by Robert Drewe

Evil among Us: The Texas Mormon Missionary Murders, by Ken Driggs

Justice: Crimes, Trials, and Punishments, by Dominick Dunne

Conspiracy of Fools: A True Story; Serpent on the Rock; and *The Informant: A True Story,* by Kurt Eichenwald

Paddy Whacked: The Untold Story of the Irish-American Gangster, by T. J. English

Trail of Blood: A Father, a Son and a Tell-Tale Crime Scene Investigation, by Wanda Webb Evans and James Dunn

Written in Blood and *Gone Forever: A True Story of Marriage, Betrayal, and Murder* (and her other work), by Diane Fanning

True Story: Murder, Memoir, Mea Culpa, by Michael Finkel

The Death of Innocents: A True Story of Murder, Medicine, and High-Stake Science, by Richard Firstman and Jamie Talan

Invisible Eden: A Story of Love and Murder on Cape Cod, by Maria Flook

Death and Justice (and his other work), by Mark Fuhrman

Never Leave Me: A True Story of Marriage, Deception, and Brutal Murder (and his other work), by John Glatt

Zodiac (and his other work), by Robert Graysmith

The Innocent Man: Murder and Injustice in a Small Town, by John Grisham

Going Up the River: Travels in a Prison Nation, by Joseph Hallinan

A Civil Action, by Jonathan Harr

The Cyanide Canary, by Joseph Hilldorfer and Robert Dugoni

Black Dahlia Avenger: The True Story, by Steve Hodel

The Restless Sleep: Inside New York City's Cold Case Squad, by Stacy Horn

Desire Street: A True Story of Death and Deliverance in New Orleans, by Jed Horne

No Matter How Loud I Shout: A Year in the Life of Juvenile Court and *Mean Justice,* by Edward Humes

All She Wanted (and her other work), by Aphrodite Jones

The Other Side of the River: A Story of Two Towns, a Death, and America's Dilemma, by Alex Kotlowitz

Under the Banner of Heaven: A Story of Violent Faith, by Jon Krakauer

Burning Rainbow Farm: How a Stoner Utopia Went Up in Smoke, by Dean Kuipers

Bad Boy: The True Story of Kenneth Allen McDuff, the Most Notorious Serial Killer in Texas History (and his other work), by Gary M. Lavergne

Our Guys: The Glen Ridge Rape and the Secret Life of the Perfect Suburb, by Bernard Lefkowitz

Black Mass: The True Story of an Unholy Alliance between the FBI and the Irish Mob, by Dick Lehr and Gerard O'Neill

Judgment Ridge: The True Story behind the Dartmouth Murders, by Dick Lehr and Mitchell Zuckoff

Conviction: Solving the Moxley Murder, by Leonard Levitt

Underboss (and his other work), by Peter Maas

Killing for Company: The Story of a Man Addicted to Murder, by Brian Masters

Blind Faith and *Fatal Vision* (and his other work), by Joe McGinniss

Evil Eyes (and his other work), by Corey Mitchell

The Wrong Man: The Final Verdict on the Dr. Sam Sheppard Murder Case, by James Neff

I: The Creation of a Serial Killer (and his other work), by Jack Olsen

Are You There Alone? The Unspeakable Crime of Andrea Yates, by Suzanne O'Malley

Missing: The Oregon City Girls, by Linda O'Neal, Philip F. Tennyson, and Rick Watson

Clubland: The Fabulous Rise and Murderous Fall of Club Culture, by Frank Owen

Rothstein: The Life, Times, and Murder of the Criminal Genius Who Fixed the 1919 World Series, by David Pietrusza

Wiseguy and *Casino (Love and Honor in Las Vegas),* by Nicholas Pileggi; and see *On the Run: A Mafia Childhood,* by Gina Hill and Gregg Hill, for an account of Henry Hill from his children's perspective

Five Families: The Rise, Decline, and Resurgence of America's Most Powerful Mafia Empires, by Selwyn Raab

Green River, Running Red: The Real Story of the Green River Killer—America's Deadliest Serial Murderer (and her other work), by Ann Rule

Bestial: The Savage Trail of a True American Monster (and his other work), by Harold Schechter

Cape May Court House: A Death in the Night and *Perfect Murder, Perfect Town* (and his other work), by Lawrence Schiller

One of Ours: Timothy McVeigh and the Oklahoma City Bombing, by Richard A. Serrano

Shattered: Reclaiming a Life Torn Apart by Violence, by Debra Puglisi Sharp, with Marjorie Preston

A Rose for Mary: The Hunt for the Real Boston Strangler, by Casey Sherman

Presumed Guilty: An Investigation into the Jon Benet Ramsey Case, the Media, and the Culture of Pornography and *Unholy Messenger: The Life and Crimes of the BTK Serial Killer* (and his other work), by Stephen Singular

The BTK Murders (and his other work), by Carlton Smith

Blind Eye: The Terrifying Story of a Doctor Who Got Away with Murder, by James B. Stewart

To the Last Breath: Three Women Fight for the Truth behind a Child's Tragic Murder, by Carlton Stowers

LAbyrinth: A Detective Investigates the Murders of Tupac Shakur and Notorious B.I.G., the Implication of Death Row Records' Suge Knight, and the Origins of the Los Angeles Police Scandal, by Randall Sullivan

Killer Clown: The John Wayne Gacy Murders, by Terry Sullivan, with Peter T. Maiken

The Count and the Confession: A True Murder Mystery, by John Taylor

Blood and Money (and his other work), by Thomas Thompson

May God Have Mercy: A True Story of Crime and Punishment, by John C. Tucker

Blood Washes Blood: A True Story of Love, Murder, and Redemption under the Sicilian Sun, by Frank Viviano

Son of a Grifter: The Twisted Tale of Sante and Kenny Kimes, the Most Notorious Con Artists in America, by Kent Walker, with Mark Schone

Fire Lover: A True Story (and his other work), by Joseph Wambaugh

The Medici Conspiracy: The Illicit Journey of Looted Antiquities, from Italy's Tomb Raiders to the World's Greatest Museums, by Peter Watson and Cecelia Todeschini

Pointing from the Grave: A True Story of Murder and DNA, by Samantha Weinberg

American Taboo: A Murder in the Peace Corps, by Philip Weiss

Rattlesnake Romeo, by Joy Wellman

The General: Irish Mob Boss, by Paul Williams

Heists and Capers

Catch Me If You Can: The True Story of a Real Fake, by Frank W. Abagnale

The Rescue Artist: A True Story of Art, Thieves, and the Hunt for a Missing Masterpiece, by Edward Dolnick

The Irish Game: A True Story of Crime and Art, by Matthew Hart

A Fool's Gold: A Story of Ancient Spanish Treasure, Two Pounds of Pot, and the Young Lawyer Almost Left Holding the Bag, by Bill Merritt

Ballad of the Whiskey Robber: A True Story of Bank Heists, Ice Hockey, Transylvanian Pelt Smuggling, Moonlighting Detectives, and Broken Hearts, by Julian Rubinstein

The Cuckoo's Egg: Tracking a Spy through the Maze of Computer Espionage, by Clifford Stoll

Final Confession: The Unsolved Crimes of Phil Cresta, by Brian P. Wallace and Bill Crowley

Biography, Memoir, and Personal Accounts

Dead Reckoning: The New Science of Catching Killers, by Michael M. D. Baden and Marion Roach

Death's Acre: Inside the Legendary Forensic Lab—the Body Farm—Where the Dead Do Tell Tales, by William M. Bass and Jon Jefferson

Ready for the People: My Most Chilling Cases as a Prosecutor, by Marissa N. Batt

Portraits of Guilt, by Jeanne Boylan

No Lights, No Sirens: The Corruption and Redemption of an Inner City Cop, by Robert Cea

Blue Blood, by Edward Conlon

When Corruption Was King: How I Helped the Mob Rule Chicago, Then Brought the Outfit Down, by Robert Cooley, with Hillel Levin

Prince of the City: The True Story of a Cop Who Knew Too Much, by Robert Daley

Between Good and Evil: A Master Profiler's Hunt for Society's Most Violent Predators, by Roger L. Depue

Reversal of Fortune: Inside the Von Bulow Case, by Alan M. Dershowitz

Mindhunter: Inside the FBI's Elite Serial Crime Unit; The Anatomy of Motive: The FBI's Legendary Mindhunter Explores the Key to Understanding and Catching Violent Criminals; and *Anyone You Want Me to Be: A True Story of Sex and Death on the Internet* (and his other work), by John Douglas

Indefensible: One Lawyer's Journey into the Inferno of American Justice, by David Feige

Dark Dreams: Sexual Violence, Homicide and the Criminal Mind, by Roy Hazelwood and Stephen G. Michaud

No Stone Unturned: The Story of Necrosearch International Investigators, by Steve Jackson

Cracking Cases: The Science of Solving Crimes, by Henry C. Lee, with Thomas W. O'Neil; and *Dr. Henry Lee's Forensic Files,* by Henry C. Lee and Jerry Labriola

Serpico, by Peter Maas

The Unknown Darkness: Profiling the Predators among Us, by Gregg O. McCrary and Katherine Ramsland

My Father's Gun: One Family, Three Badges, One Hundred Years in the NYPD, by Brian McDonald

Within These Walls: Memoirs of a Death House Chaplain, by Carroll Pickett, with Carlton Stowers

Donnie Brasco: My Undercover Life in the Mafia, by Joseph D. Pistone

Under and Alone: The True Story of the Undercover Agent Who Infiltrated America's Most Violent Outlaw Motorcycle Gang, by William Queen

Where the Money Is: True Tales from the Bank Robbery Capital of the World, by William J. Rehder and Gordon Dillow

Chasing the Devil: My Twenty-Year Quest to Capture the Green River Killer, by David Reichert

Whoever Fights Monsters: My Twenty Years Tracking Serial Killers for the FBI, by Robert K. Ressler and Thomas Schachtman

Why They Kill: The Discoveries of a Maverick Criminologist, by Richard Rhodes

Actual Innocence: Five Days to Execution, and Other Dispatches from the Wrongly Convicted, by Barry Scheck, Peter Neufeld, and Jim Dwyer

Homicide: A Year on the Killing Streets, by David Simon

Blood Done Sign My Name: A True Story, by Timothy B. Tyson

Inside Rikers: Stories from the World's Largest Penal Colony, by Jennifer Wynn

Resources and Awards

It is hard not to know when a major crime story breaks. Simply turn on the TV and you will hear, in an endless parade of talking heads, all the details of the crime of the day. Websites, newspapers, and magazines also keep everyone who is interested up-to-date. Still, if true crime is not your cup of tea, or even if it is, it is nice to know the best in the field and have a way of keeping up without constantly tuning in. The best way to get a sense of the subject and who is writing is to page through the yearly compendium of *The Best American Crime Writing.* This gives the readers' advisory librarian a sense of the types of writing popular each year and the various styles employed to narrate a true crime story. Another way to keep up is to see what publishing imprints such as Berkley True Crime, St. Martin's True Crime Library, and Pinnacle True Crime are focused on; each publishes books on the most sensational and news-making stories.

Readers' advisory librarians should monitor the true crime awards each year to get a sense of the best in the field and to track trends. The two most useful awards to look for are the Edgar and the Gold Dagger awards. Any nominated title should be reviewed with an eye toward both readers' advisory service and collection development. The Anthony and Macavity awards offer less consistently useful help, but when they do list a true crime book it is well worth noting.

EDGAR ALLAN POE AWARDS

The Edgars are given yearly by the Mystery Writers of America. The awards honor the most distinguished title in several categories, including best fact crime. The winning titles range from the historical to the more sensational, making this an important award to monitor since it can direct readers' advisory librarians to the best in a wide range of types. See http://www.mystery writers.org/pages/awards/index.htm.

CRIME WRITER'S ASSOCIATION

The Crime Writers' Association (UK) gives an award called the Gold Dagger for the best nonfiction crime book of the year. The winning titles must be first published in Britain, but more often than not they become big titles in the United States as well. See http://www.thecwa.co.uk.

ANTHONY AWARDS

The Anthony Awards are given at the annual Bouchercon World Mystery Convention. They are decided during the convention by a vote of registered attendees. Nominations are submitted by fans. Since this is a reader-based process, the nominations and winners each year can be diverse, but usually some true crime titles are at least nominated. Monitoring this award gives readers' advisory librarians insights on the collective mood of fans and, if examined over time, a good sense of the direction the subject is heading. Bouchercon is run by volunteers and its website changes for each conference. The best way to find all the awards is to search on Bouchercon and Anthony Awards and to look for links for each year.

MACAVITY AWARDS

The Macavity Awards are given by the members of Mystery Readers International. Similar to the Anthony Awards procedure, the members of MRI nominate and vote on the winning titles. Though more true crime titles were nominated in past years, the current trend in the nonfiction category is for reference works on mysteries. Still, this is an award worth checking, since any nonfiction true crime title nominated by this group of readers would be well worth noting. See http://www.mysteryreaders.org/macavity.html.

8

TRAVEL

Few books offer as much delight, wonder, and exhilaration as those that describe places we long to visit or explore. All sorts of readers enjoy these books, from armchair travelers to those planning an actual journey, so it is no wonder that travel books account for a huge section of nonfiction. Everyone, it seems, is eager to discover more about a locale, take a vicarious trip, or read about the missteps and wrong turns of fellow travelers.

Travel books range from those that are directly and solely focused on the destination to those that use the destination to muse on a broader range of topics. Often writers in this area have many other interests and motivations than a simple trip, and those wider aspects are reflected in their works. Travel books can encompass any manner of additional subjects: history, adventure, anthropology, personal growth, or easement of grief. It is not unusual for avid fans of this subject to find themselves pedaling ungainly along the route of the Tour de France, camping in the desert during a wind storm, or escaping the stress of sorrow by creating a new home abroad.

What Readers Enjoy in These Books

Many reading pleasures are richly realized in these books. Readers enjoy the romance and adventure, the social and cultural commentary, the sense of exploration and place, and the coming-of-age quality that imbues many (even if the character is over sixty when she decides to move to France, build a house, or climb a mountain). It should be no surprise, then, that the appeal elements of tone, setting, description, character, and learning/experiencing are all prevalent in these books.

Writers take great care to evoke the mood necessary to enhance the journey and to describe place as richly as possible. Because of this need to capture location and express place to a reader, these books are written in a particular and notable style. Their narrative context tends to be medium to high, and the authors' interests are often expressed through indirect story lines that meander toward a conclusion. Clear yet evocative language is often employed as the writers conjure both familiar and exotic worlds. Working hand in hand with the appeal of language, travel books are also wonderfully full of detail. Indeed, detail and description combine to create the landscape of travel books, wallpapering their pages with the elements that turn a trip to the market into a riotous mix of sights, sounds, and flavors.

Many of these books are individual accounts of the author's travels, so not only do readers get to experience that odd mix of author as character, they also get to read about a wide range of characters who are brought to vivid life by their interactions with the author. Finally, the appeal element of learning/experiencing is also a big attraction. Readers enjoy learning more about a location and its history, culture, land, and people along with the simple pleasure of experiencing a new place, point of view, or way of life.

Types of Books

In contrast to other areas in this book, the subject of travel is not as strongly divided by type. Travel books have many aspects in common, thus narrowing the type ranges. This chapter reviews three types:

- Memoir and Personal Accounts
- History, Land, and Place
- Journeys, Escapes, and Adventures

Memoirs should be expected, not only because it is a standard nonfiction type but because travel books are almost always personal stories as well as stories of journeys. History, land, and place is not as unusual a type here as one might think. Many of its elements, including focus and authorial intent, are similar to those in titles listed under the time and place type in the chapter on sports. In fact, many subject chapters have types that address a topic from a perspective of time, place, or history. Perhaps because the distinctions among travel types are so subtle, fans of this subject area read fairly widely and enjoy books in all classifications. Use these types to help guide readers to the books most applicable to their preferences at the moment.

There is often little separating a travel story from a true adventure, and many travel readers find much to appreciate in the true adventure titles listed in chapter 9. So use the information in both chapters when making suggestions to readers, and keep in mind that nature and natural history titles (such as those in chapter 4) can also be good suggestions for travel readers.

Benchmark Books to Read and Suggest

Travel is such a rich subject area that readers' advisory librarians have little difficulty finding books readers enjoy. It is important, however, to reason out why a reader enjoys a book. Location and description drive some books; history and understanding drive others. Readers enjoy a wide range of titles but may not be able to express the differences between them. Readers' advisory librarians should, despite the fine distinctions between travel types, strive to recognize these differences in order to make suggestions best fitting a reader's interests.

Memoir and Personal Accounts

These titles are particularly moored in the personal realm. Writers have traveled to places to settle or to escape, but whatever the motivation, the journey is as much inward as outward. These books are popular not only for their expressions of locale but for the adult coming-of-age story they often tell. They are typically highly narrative and character focused and can be endlessly funny as well as quite poignant.

Eat, Pray, Love: One Woman's Search for Everything across Italy, India, and Indonesia, **by Elizabeth Gilbert**
Elizabeth Gilbert had a slow and heartbreaking realization: she did not want to be married, and she was more excited about writing a story on giant squid than about having a baby. The result of this insight was a divorce, lots of sadness, and a decision to take a year off. She would visit three places—Italy, India, and Indonesia—and attempt to find pleasure, spiritual growth, and balance. The result is a travel story that mixes the chick lit charm of Bridget Jones with the flat-out honesty and questing nature of Anne Lamott. In Italy she learns to speak the language and travels around, mostly eating. In India she goes to an ashram and experiences its practice and discipline; it is a long way from rich sheets of pasta swimming in olive oil. Here she finds some peace in middle-of-the-night devotions, hours of chanting, and a landscape and people that offer her solace and rest. Indonesia is character filled, almost overflowing with the names of people she meets and grows to treasure. Indonesia is also filled with love, because it is here she meets Felipe. After a year

of travel, Gilbert finds something of what she needs, and in writing this book she offers the reader a great souvenir.

Read this book because, though it is a fresh take on the type, it is also a work that illustrates its key elements: it is location specific and full of characters met along the journey, it is begun as an escape and ends as a refuge, and it is personal, funny, and reflective.

Suggest this book to chick lit fans looking for something new and to travel fans willing to read a mix of spiritual quest and travel tale. It works well with *Dear Exile: The True Story of Two Friends Separated (for a Year) by an Ocean*, by Hilary Liftin and Kate Montgomery, because the two books have a similar hip and self-aware feel. For readers more interested in Gilbert's quest than her travels, suggest *Traveling Mercies: Some Thoughts on Faith*, by Anne Lamott.

History, Land, and Place

Books that combine history with location, or focus on the landscape as well as the journey, make up another large section of travel books. These titles tend to be elegantly written, weaving an array of threads into the story of place.

Angry Wind: Through Muslim Black Africa by Truck, Bus, Boat, and Camel, by Jeffrey Tayler

The Sahel is the area of the lower Sahara where such sites as Timbuktu and Mopti can be found. It is a place of harsh landscape and even harsher history, ruled by poverty and Islamic fundamentalism. Tayler's portrait of this land, its people, and its history is keenly observant. He writes in a vivid yet restrained manner, mixing violent images of a sunset with pragmatic descriptions of making camp. He is particularly arresting when he describes the desert and its billowing shapes, the dust-covered people and cities, busy markets, and lost greatness of a fading sultan. Along his travels he encounters much danger (land mines) and frustration (corrupt governments), but also scores of fascinating people. He has ventured into a land foreign to most Americans, shortly after September 11 and on the eve of the Iraq war. He finds plenty to talk about. Tayler is horrified by some of what he sees and guilt ridden by much else, but most of all he is a brilliant chronicler of one of the world's forgotten corners.

Read this book because it sheds light on a part of the earth that has been too long ignored, illustrates the learning/experiencing inherent in this type of travel book, and provides an excellent example of the cultural connectivity at which history, land, and place books excel.

Suggest this book to readers interested in the Sahara as well as those who enjoy active and reflective travel stories. Consider pairing it with *An Unexpected Light: Travels in Afghanistan,* by Jason Elliot, which, although it is about a different location, has much of the same rigorous reporting on land and history. *The Places in Between,* by Rory Stewart, is another good suggestion for similar reasons. Readers also might enjoy *Cruelest Journey: Six Hundred Miles to Timbuktu,* by Kira Salak, which has some of the same points of destination and struggles, from a different point of view, and many of the same themes and issues.

Journeys, Escapes, and Adventures

Many travel books focus on the trip, the step-by-step journey from one point on a map to another. Along the way there is much to delight and confound—both the traveler and the reader. These books are story and character rich and are often the type of book many readers think of as armchair travel. They can be funny, thrilling, evocative, or musing, but they are always richly rewarding.

A Walk in the Woods: Rediscovering America on the Appalachian Trail, by Bill Bryson

One day in March, Bill Bryson started walking the Appalachian Trail, a 2,100-mile path in the woods running from Georgia to Maine. He took with him an old college friend, Stephen Katz, and together the two out-of-shape wilderness know-nothings set forth. With his trademark mix of humor and elegant observation, Bryson details the hike. He enjoys patches of Skyline Drive because it is nice to walk on pavement for a while. Here he riffs on the beauty of the parkway and considers it, the Hoover Dam, and Mount Rushmore the three places in America were man has complemented the landscape. He likes to riff and does so to great and charming effect as he passes anything interesting. As he and Stephen walk they encounter a bear (well, maybe), inept Boy Scouts, and assorted hiker types. Bryson is a great travel companion; he provides diversions, descriptions, and lots and lots of humor. His story of the trail, its creation, and those who walk it and work on it is delightful.

Read this book to get a good sense of the funny branch of armchair travel and to experience the work of one of its best practitioners.

Suggest this book to anyone interested in hiking, funny trips, or books that are well paced but rambling. Consider paring it with *Travels with My Donkey: One Man and His Ass on a Pilgrimage to Santiago,* by Tim Moore, *Lost in My Own Backyard: A Walk in Yellowstone National Park,* by Tim Cahill, and *Round Ireland with a Fridge,* by Tony Hawks.

Key Authors

Travel writing has some well-established authors, and it is usually easy to understand both their style and appeal. Yet, no matter how easy it may be, it is often hard to have more than three or four names readily available to suggest to patrons. The authors listed below are reliable travel writers who span a range of approaches. This list can also be used to plan a personal reading program, build a sure-bet cart, create a booklist or display, or help inform collection purchases.

Bill Bryson	William Least Heat-	Tim Moore
Tim Cahill	Moon	Jan Morris
Bruce Chatwin	Peter Hessler	Eric Newby
Nicholas Clapp	Tony Horwitz	Redmond O'Hanlon
William Dalrymple	Pico Iyer	Jonathan Raban
Lawrence Durrell	Peter Jenkins	Tim Severin
Jason Elliot	Robert D. Kaplan	Tahir Shah
Fergus Fleming	Norman Lewis	Jeffrey Tayler
Ian Frazier	Peter Matthiessen	Paul Theroux
Eric Hansen	Frances Mayes	Colin Thubron
Tony Hawks	Peter Mayle	J. Maarten Troost

Selected Bibliography of Travel Books to Read and Suggest

Memoir and Personal Accounts

Wrong about Japan: A Father's Journey with His Son, by Peter Carey

My 'Dam Life: Three Years in Holland, by Sean Condon

Around the World in 80 Dates, by Jennifer Cox

Fair Wind and Plenty of It: A Modern-Day Tall Ship Adventure, by Rigel Crockett

The Olive Farm: A Memoir of Life, Love, and Olive Oil in the South of France, by Carol Drinkwater

A Time of Gifts and *Between the Woods and the Water,* by Patrick Leigh Fermor

You Can't Get There from Here: A Year on the Fringes of a Shrinking World, by Gayle Forman

Scribbling the Cat: Travels with an African Soldier, by Alexandra Fuller

Tales of a Female Nomad: Living at Large in the World, by Rita Golden Gelman

Eat, Pray, Love: One Woman's Search for Everything across Italy, India, and Indonesia, by Elizabeth Gilbert

Monkey Dancing: A Father, Two Kids, and a Journey to the Ends of the Earth, by Daniel Glick

Paris to the Moon, by Adam Gopnik

Shopping for Buddhas, by Jeff Greenwald

Extra Virgin: A Young Woman Discovers the Italian Riviera Where Every Month Is Enchanted, by Annie Hawes

A Moveable Feast, by Ernest Hemingway

River Town: Two Years on the Yangtze, by Peter Hessler

Snowball Oranges: A Winter's Tale on a Spanish Isle (and his other work), by Peter Kerr

Ella in Europe: An American Dog's International Adventures, by Michael Konik

Up the Amazon without a Paddle, by Doug Lansky

Dear Exile: The True Story of Two Friends Separated (for a Year) by an Ocean, by Hilary Liftin and Kate Montgomery

Holy Cow: An Indian Adventure, by Sarah Macdonald

The Stone Boudoir: Travels through the Hidden Villages of Sicily, by Theresa Maggio

The Hills of Tuscany, by Ferenc Mate

Under the Tuscan Sun (and her other work), by Frances Mayes

A Year in Provence (and his other work), by Peter Mayle

Japanland: A Year in Search of Wa, by Karin Muller

Pasquale's Nose: Idle Days in an Italian Town, by Michael Rips

Stolen Figs, and Other Adventures in Calabria, by Mark Rotella

On Persephone's Island: A Sicilian Journal, by Mary Taylor Simeti

Driving over Lemons: An Optimist in Spain, by Chris Stewart

The Summer of My Greek Taverna, by Tom Stone

Dinner with Persephone: Travels in Greece, by Patricia Storace

My Love Affair with England: A Traveler's Memoir (and her other work), by Susan Allen Toth

The Sex Lives of Cannibals: Adrift in the Equatorial Pacific and *Getting Stoned with Savages: A Trip through the Islands of Fiji and Vanuatu,* by J. Maarten Troost

Almost French: Love and a New Life in Paris, by Sarah Turnbull

An Embarrassment of Mangoes: A Caribbean Interlude, by Ann Vanderhoof

Vietnam and *Where the Pavement Ends: One Woman's Bicycle Trip through Mongolia, China, and Vietnam,* by Erika Warmbrunn

Hearing Birds Fly: A Nomadic Year in Mongolia, by Louisa Waugh

Beyond the Sky and the Earth: A Journey into Bhutan, by Jamie Zeppa

History, Land, and Place

The City of Falling Angels, by John Berendt

30 Days in Sydney: A Wildly Distorted Account, by Peter Carey

In Patagonia and *The Songlines,* by Bruce Chatwin; and consider *Bruce Chatwin: A Biography,* by Nicholas Shakespeare

The Road to Ubar: Finding the Atlantis of the Sands and *Sheba: Through the Desert in Search of the Legendary Queen,* by Nicholas Clapp

Land's End: A Walk in Provincetown, by Michael Cunningham

From the Holy Mountain: A Journey among the Christians of the Middle East and *City of Djinns: A Year in Delhi,* by William Dalrymple

Lawrence Durrell Travel Reader, by Lawrence Durrell

An Unexpected Light: Travels in Afghanistan, by Jason Elliot

The Sword and the Cross: Two Men and an Empire of Sand (and his other work), by Fergus Fleming

Great Plains (and his other work), by Ian Frazier

Theatre of Fish: Travels through Newfoundland and Labrador and *At the Tomb of the Inflatable Pig: Travels through Paraguay,* by John Gimlette

Downtown: My Manhattan, by Pete Hamill

Orchid Fever: A Horticultural Tale of Love, Lust, and Lunacy, by Eric Hansen; and consider pairing with *The Orchid Thief,* by Susan Orlean

Seven Years in Tibet, by Heinrich Harrer

Oracle Bones: A Journey between China's Past and Present, by Peter Hessler

A Northern Front: New and Selected Essays, by John Hildebrand

Baghdad without a Map, and Other Misadventures in Arabia and *Blue Latitudes: Boldly Going Where Captain Cook Has Gone Before* (and his other work), by Tony Horwitz

Balkan Ghosts: A Journey through History; Mediterranean Winter: The Pleasures of History and Landscape in Tunisia, Sicily, Dalmatia, and Greece; and *The Ends of the Earth: From Togo to Turkmenistan, from Iran to Cambodia, a Journey to the Frontiers of Anarchy* (and his other work), by Robert D. Kaplan

Subwayland: Adventures in the World beneath New York, by Randy Kennedy

Never a City So Real: A Walk in Chicago, by Alex Kotlowitz

Sahara Unveiled: A Journey across the Desert, by William Langewiesche

The Tomb in Seville and *Golden Earth: Travels in Burma* (and his other work), by Norman Lewis

Cloud Forest, by Peter Matthiessen

Wandering Home: A Long Walk across America's Most Hopeful Landscape: Vermont's Champlain Valley and New York's Adirondacks, by Bill McKibben

Jack Ruby's Kitchen Sink: Offbeat Travels through America's Southwest and *The Panama Hat Trail,* by Tom Miller

The Shark God: Encounters with Ghosts and Ancestors in the South Pacific, by Charles Montgomery

A Turn in the South, by V. S. Naipaul

Istanbul: Memories and the City, by Orhan Pamuk

Old Glory: A Voyage down the Mississippi; Hunting Mister Heartbreak: A Discovery of America; and *Bad Land: An American Romance* (and his other work), by Jonathan Raban

Iron and Silk, by Mark Salzman

A Fez of the Heart: Travels around Turkey in Search of a Hat; The Wreck at Sharpnose Point; and *Nicholas: The Epic Journey from Saint to Santa Claus,* by Jeremy Seal

Ciao, America! An Italian Discovers the U.S., by Beppe Severgnini

Americana: Dispatches from the New Frontier, by Hampton Sides

The Places in Between and *The Prince of the Marshes, and Other Occupational Hazards of a Year in Iraq,* by Rory Stewart

Chasing Che: A Motorcycle Journey in Search of the Guevara Legend, by Patrick Symmes

River of No Reprieve: Descending Siberia's Waterway of Exile, Death, and Destiny; Angry Wind: Through Muslim Black Africa by Truck, Bus, Boat, and Camel; and *Glory in a Camel's Eye: A Perilous Trek through the Greatest African Desert,* by Jeffrey Tayler

Among the Russians and *Behind the Wall: A Journey through China* (and his other work), by Colin Thubron

Bayou Farewell: The Rich Life and Tragic Death of Louisiana's Cajun Coast, by Mike Tidwell

Assassination Vacation, by Sarah Vowell

Terra Incognita: Travels in Antarctica (and her other work), by Sara Wheeler

Seasons in Basilicata: A Year in a Southern Italian Hill Village, by David Yeadon

Journeys, Escapes, and Adventures

Men of Salt: Crossing the Sahara on the Caravan of White Gold, by Michael Benanav

Chasing the Sea: Lost among the Ghosts of Empire in Central Asia, by Tom Bissell

A Walk in the Woods: Rediscovering America on the Appalachian Trail and *In a Sunburned Country* (and his other work), by Bill Bryson

The Road to Oxiana, by Robert Byron

Road Fever; Hold the Enlightenment: More Travel, Less Bliss; and *A Wolverine Is Eating My Leg* (and his other work), by Tim Cahill

In Xanadu: A Quest, by William Dalrymple

Tracks, by Robyn Davidson

Yoga for People Who Can't Be Bothered to Do It, by Geoff Dyer

The 8:55 to Baghdad: From London to Iraq on the Trail of Agatha Christie and the Orient Express, by Andrew Eames

Race to the Pole: Tragedy, Heroism, and Scott's Antarctic Quest, by Ranulph Fiennes

Rowing to Latitude: Journeys along the Arctic's Edge, by Jill Fredston

Time's Magpie, by Myla Goldberg

The Gentleman from Finland: Adventures on the Trans-Siberian Express, by Robert M. Goldstein

Kite Strings of the Southern Cross: A Woman's Travel Odyssey, by Laurie Gough

Size of the World, by Jeff Greenwald

Braving Home: Dispatches from the Underwater Town, the Lava-Side Inn, and Other Extreme Locales, by Jake Halpern

The Bird Man and the Lap Dancer: Close Encounters with Strangers and *Stranger in the Forest: On Foot across Borneo* (and his other work), by Eric Hansen

Mississippi Solo, by Eddy L. Harris

The Zanzibar Chest: A Story of Life, Love, and Death in Foreign Lands, by Aidan Hartley

Round Ireland with a Fridge and *Playing the Moldovans at Tennis*, by Tony Hawks

Blue Highways: A Journey into America (and his other work), by William Least Heat-Moon

Sun after Dark: Flights into the Foreign and *Video Night in Kathmandu, and Other Reports from the Not-So-Far East* (and his other work), by Pico Iyer

Walk across America (and his other work), by Peter Jenkins

McCarthy's Bar: A Journey of Discovery in Ireland, by Pete McCarthy

Long Way Round: Chasing Shadows across the World, by Ewan McGregor and Charley Boorman

Roads: Driving America's Great Highways, by Larry McMurtry

Uncommon Carriers, by John McPhee

Travels with My Donkey: One Man and His Ass on a Pilgrimage to Santiago (and his other work), by Tim Moore

The World: Life and Travel, 1950–2000 and *Trieste and the Meaning of Nowhere* (and her other work), Jan Morris

Rounding the Horn: Being the Story of Williwaws and Windjammers, Drake, Darwin, Murdered Missionaries and Naked Natives, a Deck's Eye View of Cape Horn, by Dallas Murphy

In Ethiopia with a Mule (and her other work), by Dervla Murphy

Departures and Arrivals and *A Short Walk in the Hindu Kush* (and his other work), by Eric Newby

Take Me with You: A Round-the-World Journey to Invite a Stranger Home, by Brad Newsham

Trawler, No Mercy: A Journey to the Heart of the Congo and *Into the Heart of Borneo* (and his other work), by Redmond O'Hanlon

My Kind of Place: Travel Stories from a Woman Who's Been Everywhere, by Susan Orlean

Michael Palin's Hemingway Adventure (and his other work), by Michael Palin

Cork Boat, by John Pollack

Imagined London: A Tour of the World's Greatest Fictional City, by Anna Quindlen

The Cruelest Journey: Six Hundred Miles to Timbuktu, by Kira Salak

In Search of Genghis Khan: An Exhilarating Journey on Horseback across the Steppes of Mongolia (and his other work), by Tim Severin

The Caliph's House: A Year in Casablanca and *In Search of King Solomon's Mines* (and his other work), by Tahir Shah

Sacred Monkey River: A Canoe Trip with the Gods, by Christopher Shaw

Life on the Ice: No One Goes to Antarctica Alone, by Roff Smith

Travels with Charley: In Search of America, by John Steinbeck

Night Train to Turkistan: Modern Adventures along China's Ancient Silk Road, by Stuart Stevens

Cross Country: Fifteen Years and 90,000 Miles on the Roads and Interstates of America with Lewis and Clark, a Lot of Bad Motels, a Moving Van, Emily Post, Jack Kerouac, My Wife, My Mother-in-Law, Two Kids, and Enough Coffee to Kill an Elephant. . . , by Robert Sullivan

Facing the Congo: A Modern-Day Journey into the Heart of Darkness (and his other work), by Jeffrey Tayler

The Great Railway Bazaar: By Train through Asia; Dark Star Safari: Overland from Cairo to Cape Town; and *Riding the Iron Rooster* (and his other work), by Paul Theroux

The White Rock: An Exploration of the Inca Heartland, by Hugh Thomson

The Last Opium Den, by Nick Tosches

Venture to the Interior, by Laurens van der Post

The River at the Center of the World: A Journey up the Yangtze, and Back in Chinese Time, by Simon Winchester

The Back of Beyond: Travels to the Wild Places of the Earth (and his other work), by David Yeadon

Resources and Awards

The best way to get a sense of the subject is to page through magazines such as *Outside* and *National Geographic Traveler.* There is also a yearly selection of the best articles on travel published each year in the Best American Travel

Writing series, which makes a fast and enjoyable way to see the range of travel writing and provides a good place to start exploring the subject.

In addition, several publishers have created series of books on travel. Among the best are Vintage Departures; National Geographic Directions; Bloomsbury's The Writer and The City series; Crown Journeys (for well-known authors writing about travel and place); and Lonely Planet Journeys (for slightly less-known writers writing on all sorts of travel topics). Some titles from these series are included in this book, but all the titles are worth considering for both collection development and readers' advisory purposes.

THOMAS COOK TRAVEL BOOK AWARD

Not many awards have as their mission the selection of travel books. The best known and most focused is the Thomas Cook Travel Book Award, which honors literary travel writing. See http://www.thomascookpublishing.com/travelbookawards.htm.

NOTABLE BOOK LIST

Readers' advisory librarians should always consider the Notable Book List. If a wonderful literary travel book has been published during the year, the odds are good that it will be listed by ALA's Notable Books Council. Titles date back to 1993, and from 1997 forward all titles are annotated. It is worth the effort of scanning the site to locate excellent examples of the genre. See http://www.ala.org/ala/rusa/rusaprotools/rusanotable/notablebooks.htm.

9

TRUE ADVENTURE

True adventures, whether deliberate or dangerously unexpected, are the adrenaline side of nonfiction, the X Games of the reading world. This group of books is perhaps the least amenable to classification, since most of them could well be placed in history, biography, travel, and even science. But this is also one of the most compulsively readable subject areas, making it an important section to consider on its own.

Flying high over an unexplored jungle in a plane that just lost both engines, sailing a small fishing trawler into a storm, climbing a mountain during a blizzard, or kayaking down an unnavigable river all seem like vacation options most of us would never consider. But for some, such outings are just warm-ups for the next great adventure, and for others they are job assignments.

True adventure also contains books that are solemn witness to tragedy, beautifully written elegies to those who have died or been horribly injured in their dangerous line of work or while on an adventure gone bad. In these cases, the X Game aspects become muted to the stark reality of the laws of gravity, the inescapable need for oxygen, and the frailty of the human body—even as they stand as testament to the unyielding nature of the sprit.

Whether celebrating the undaunted nature of adventurers or eulogizing the dead, true adventure books make for compelling reading.

What Readers Enjoy in These Books

The main appeal points in this subject tend to be the description of the event (learning/experiencing) and the characters. The event can be a modern-day expedition or a historical recounting. Contemporary adventures are typically described in an engaging and gripping manner. Historical adventures focus on the intrepid men and women of days gone by, those lured by the shadowy spaces of undrawn maps. Their stories tend to fall in the medium range of the narrative continuum and combine exciting tales with fascinating history.

Whether contemporary or historical, the characters that answer the addictive call of the unknown are fascinating. Readers enjoy these character-centered accounts because they are interested in the people who undertake these adventures or who get caught in a situation they were not expecting. Readers enjoy learning about the motivations, thoughts, and philosophies of those who venture beyond the edge. The characters are varied and can be inspiring, irritating, quirky, doomed, or uncannily competent.

The philosophy of adventure is a parallel attraction. Many adventure books have a certain ethos that readers enjoy. The elements of humans pitted against their own limitations, pushing the edges of the laws of physics, daring those laws to apply this time, in this situation, or fighting against fate create a battlelike atmosphere many find compelling. The strong focus on the majesty of nature, the exploration of the planet, and the resulting exploration of self also hold great appeal for many readers. Despite the fast pace, many of these books are beautifully wrought, with grace and compassion for those who did not survive and with awe and respect for those who did.

Finally, readers enjoy the myriad details contained in these books. Fans enjoy reading about places, cultures, gear, skills, what goes into planning and training for an adventure, and often what goes into planning the rescue or escape effort.

Types of Books

True adventure is one of the most absorbing of subjects because of the range of types it contains:

- Biography and Memoir
- Historical Accounts
- History in Retrospect
- Adventures and Catastrophes

Biographies and memoirs are a type almost universal to nonfiction. The adventures and catastrophes type, like the journeys, escapes, and adventures type in the travel chapter, is the utilitarian heart of the subject. There are also two types unique to this subject area: historical accounts and history in retrospect.

A most fascinating aspect of type is that it encapsulates what is distinct about a group of books within a larger subject. In this case the distinctiveness is of perspective and approach. Historical accounts capture the first journeys of intrepid travelers to places unexplored by outsiders. These books could be considered historical and therefore fit in the history chapter, but since they are specifically adventure accounts of and by travelers long ago, in the spirit in which they were written I include them here. In keeping with the times in which these travels took place, both the construction of the story and the literary style are more formal and, perhaps to some readers, therefore less easy to read. Yet despite, or perhaps because of, those differences from contemporary style, these books are fascinating and distinctive. Complementing them is the other unique type in true adventure, history in retrospect. Obviously, many writers are as beguiled as readers with the first travels of explorers, both intrepid and accidental, and they have written wonderful books on those expeditions. These books are well researched, elegant, and engaging. Together, these two true adventure types provide even non-adrenaline junkies a reason to savor this subject area.

Benchmark Books to Read and Suggest

Reading books in this subject area is great fun. Even if we are not likely to brave much more than the too-tall grass in our backyards, reading about others who survive disaster and plan great feats of derring-do is a sheer pleasure akin to the best action fiction. Deep down, many of us want to be as intrepid as Meriwether Lewis and William Clark, and these books allow us all the opportunity to pretend from a safe distance. For those brave but deskbound among us, and for our readers, they supply endless hours of vicarious pleasures and thrills. The books below represent some of the best and most satisfying writing of their subject classification.

Biography and Memoir

The study of the men and women who undertake grand adventures is quite appealing. These books dig deeper into the motivations and provide more of the story than just the facts surrounding an epic trip or deadly undertaking. They tend to be character centered and fall in the medium-to-high range on the narrative continuum.

Miracle in the Andes: 72 Days on the Mountain and My Long Trek Home,
by Nando Parrado

The story of the 1972 Uruguayan rugby team that crashed in the Andes is a grim one. The plane went down in one of the most remote and inhospitable places on earth, the barren pack ice of freezing high mountains. Many people died in the crash, others died at the site, and the rest were left without food, water, or adequate clothing. They were abandoned to their deaths and knew it, courtesy of a failing radio. At first they struggled along—swallowing handfuls of ice until their lips were raw and open sores. They foraged the plane for what food they could find, fixed up what could laughingly be called a base camp, and found a way to barely sustain themselves. They crafted basins to collect enough melted snow to stay just hydrated and stoically decided to eat the flesh of the dead. After two months of struggle, a few of the teammates left the crash site and fought through the Andes to find help. All told, the survivors were on the mountain for seventy-two days. Nando Parrado lost his mother and sister in the crash and led the way through the Andes to rescue. He writes his sad story with a clear and sensitive voice, relating the horror of his tragedy and the surreal routine that became everyday life for the crash survivors. He also writes about his life and the life of his teammates, elevating what could be seen as just a brutal and horribly fascinating nightmare into a sensitive story of hope and friendship.

Read this book because it is a classic story of survival and includes many features readers look for: a you-are-there sensibility, lots of relevant and interesting details of how people survive, and a sense of context about both the catastrophe and the life after rescue.

Suggest this book to readers who enjoy detailed accounts of epic fights to stay alive. It pairs perfectly with *Alive: The Story of the Andes Survivors,* by Piers Paul Read, which relates the same event from a different perspective. Also consider *Between a Rock and a Hard Place,* by Aron Ralston, and *Into the Wild,* by Jon Krakauer.

Historical Accounts

Written during or soon after the event, these are reports of travel and exploration during a time when even the shortest of trips was an adventure. The books in this type are firsthand accounts and took place when journeys could still be grand and seemingly impossible. Although the writing may sometimes seem overly formal, beneath is a landscape of worlds still to be discovered and the evocative and frightening dream of the unknown. It is well worth reading the work of the men and women who explored the globe when the earth was still a strange and uncharted land.

The Worst Journey in the World, by Apsley Cherry-Garrard

Cherry-Garrard was the youngest of Robert Falcon Scott's crew when he set off in 1911 on Scott's expedition to the South Pole. Scott was racing Roald Amundsen to be the first man to reach the pole. While on the expedition, Cherry-Garrard set forth on his own journey to collect emperor penguin eggs. It was an adventure that took five weeks in the near-constant darkness of the polar winter. Cherry-Garrard was also a member of the search party that went looking for Scott, who had been beaten to the pole by a month. On the return journey, Scott and his crew died tragically. Cherry-Garrard had been sent to meet them, and though he waited longer than he should have, his own supplies dwindling, he tortured himself for years that if he had gone just a bit farther he could have saved them. Using his own journal and those of his shipmates, Cherry-Garrard wrote this account of one of the most famous expeditions of history soon after he returned from fighting in World War I, exhausted and sad. His detailed account of life during that time and the motivations of Scott and his crew, along with his summation of why men explore, are simply glorious.

Read this book because it is a classic work of historical adventure and illustrates the tone, detail, and approach many readers look for in this type.

Suggest this book to readers who want to learn more about the Scott expedition or are interested in firsthand historical accounts of adventure. It pairs well with *The South Pole: An Account of the Norwegian Antarctic Expedition in the* Fram, *1910–1912,* by Roald Amundsen; *Scott's Last Expedition: The Journals,* by Robert Falcon Scott; *Race to the Pole: Tragedy, Heroism, and Scott's Antarctic Quest,* by Ranulph Fiennes; *A First Rate Tragedy: Robert Falcon Scott and the Race to the South Pole,* by Diana Preston; and *Scott, Shackleton and Amundsen: Ambition and Tragedy in the Antarctic,* by David Thomson. Readers willing to leave the icy polar region might also enjoy Owen Chase's *Shipwreck of the Whaleship* Essex or *Wind, Sand and Stars,* by Antoine de Saint-Exupery.

History in Retrospect

One of the most appealing areas of nonfiction for many is the merging of history and adventure. These books tell the stories of great quests with the perspective of time and the benefit of research. Merging the skills of the historian with the soul of adventure writing, the authors can be both pointedly critical and utterly engaging. These books make great reading on their own and can be paired with historical accounts for dual takes on the same adventure.

Sea of Glory: America's Voyage of Discovery, the U.S. Exploring Expedition, 1838–1842, by Nathaniel Philbrick

The U.S. Exploring Expedition, better known as the Ex-Ex, sailed on a mission as grand and adventurous as that of Lewis and Clark. The work of Ex-Ex was arguably as important as well; among other things Capt. Charles Wilkes and his crew confirmed the existence of Antarctica, laid claim to the Columbia River and Puget Sound, mapped the coast of what would become Oregon and Washington, and collected thousands of species that founded the collection of the Smithsonian Institution. It was a journey filled with almost every adventure motif there is: the crew struggled with ice and cold, they were the first westerners to see many new animal and plant species, they fought cannibals and were threatened with dwindling food supplies. Yet today few people know of the Ex-Ex's accomplishments. Philbrick explores not just their adventures but the reasons they have faded from the limelight of history. Largely this was because of Wilkes and the just castigation by his crew once the expedition was over. Wilkes was not ready to lead such a journey and was given neither the rank nor the authority to do his job fully. Nor was he a capable leader. As much as went right on the trip, even more went wrong, and when the expedition was over, his men cast Wilkes into the hands of a bitter fate; he died in obscurity, taking the work of the Ex-Ex with him.

Read this book because Philbrick is a master at creating adventure stories wrapped in brilliant research and because his work typifies what many readers look for in this area: an adventurous yet serious tone, a medium level of narrative writing full of well-drawn characters, and quite a bit of detail and description about the journey.

Suggest this book to readers who enjoy a mix of story and character as well as research and history. In addition to Philbrick's other works, the title pairs well with *The* Bounty: *The True Story of the Mutiny on the* Bounty, by Caroline Alexander; *Barrow's Boys: A Stirring Story of Daring, Fortitude, and Outright Lunacy*, by Fergus Fleming; *The Mapmaker's Wife: A True Tale of Love, Murder, and Survival in the Amazon*, by Robert Whitaker; and *Undaunted Courage: Meriwether Lewis, Thomas Jefferson, and the Opening of the American West*, by Stephen Ambrose.

Adventures and Catastrophes

This is the modern heart of the subject area. One would think, after reading about the glory of historical expeditions, that there is not much new to do. Well, the men and women in these books prove that there are many more explorations waiting for the brave or foolhardy to undertake them. There are still waterways to be mastered and lands to be trekked. Included here are the contemporary books of climbing mountains, rafting unknown rivers, fighting nature, and defying physics.

The Last River: The Tragic Race for Shangri-la, by Todd Balf

In 1998 five kayakers, Wick Walker, Tom and Jamie McEwan, Doug Gordon, and Roger Zbel, set out on an epic quest to be the first men to run the Yarlung Tsangpo River. Twelve days into the expedition, one of them was dead. Blending the stories of Wick, who set out over land, and the four expeditionary paddlers, Balf provides readers with a blow-by-blow account of the attempted navigation of a waterway known as the Everest of rivers, in a land shrouded in myth. The Tsangpo headwaters are in Tibet, in the fabled land of Shangri-la, and the river runs through the deepest gorge on the planet. The water seethes and roils and has deep holes. The men were ready for it. Wick and Tom had dreamed about it for years, and all of them were expert paddlers with high levels of experience. They knew what they were doing. They also knew that experience, at the level they worked, was not the issue. The river and the kayaker simply met. In the end the danger could not be avoided, but simply chosen and faced. Balf tells their story in a gripping yet respectful narrative that captures the character of the land and the nature of the men and relates something of what it must feel like to stand on the edge of a thundering waterfall and decide to jump in.

Read this book because it is a wonderful example of the best aspects of this type—full of well-described characters and their motivations, grippingly paced, respectful of the land and the people, and detailed in the description of the adventure.

Suggest this book to readers who like fast-paced yet reflective adventures or who are interested in kayaking. It works well with the movie *Into the Tsangpo Gorge,* directed by Dustin Knapp, even though the movie recounts a latter attempt to run this river, and *Hell or High Water: Surviving Tibet's Tsangpo River,* by Peter Heller, which recounts that later attempt. Other books to consider include *Lost in Mongolia: Rafting the World's Last Unchallenged River,* by Colin Angus, which has the same expeditionary feel, and *At the*

Mercy of the River: An Exploration of the Last African Wilderness, by Peter Stark, which provides a different perspective on paddling expeditions.

Key Authors

Although there will be no new books by Gertrude Bell or Aspley Cherry-Garrard, it is still important to know their names—to help make suggestions, understand the development of the subject area, and weed the collection. The modern-day world of adventure writing is always changing as new treks are undertaken, old expeditions uncovered, and tragedies unfold. Below is a list of current writers, past adventures, and key authors whose work defines the subject. The works by these authors are reliable to suggest to readers, can be used in displays and booklists, and can fill a sure-bet cart. Collection development librarians should be sure that the authors listed below are purchased, retained in the collection, and kept in mind as any new works are published.

Caroline Alexander	Linda Greenlaw	Nathaniel Philbrick
Roald Amundsen	Maurice Herzog	Piers Paul Read
Colin Angus	Joe Jackson	Antoine de Saint-Exupery
Todd Balf	Sebastian Junger	Robert Falcon Scott
Gertrude Bell	Joe Kane	Ernest Shackleton
Isabella Bird	Gary Kinder	Joe Simpson
Apsley Cherry-Garrard	Dean King	Joshua Slocum
Isak Dinesen	Jon Krakauer	Freya Stark
Martin Dugard	Robert Kurson	Wilfred Thesiger
Ranulph Fiennes	Jack London	Mark Twain
Fergus Fleming	Derek Lundy	Robert Whitaker
Graham Greene	Norman Maclean	F. A. Worsley
	Jennifer Niven	

Selected Bibliography of True Adventure Writing to Read and Suggest

Many true adventure books share appeal points with the travel book types history, land, and place and journeys, escapes, and adventures (chapter 8) and also with the science type nature and natural history (chapter 4), and thus reference advisory librarians should consider all three subject areas when making suggestions and look for cross-subject possibilities.

Biography and Memoir

Red Sky in Mourning: A True Story of Love, Loss, and Survival at Sea, by Tami Oldham Ashcraft and Susea McGearhart

The Heart of the World: A Journey to the Last Secret Place, by Ian Baker

The Lost River: A Memoir of Life, Death, and Transformation on Wild Water, by Richard Bangs

The Last Season, by Eric Blehm

The Mountains of My Life, by Walter Bonatti

High Exposure: An Enduring Passion for Everest and Unforgiving Places, by David Breashears

Good Morning Midnight: Life and Death in the Wild, by Chip Brown

The Silent World, by Jacques Cousteau

Heart of the Storm: My Adventures as a Helicopter Rescue Pilot and Commander, by Edward L. Fleming

Off the Map: Tales of Endurance and Exploration, by Fergus Fleming

The Secret Lives of Alexandra David-Neel: A Biography of the Explorer of Tibet and Its Forbidden Practices, by Barbara Foster and Michael Foster

Snowstruck: In the Grip of Avalanches, by Jill Fredston

Passionate Nomad: The Life of Freya Stark, by Jane Geniesse

Danger My Ally, by F. A. Mitchell Hedges

My Life as an Explorer (and his other work), by Sven Anders Hedin

Captain James Cook, by Richard Hough

Shackleton and *The Last Place on Earth*, by Roland Huntford

Into the Wild, by Jon Krakauer

The Last Gentleman Adventurer: Coming of Age in the Arctic, by Edward Beauclerk Maurice

Fatal Passage: The True Story of John Rae, the Arctic Hero Time Forgot, by Kenneth McGoogan

Miracle in the Andes: 72 Days on the Mountain and My Long Trek Home, by Nando Parrado; see also *Alive: The Story of the Andes Survivors*, by Piers Paul Read

Seaworthy: Adrift with William Willis in the Golden Age of Rafting, by T. R. Pearson

A Pirate of Exquisite Mind: Explorer, Naturalist, and Buccaneer: The Life of William Dampier, by Diana Preston and Michael Preston

Between a Rock and a Hard Place, by Aron Ralston

Captain Sir Richard Francis Burton: The Secret Agent Who Made the Pilgrimage to Mecca, Discovered the "Kama Sutra," and Brought the "Arabian Nights" to the West, by Edward Rice

On the Ridge between Life and Death: A Climbing Life Reexamined, by David Roberts

A Sense of the World: How a Blind Man Became History's Greatest Traveler, by Jason Roberts

To the Heart of the Nile: Lady Florence Baker and the Exploration of Central Africa, by Pat Shipman

Treasure Islands: Sailing the South Seas in the Wake of Fanny and Robert Louis Stevenson, by Pamela Stephenson

Big Weather: Chasing Tornadoes in the Heart of America, by Mark Svenvold

To Conquer the Air: The Wright Brothers and the Great Race for Flight, by James Tobin

The Strange Last Voyage of Donald Crowhurst, by Nicholas Tomalin and Ron Hall

Touch the Top of the World, by Erik Weihenmayer

American Traveler: The Life and Adventures of John Ledyard, the Man Who Dreamed of Walking the World, by James Zug

Historical Accounts

In the Land of White Death, by Valerian Albanov

The South Pole: An Account of the Norwegian Antarctic Expedition in the Fram, *1910–1912*, by Roald Amundsen

The Desert and the Sown: The Syrian Adventures of the Female Lawrence of Arabia and *Gertrude Bell: The Arabian Diaries, 1913–1914*, by Gertrude Bell; and consider *Desert Queen: The Extraordinary Life of Gertrude Bell: Adventurer, Adviser to Kings, Ally of Lawrence of Arabia*, by Janet Wallach

Inca Land: Explorations in the Highlands of Peru, by Hiram Bingham

A Lady's Life in the Rocky Mountains; Six Months in the Sandwich Islands; and Unbeaten Tracks in Japan, by Isabella Bird

The Mutiny on Board H. M. S. Bounty: *The Captain's Account of the Mutiny and His 3,600 Mile Voyage in an Open Boat,* by William Bligh, and *The* Bounty Mutiny, by William Bligh and Edward Christian

The Lake Regions of Central Africa: From Zanzibar to Lake Tanganyika, by Richard Francis Burton

Alone: The Classic Polar Adventure, by Admiral Richard E. Byrd

Shipwreck of the Whaleship Essex, by Owen Chase

The Worst Journey in the World, by Apsley Cherry-Garrard; and see *Cherry: A Life of Apsley Cherry-Garrard,* by Sara Wheeler

The Journals of Captain Cook, by James Cook

Two Years before the Mast: A Personal Narrative of Life at Sea, by Richard Henry Dana Jr.

My Journey to Lhasa, by Alexandra David-Neel

The Journals of Lewis and Clark, edited by Bernard DeVoto

Out of Africa, by Isak Dinesen

Prisoner of Dunes, by Isabelle Eberhardt

Brazilian Adventure (and his other work), by Peter Fleming; and see *Exploration Fawcett,* by Percy Harrison Fawcett

Journey without Maps and *The Lawless Roads,* by Graham Greene

Exploration of the Valley of the Amazon, by William Lewis Herndon

The American Scene, by Henry James

Travels in West Africa, by Mary Kingsley

The Spirit of St. Louis, by Charles A. Lindbergh

The Cruise of the Snark, by Jack London

West with the Night, by Beryl Markham

Home of the Blizzard, by Douglas Mawson

The Last Voyage of the Karluk: *A Survivor's Memoir of Arctic Disaster,* by William Laird McKinlay

In Search of England (and his other work), by H. V. Morton

Farthest North: The Exploration of the Fram, *1893–1896,* by Fridjtof Nansen

The Oregon Trail, by Francis Parkman

The Travels of Marco Polo, by Marco Polo, translated by Ronald Latham

Sufferings in Africa: The Astonishing Account of a New England Sea Captain Enslaved by North African Arabs, by James Riley

Wind, Sand and Stars, by Antoine de Saint-Exupery

Scott's Last Expedition: The Journals, by Robert Falcon Scott

The Heart of the Antarctic: Being the Story of the British Antarctic Expedition, 1907–1909 and *South: The Last Antarctic Expedition of Shackleton and the Endurance* (and his other work), by Ernest Shackleton

Sailing Alone around the World, by Joshua Slocum

Through the Dark Continent, by Henry M. Stanley

The Valleys of the Assassins, and Other Persian Travels and *Riding to the Tigris,* by Freya Stark; also suggest *Passionate Nomad: The Life of Freya Stark,* by Jane Geniesse

In the South Seas, by Robert Louis Stevenson

Arabian Sands, by Wilfred Thesiger

The West Indies and the Spanish Main, by Anthony Trollope

The Innocents Abroad; Following the Equator; and *Roughing It,* by Mark Twain

Waugh Abroad: The Collected Travel Writing, by Evelyn Waugh

Black Lamb and Grey Falcon: A Journey through Yugoslavia, by Rebecca West

Shackleton's Boat Journey: The Narrative of the Captain of the Endurance and Endurance: *An Epic of Polar Adventure,* by F. A. Worsley

History in Retrospect

The Bounty: *The True Story of the Mutiny on the* Bounty and *The* Endurance: *Shackleton's Legendary Antarctic Expedition,* by Caroline Alexander

The Darkest Jungle: The True Story of the Darien Expedition and America's Ill-Fated Race to Connect the Seas and *The Last River: The Tragic Race for Shangri-la,* by Todd Balf

Over the Edge of the World: Magellan's Terrifying Circumnavigation of the Globe, by Laurence Bergreen

The Arctic Grail: The Quest for the Northwest Passage and the North Pole, 1818–1909, by Pierre Berton

Mawson's Will: The Greatest Polar Survival Story Ever Written and *Shackleton's Forgotten Men: The Untold Tale of an Antarctic Tragedy,* by Lennard Bickel

Ice Blink: The Tragic Fate of Sir John Franklin's Lost Polar Expedition, by Scott Cookman

The Lady and the Panda: The True Adventures of the First American Explorer to Bring Back China's Most Exotic Animal, by Vicki Croke

Into Africa: The Epic Adventures of Stanley and Livingstone and *The Last Voyage of Columbus: Being the Epic Tale of the Great Captain's Fourth Expedition, Including Accounts of Swordfight, Mutiny, Shipwreck, Gold, War, Hurricane, and Discovery* (and his other, less historical work), by Martin Dugard

Race to the Pole: Tragedy, Heroism, and Scott's Antarctic Quest, by Ranulph Fiennes

Ninety Degrees North: The Quest for the North Pole and *Barrow's Boys: A Stirring Story of Daring, Fortitude, and Outright Lunacy,* by Fergus Fleming

Ghosts of Cape Sabine: The Harrowing True Story of the Greely Expedition, by Leonard F. Guttridge

True North: Peary, Cook, and the Race to the Pole, by Bruce Henderson

We Die Alone: A WWII Epic of Escape and Endurance, by David Howarth

Bold Spirit: Helga Estby's Forgotten Walk across Victorian America, by Linda Lawrence Hunt

A Furnace Afloat: The Wreck of the Hornet *and the Harrowing 4,300-Mile Voyage of Its Survivors,* by Joe Jackson

Skeletons on the Zahara: A True Story of Survival, by Dean King

The Race for Timbuktu: In Search of Africa's City of Gold, by Frank T. Kryza

The Longest Winter: The Incredible Survival of Captain Scott's Lost Party, by Katherine Lambert

Endurance: *Shackleton's Incredible Voyage,* by Alfred Lansing

The Last Expedition: Stanley's Mad Journey through the Congo, by Daniel Liebowitz and Charles Pearson

Weird and Tragic Shores: The Story of Charles Francis Hall, Explorer, by Chauncey Loomis

A Night to Remember, by Walter Lord

The River of Doubt: Theodore Roosevelt's Darkest Journey, by Candice Millard

The Ice Master: The Doomed 1913 Voyage of the Karluk, by Jennifer Niven

In the Heart of the Sea: The Tragedy of the Whaleship Essex and *Sea of Glory: America's Voyage of Discovery, the U.S. Exploring Expedition, 1838–1842,* by Nathaniel Philbrick

A First Rate Tragedy: Robert Falcon Scott and the Race to the South Pole, by Diana Preston

Shackleton's Forgotten Expedition: The Voyage of the Nimrod, by Beau Riffenburgh

Caliban's Shore: The Wreck of the Grosvenor *and the Strange Fate of Her Survivors*, by Stephen Taylor

Cook: The Extraordinary Voyages of Captain James Cook, by Nicholas Thomas

Scott, Shackleton and Amundsen: Ambition and Tragedy in the Antarctic, by David Thomson

Captain Bligh's Portable Nightmare, by John Toohey

The Lost Men: The Harrowing Saga of Shackleton's Ross Sea Party, by Kelly Tyler-Lewis

The Mapmaker's Wife: A True Tale of Love, Murder, and Survival in the Amazon, by Robert Whitaker

Adventures and Catastrophes

Lost in Mongolia: Rafting the World's Last Unchallenged River and *Amazon Extreme: Three Ordinary Guys, One Rubber Raft and the Most Dangerous River on Earth*, by Colin Angus

The Last River: The Tragic Race for Shangri-la, by Todd Balf

Sailing into the Abyss: A True Story of Extreme Heroism on the High Seas, by William R. Benedetto

No Picnic on Mount Kenya: A Daring Escape, a Perilous Climb, by Felice Benuzzi

Adrift: Seventy-six Days Lost at Sea, by Steven Callahan

Death in the Long Grass, by Peter H. Capstick

The Last Dive: A Father and Son's Fatal Descent into the Ocean's Depths, by Bernie Chowdhury

Expedition Whydah: *The Story of the World's First Excavation of a Pirate Treasure Ship and the Man Who Found Her*, by Barry Clifford

The Cloud Garden: A True Story of Adventure, Survival, and Extreme Horticulture, by Tom Hart Dyke and Paul Winder

Mind over Matter: The Epic Crossing of the Antarctic Continent (and his other work), by Ranulph Fiennes; then read *Shadows on the Wasteland: Crossing Antarctica with Ranulph Fiennes*, by Mike Stroud, who took the trip with Fiennes

Heart of the Amazon, by Yossi Ghinsberg

The Hungry Ocean: A Swordboat Captain's Journey, by Linda Greenlaw

Hell or High Water: Surviving Tibet's Tsangpo River, by Peter Heller

Annapurna, by Maurice Herzog

Kon-Tiki: *Across the Pacific by Raft*, by Thor Heyerdahl

K2, the Savage Mountain, by Charles H. Houston and Robert H. Bates

To Timbuktu, by Mark Jenkins

Savage Summit: The True Stories of the First Five Women Who Climbed K2, the World's Most Feared Mountain, by Jennifer Jordan

The Perfect Storm: A True Story of Men against the Sea, by Sebastian Junger

Running the Amazon, by Joe Kane

Ship of Gold in the Deep Blue Sea, by Gary Kinder; and consider *Exploration of the Valley of the Amazon*, by William Lewis Herndon, the man featured in Kinder's book

Lords of Sipan: A True Story of Pre-Inca Tombs, Archaeology, and Crime, by Sidney D. Kirkpatrick

Into Thin Air: A Personal Account of the Mt. Everest Disaster (and his other work), by Jon Krakauer; see also *The Climb: Tragic Ambitions on Everest*, by Anatoli Boukreev

Shadow Divers: The True Adventure of Two Americans Who Risked Everything to Solve One of the Last Mysteries of World War II, by Robert Kurson

The Last Run: A True Story of Rescue and Redemption on the Alaska Seas, by Todd Lewan

Godforsaken Sea: The True Story of a Race through the World's Most Dangerous Waters, by Derek Lundy

The Terrible Hours, by Peter Maas

Young Men and Fire, by Norman Maclean

Shattered Air: A True Account of Catastrophe and Courage on Yosemite's Half Dome, by Bob Madgic

Lost Tribe: A Harrowing Passage into New Guinea's Heart of Darkness, by Edward Marriott

Extremes: Surviving the World's Harshest Environments and *Going to Extremes: Mud, Sweat and Frozen Tears*, by Nick Middleton

The Long Way, by Bernard Moitessier

Fatal Storm: The Inside Story of the Tragic Sydney–Hobart Race, by Rob Mundle; and see *The Proving Ground,* by G. Bruce Knecht, about the same ill-fated race

A Voyage for Madmen and *Sea Change: Alone across the Atlantic in a Wooden Boat* (and his other work), by Peter Nichols

Alive: The Story of the Andes Survivors, by Piers Paul Read

Touching the Void: The True Story of One Man's Miraculous Survival and *The Beckoning Silence,* by Joe Simpson

At the Mercy of the River: An Exploration of the Last African Wilderness, by Peter Stark

8 Men and a Duck: An Improbable Voyage by Reed Boat to Easter Island, by Nick Thorpe; and consider pairing with Kon-Tiki: *Across the Pacific by Raft,* by Thor Heyerdahl

Resources and Awards

Outside Magazine is the single best resource to keep up with true adventure books. It reports on the adventure before it begins and reviews or features the book after it is over. For unplanned events that turn into either adventures or disasters, its reporting has the perspective and depth readers of these book types are looking for, and staff writers for the magazine go on to write books based on their reporting. In addition to the single issues, there are also wonderful collections to browse: *The Best of Outside: The First 20 Years; Outside 25: Classic Tales and New Voices from the Frontiers of America;* and *Out of the Noosphere: Adventure, Sports, Travel, and the Environment.*

Men's Journal* is another fine resource from the magazine world. *Wild Stories: The Best of Men's Journal* is a collection of essays ranging from the high octane to the more pensive and makes for a great introduction to the field. Readers' advisory librarians may also want to page through *National Geographic* as well as *National Geographic Adventure; Adventure Sport;* and *Smithsonian* magazines.

For book suggestions and retrospective collection building, librarians can turn to back issues of all these magazines, the list in this chapter, and several great collected surveys available on the web:

National Geographic Adventure Magazine's Extreme Classics: The 100 Greatest Adventure Books of All Time: http://www.nationalgeographic.com/adventure/0404/adventure_books_1-19.html.

Outside Magazine's List of the 25 (Essential) Books for the Well-Read Explorer: http://outside.away.com/outside/features/200301/200301_adventure_canon_1.html.

The Outside Canon, which mixes fiction and nonfiction and is useful not only for collection building and as a source of suggestions but also for creating booklists on a range of specialized topics: http://outside.away.com/magazine/bookstore/outside_canon.html#outside.

There are also two book series worth noting. The Modern Library Exploration series brings classics of the subject back into print, as does National Geographic Adventure Classics. National Geographic is a good source and has also published a collection of early travel tales: *Worlds to Explore: Classic Tales of Travel and Adventure from National Geographic,* edited by Mark Jenkins. For more on historical adventures, consider *Points Unknown: The Greatest Adventure Writing of the Twentieth Century,* edited by David Roberts, and *Dead Reckoning: Great Adventure Writing from the Golden Age of Exploration, 1800–1900,* edited by Helen Whybrow.

There are no specific subject awards for adventure, but some National Book Award nominees and winners occasionally fit into the history in retrospect category. http://www.nationalbook.org/index.html.

And, as always, the ALA Notable Book Council is a great resource for readers' advisory librarians. The council often includes books in almost all the categories covered in this section (with the exception of historical accounts). The winning books are listed on the council's site back to 1993. http://www.ala.org/ala/rusa/rusaprotools/rusanotable/notablebooks.htm.

10

HISTORY AND HISTORICAL BIOGRAPHY

The number of books falling into the history classification is seemingly end-less, representing a wide range of approaches on a variety of topics. Thou-sands of wonderful history titles are available to readers. Some of these readers are avid, almost lay scholars in an area, and others are casual read-ers who have developed an interest in an event or person. Many readers make a lifelong study of history; many more are momentarily drawn to these books through the publicity buzz surrounding blockbuster titles or the many movies and TV shows highlighting epic events. Whatever their motivation, readers have a wealth of wonderful titles from which to choose. From every human conflict to every human discovery, from tiny personal moments to grand nation-building efforts, history books cover it all in sweeping epics and small treasures. Historical biography is included here because history almost always boils down to the individuals who create it, and biography is integral to history's very weft and weave.

What Readers Enjoy in These Books

The allures of history and historical biography are manifold. History itself is a driving reason for readers to read a particular book, and therefore the subject and story line are important. Great historians and biographers bring events to life, make them real, put them in context, and let readers see not just the "what" of an event but the "why" of it as well. The contextualizing or sense making history and biography provide is critical. These books allow readers to work through the worst horrors of human history or to experience vicariously the best, most heroic, side of human nature.

Character development and a strong sense of the personalities of the past are also hallmarks in this subject area, and many readers enjoy both his-tory and historical biography for the wonderful character studies they offer.

Bringing historical personalities to life is a skill historians and biographers share; in fact, many of the best writers in the field write both forms of history. The strongly character-centered nature of the work provides readers with a sense of connection to great historical figures as well as to less august, but no less worthy, characters from an everyday world gone by. Readers enjoy characters facing challenges, debating moral dilemmas, struggling with the right course of action, and being smart, creative, brave, and heroic or idiotic, cowardly, and craven. Readers find great enjoyment in reading about the development of the character and how he or she changes in reaction to life's events. They also enjoy rubbing elbows with the same circle of friends, family, and acquaintances as did the distinguished figures they learned about in school.

Those who read for such elements as detail and description also find these works to be a rich source of enjoyment, providing an array of depictions of dress, secret deals, correspondence, battle movements, and a litany of other such elements as well. These details provide readers a vivid sense of the times, setting, personalities, and events of the age.

Much of nonfiction is enjoyed for what a reader learns while spending time with a writer. In the case of history and historical biography, the learning becomes grand in scale and is one of the major reasons readers enjoy these books. This is true for the more narrative history as well as the less narrative account. Regardless of the method employed to relate the facts, readers work through a book because they know it will lead to understanding and illumination, making learning/experiencing a critical element for history fans.

Types of Books

It is futile to attempt to gather all the best history and historical biography titles into the pages of any one book. The subject world is too large and the writing too good to attempt any sort of complete listing. What is possible is to understand the different types and to get a sense of who is writing what. There are seven different history types reviewed in this chapter:

- Historical Explanations
- Historical Biography
- History of War and Military History
- Pivot Points
- Social and Cultural History

- Disaster History
- Micro History

Most readers, however, approach staff with a particular subject or historical period in mind; that is the most common access point within the subject. In fact, outside military history and historical biography, few readers ever directly mention one of these types by name. But they do tell us they are looking for a book that explains the Crusades or helps them better understand what life was like during the beginning of the civil rights movement in America. They will be asking for an explanation or a work of social and cultural history, and it is important for us to know that going into the conversation.

Type may not, however, be the most important thing. The intertwined elements of nonfiction—narrative nature, subject, type, and appeal—work as a framework to interpret patrons' approaches to the books they love and as a guide for readers' advisory librarians seeking to help patrons find additional books to enjoy. It is not a balanced set of elements, all equal in importance, all of the time. In history in particular (and as was noted for sports), sometimes the subject or time period is the most important thing.

This chapter might be easier to use if it were broken by subject or time period, but the library catalog can do that for you. By considering titles by type, readers' advisory librarians can contextualize the collection in a way that is more flexible than subject or time period alone and see why disparate books can be good matching suggestions. Both time period and subject do matter a great deal, but they have built-in limitations. Although there are a great many books on the American Revolution or World War II (more than there are on quarks, for example), there is an end to them, and all books on a given subject are not the same. Thinking about a book as being only about a specific time or subject is limiting—to the reader, to our collections, and to our duties as readers' advisory librarians. We need a way to think about connections between books that are above these limitations. Type provides that and gives a framework readers can consider and react to that goes beyond the restrictions of period or subject.

Keep in mind that prolific historians and biographers often write on more than one subject or about more than one period, so fans of a writer are already reading, and looking to read more, in myriad directions based on the types they already associate with their favorite writers. History and biography is therefore a wonderful place to launch all sorts of cross-subject reading suggestions. For example, history readers may enjoy some of the true crime books that focus more on the sense of place and time, such as those by

Erik Larson. Titles from the sciences appeal when they have a strong focus on the characters, natural disasters, or scientific development. Historically set sports books can make good suggestions, such as *Seabiscuit: An American Legend,* as can the more direct matches in both travel and true adventure, such as *In the Heart of the Sea: The Tragedy of the Whaleship* Essex, by Nathaniel Philbrick, or *The* Endurance: *Shackleton's Legendary Antarctic Expedition,* by Caroline Alexander.

Benchmark Books to Read and Suggest

Reading in this area can lead to a life of pleasure, inquiry, and learning, but readers' advisory librarians do not have to read a huge range of titles to get a sense of the subject. These seven titles illustrate the range of approaches and styles and suggest reasons both to read the books and to offer them to patrons. Reading these books help readers' advisory librarians become comfortable with the various types of books in the field and get a sense of how the classifications within the field vary. As you read these books, try to articulate the differences between the type classifications; this will help when dealing with patrons who, though they may not be able to articulate it, are searching for a particular type of book as well as for a specific subject.

Historical Explanations

The largest section of history works is historical explanations. These are books that explain what happened, why it occurred, and why it mattered. Readers new to history or those without an abiding interest in a particular area more than likely see all history as historical explanations. These works are written for the general reader but range in narrative styles. Some are highly story based; others are more fact based and scholarly.

Rough Crossings: Britain, the Slaves and the American Revolution, by Simon Schama

With great narrative skill, Schama relates the quasi freedom of slaves during the birth of America. He is a compelling writer and paints vivid portraits of both characters and landscape as he reveals the motivations of key players in this sad, but little noted, saga. During the American Revolution, the last British governor of Virginia declared that any slave who would serve in the British army would be granted freedom. Thousands of slaves escaped, making their way to British camps all over the colonies, where they again risked their lives—acting as spies, nurses, laborers, and soldiers. Near the end of the war many of them were subsequently transported off American shores. Some were betrayed and resold in the West Indies; others were shipped to a fledgling new home in Nova Scotia. In the cold and harsh climate of Canada, many ex-slaves were given land and freedom. But it was hard to live off the thin and icy dirt, and the white loyalists who also fled to Canada were not happy with the freedoms granted to those they still considered slaves. Sierra Leone looked to be a promised land, and thus a new idea was born and a great transport to Africa began. Schama's sweeping narrative follows the journey and recounts the efforts of abolitionists Granville Sharp and Thomas and John Clarkson.

Read this book because it illustrates the perfect blending of story and history and of narration and facts, and because it typifies much of what readers look for in these book types: it puts facts into context, uses character to make history real, has a strong steady pace, and is both engrossing and rigorous.

Suggest this book to readers who want something moderately paced that brings history vividly to life with many story lines and characters. It matches well with *Bury the Chains: Prophets and Rebels in the Fight to Free an Empire's Slaves* and *King Leopold's Ghost: A Story of Greed, Terror, and Heroism in Colonial Africa,* by Adam Hochschild, as well as *New York Burning: Liberty, Slavery, and Conspiracy in Eighteenth-Century Manhattan,* by Jill Lepore.

Historical Biography

Biographies about individuals who created history or were caught up in the sweep of history are included here. These books are almost addictively enjoyable, since seeing the arc of history through the eyes of those who lived it, even created it, is as close to being there as we can get. The added context readers gain about the social and political landscape is also a big draw, for these books illuminate history and character in rich and endlessly textured ways. The best biographies not only capture the lives of their subjects but place those subjects in the context of their times and blend strong narratives with great scholarship.

A Perfect Union: Dolley Madison and the Creation of the American Nation, by Catherine Allgor

In this beautifully written and observant book, Allgor blends the finest elements of historical biography into a great reading experience. The work is both history and rich story, full of detail, description, and well-crafted characters that combine in a fascinating way to enliven not just Dolley Madison but also the society, culture, and political world in which she lived and reigned. During the War of 1812 and the growth and definition of the new American republic, Dolley Madison had a unifying effect on the nation. She forged, in the home of the president, a Washington social scene and used her drawing room as a focal point of political power, nation building, and charming persuasion. In an age when women were legally without power, Dolley Madison wielded a great deal of clout, and Allgor explores her motivations and actions and explains her effect on the nation with keen insight and an elegant hand.

Read this book because it brings history to life through biography. It has a great mix of appeal elements (fascinating characters, rich historical detail, and an intelligent and inviting style), helping readers' advisory librarians understand the force of appeal in reading. It also ably illustrates how biography can blend story, place, and personality.

Suggest this book to readers who want biographies of strong women, enjoy elegant and observant writing, and prefer engaging narratives that blend story with history. Consider pairing it with *Georgiana: Duchess of Devonshire,* by Amanda Foreman, or *Queen of Fashion: What Marie Antoinette Wore to the Revolution,* by Caroline Weber. Readers who like story, context, and history in biography should be directed toward David McCullough, and those who appreciate both scholarship and elegant construction might consider the work of Stacy Schiff.

History of War and Military History

Historical accounts of war are among the most popular individual subjects under the large umbrella of history. Works range from detailed accounts of battles to broad overviews of entire wars. These books can focus on the activities of war, use the personalities caught up in war to tell their stories, or contextualize a war. They range from the highly narrative and character filled to the scholarly, somewhat distant, account. If the war is recent enough, titles can also be personal stories, adding even more immediacy and emotion to the telling. Readers come to these works out of casual or fervent interest, sometimes looking for context or an understanding of what a loved one experienced. Reader motivation often drives the level of narrative needed. Popular media also drive interest in these books, many of which become hot topics as soon as they are published. The subsequent tide of interest that surrounds these books slowly attracts readers who normally would have no interest in reading a 350-page work on one group of soldiers.

Band of Brothers: E Company, 506th Regiment, 101st Airborne from Normandy to Hitler's Eagle's Nest, **by Stephen E. Ambrose**

Band of Brothers traces the story of Easy Company from their brutal training to their triumph in seizing Hitler's crown jewel. Detailing the entire span of the European front of World War II, Ambrose melds character and story with battle movement and history to create a work that resonates deeply with a huge number of readers—not all of them typically history or battle book readers. Partly this follows from the way Ambrose handles the history, blending it into the story so skillfully that it is barely discernable yet still remains robust and rigorous. Partly it is because of the way Ambrose writes. He has an addictively confident and subtly forceful way—pulling readers along not just by the compelling story but by the seductively easy writing. Ambrose makes readers feel as if they already know the story and are participating in the retelling. He is talking about our grandfathers in the same way they talked to us. In capturing the memories and actions of Easy Company, he has written one of the key texts of the narrative of World War II.

Read this book because it is a classic work in the subject area and can be used as a touchstone with readers.

Suggest this book to readers who want to understand the sweep of World War II, readers who enjoy strongly narrative works, and those who want more personal explanations of war. Ambrose has several other titles on the history of the war that should be considered by any reader who started with *Band of Brothers.* For works by others on World War II, consider *The Greatest Generation,* by Tom Brokaw; *An Army at Dawn: The War in Africa, 1942–1943,* by Rick Atkinson; and *The Bedford Boys: One American Town's Ultimate D-Day Sacrifice,* by Alex Kershaw. Beyond the subject of World War II, *1776,* by David McCullough, might work for many readers because it has the same inviting tone and a similar character-based story.

Pivot Points

Pivot points are books that focus on pivotal moments in history. They are often about a specific event, but they can also focus on the longer lead-up to a huge change in history, putting a contextual spin on the rising tides of change. For the most part, these books tend to be moderately narrative in nature and character based. But even when they are not, readers get caught up in the history-changing moments these books evoke. Pivot point books can also be military titles and thus span two types.

Nelson's Trafalgar: The Battle That Changed the World, **by Roy Adkins**

This is a work of history that blends moments of medium narrative with less story-based sections and uses selections of primary documents to make its points. It is an excellent account of one of the pivotal moments in history. Trafalgar launched Britain as ruler of the sea-trading routes and set it up as a colonial power, which changed the face of the world. Adkins supplies a detailed account of the battle and its aftermath, tracing the five-hour engagement from the French, Spanish, and British sides in almost cannon-shot-by-cannon-shot detail. Aspects of naval operations and tactics, seamanship, boat construction, and shipboard life are all vividly described as well, down to uniforms and gruesome explanations of shipboard medical care. The death of Nelson, the fierce storms that ravaged all sides after the battle, and the politics that followed are included, making this an excellent introduction to the battle and its meaning.

Read this book because it illustrates the less narrative side of history and shows how fact-based research can still create compelling reading. It also helps readers' advisory librarians see how works can bridge different types, since this is not only a pivot point book but also a work of military history.

Suggest this book to readers interested in the era or the battle itself or who enjoy works that allow them to read primary source materials as well as contextual explanations. It works well with *Seize the Fire: Heroism, Duty, and the Battle of Trafalgar,* by Adam Nicolson, and *Nelson: A Dream of Glory, 1758–1797,* by John Sugden, and together the two illustrate how subjects span type and how readers' advisory librarians can work with readers to expand selections in many directions. The title also works well with fiction by Patrick O'Brian, C. S. Forester, and Bernard Cornwell. Start with *Master and Commander; Mr. Midshipman Hornblower;* and *Sharpe's Tiger,* respectively.

Social and Cultural History

These works set history into its cultural context and capture a particular time. Like many history types, the works range widely on the narrative continuum. Some are story based, others are more fact driven, but all are richly detailed and explanatory of the cultural and societal aspects of history.

The Wreckers: A Story of Killing Seas, False Lights, and Plundered Shipwrecks, **by Bella Bathurst**

In this captivating and lyrical social history, Bathurst relates the culture of seamen and the wreckers who preyed off their misfortunes. She focuses on the eighteenth and nineteenth centuries when wrecking was at its height but also considers twentieth-century evolutions. In places all over Britain, men, women, and children participated in wrecking—either from the deliberate luring of a ship to ruin or by taking advantage of ships floundering near shore. The British coast was a treacherous place, bordered by the icy cold Pentland Firth in northern Scotland, the jagged rocks and crowded seas of Cornwall in the south, the looming sandbars off the easterly coast, and the whirlpools of the Gulf of Corrievreckan in the high west. It was a tough business making port in these locations, and in houses all along the water's edge was pilfered booty taken from ships that found unsafe harbor. Bathurst tells the history of all sides of these struggles: the sailors trying to earn a living, the wreckers trying to steal it, and the brave rescuers focused on saving lives. Her stories are enchanting, funny, and melancholy by turn and ensnare the reader in the unique sea culture of a rapidly fading time.

Read this book because it illustrates the type well and shows clearly the way researchers can frame culture and society with the facts of history.

Suggest this book to readers interested in story-rich history of a particular place, culture, and time. Another of Bathurst's books, *The Lighthouse Stevensons: The Extraordinary Story of the Building of the Scottish Lighthouses by the Ancestors of Robert Louis Stevenson*, makes for good reading in conjunction with the history of wrecking. Readers might also enjoy the novel *Jamaica Inn*, by Daphne du Maurier, or the book and movie *Whiskey Galore*, by Compton MacKenzie, in which a small Scottish town is treated to thousands of cases of whiskey from a capsized ship—a tale included in *The Wreckers*.

Disaster History

Books on the disasters of history—ships sinking, floods, influenzas, fires, and other traumatic events—are in constant demand. These books are typically character focused and moderately to strongly narrative as they tell the story of individuals caught up in deadly events. There are also related titles in the science chapter, and readers' advisory librarians should consider those titles as well.

Curse of the Narrows: The Halifax Disaster of 1917, by Laura M. Mac Donald

With riveting writing and a fine eye for detail and story, Laura Mac Donald relates the disaster of the *Mont Blanc* explosion in Halifax harbor—an explosion so devastating that Robert Oppenheimer later studied it to see the possible effects of the atomic bomb. During the buildup of World War I, the French munitions ship *Mont Blanc* carried a deadly mix of explosives and petroleum products into the mouth of the Narrows, where the Belgian relief ship *Imo* collided into its specially constructed hull, setting off an explosion that devastated the city. Mac Donald details the explosion and the resulting tsunami in exquisite prose, keeping the timeline in check yet still illustrating the horrible majesty in a play-by-play account. She then sets forth on an exploration of disaster and recovery. She follows, among others, three families to bring to human scale such a gigantic disaster. She uses the members of the Boston rescue team to illustrate the fledgling formation of a quick response unit, one caught in what scientists call an Eastern Seaboard Bomb, in which a huge amount of snow can fall in a short period. The snow bomb hit Halifax, adding more misery to an already grim situation and slowing rescue attempts and relief efforts. All told, more than 1,600 people died and thousands more were injured. Mac Donald's history is a testament to them all.

Read this book because it includes all the elements of disaster history that readers look for: strong story, character focus, and attention to the historical importance of the event—in this case medical and relief aspects.

Suggest this book to readers looking for a highly narrative story of disaster and recovery that includes both personal history and much well-researched detail. Readers might also enjoy *A Crack in the Edge of the World: America and the Great California Earthquake of 1906,* by Simon Winchester; *The Circus Fire: A True Story of an American Tragedy,* by Stewart O'Nan; and *Isaac's Storm: A Man, a Time, and the Deadliest Hurricane in History,* by Erik Larson. Readers who appreciate Mac Donald's book for its insights on disaster recovery may find that such works as *The Great Deluge: Hurricane Katrina, New Orleans, and the Mississippi Gulf Coast,* by Douglas Brinkley, and *Breach of Faith: Hurricane Katrina and the Near Death of a Great American City,* by Jed Horne, make illuminating parallel reading.

Micro History

Micro histories are in-depth studies that focus on a narrow topic. They are historical, but that is often not the point of the book, and they frequently span two types—micro history and whatever subject-specific type is most relevant. Therefore, micro history titles can be found throughout this book under other subjects and types. For example, I classify *Longitude: The True Story of a Lone Genius Who Solved the Greatest Scientific Problem of His Time,* by Dava Sobel, the book that perhaps can be credited with starting the new trend of micro histories, in the science chapter under the type literary or historical slants; in the context of science, this classification helps readers' advisory librarians get closer to the information needed when looking to match a book (narrative nature, subject, type, and appeal) than does the collective category of micro history. Similarly, *The Portland Vase: The Extraordinary Odyssey of a Mysterious Roman Treasure,* by Robin Brooks, is listed under art in the general nonfiction chapter, and *Robbing the Bees: A Biography of Honey—The Sweet Liquid Gold That Seduced the World,* by Holley Bishop, is listed as a nature and natural history type in the science chapter.

No matter where these books appear, they tend to be highly narrative, full of characters, description, and detail, and good sources of contextualized learning. They make wonderful suggestions for readers just looking for something "good" to read or as an introduction to a broader subject.

Zarafa: A Giraffe's True Story, from Deep in Africa to the Heart of Paris, by Michael Allin

The first giraffe ever to take a long-legged step on French soil was a bribe thought up by the tomb-raiding Bernardino Dravetti, French council and private advisor to Muhammad Ali, the Ottoman viceroy of Egypt. Ali wanted to distract the king of France from the Egyptian war with Greece and hoped the giraffe would be sufficient inducement. It was not, but as an event and beloved curiosity Zarafa was a huge success. Her story is a sad yet magical one, the stuff of Arthur Rackham illustrations. She was captured in Ethiopia and sailed down the Nile with the meat from her mother. She landed in Alexandria and crossed the Mediterranean on a boat with a hole cut in its deck for her head. She arrived in Marseilles and walked 550 miles to Paris, where she became a beloved resident of the menagerie of the Jardin des Plantes. Along the way, thousands of people came to see her, and she inspired fashions, hairstyles, and hats. Her story alone would be worth reading, but Allin, with a deft touch, relates all manner of tangential history related to her journey, from the fascinations of Napoleon with Egypt to the scientific discoveries of the age.

Read this book because it is a delightfully charming example of micro history and illustrates the tone and construction many readers associate with the type.

Suggest this book to readers looking for strongly narrative history with an accessible approach and a mix of historical threads. It pairs well with works such as *Longitude: The True Story of a Lone Genius Who Solved the Greatest Scientific Problem of His Time,* by Dava Sobel, because of the similar approach and tone, and with *The Medici Giraffe,* by Marina Belozerskaya, which has the same weaving of historical fact into multiple story lines about obsessions with animals.

Key Authors

The world of history and historical biography is large. There are current writers for which every book is a major milestone. There are still others who are no longer writing but who penned classic works well worth remembering. It can be hard to keep up with all the names, but this list can help. It can be used to develop a personal reading plan, to help patrons, to build displays and booklists, and to build and weed collections.

Stephen E. Ambrose	Shelby Foote	Giles Milton
Rick Atkinson	Antonia Fraser	Adam Nicolson
Bella Bathurst	Flora Fraser	James T. Patterson
Daniel J. Boorstin	Doris Kearns Goodwin	Nathaniel Philbrick
Fergus Bordewich	David Halberstam	Diana Preston
James Bradley	Neil Hanson	Alexander Rose
Taylor Branch	Adam Hochschild	Simon Schama
H. W. Brands	John Keegan	Stacy Schiff
Thomas Cahill	Alex Kershaw	Stephen W. Sears
Robert A. Caro	Mark Kurlansky	Hampton Sides
Iris Chang	Jill Lepore	Hew Strachan
Ron Chernow	Bernard Lewis	Barbara W. Tuchman
Robert Dallek	Pauline Maier	Stanley Weintraub
Joseph J. Ellis	Mark Mazower	Alison Weir
Niall Ferguson	David McCullough	Garry Wills
David Hackett Fischer	James M. McPherson	Simon Winchester
Thomas Fleming	Robert Middlekauff	Gordon S. Wood

Selected Bibliography of History Titles to Read and Suggest

Historical Explanations

From Dawn to Decadence: 500 Years of Western Cultural Life, 1500 to the Present, by Jacques Barzun

The Discoverers: A History of Man's Search to Know His World and Himself; The Creators: A History of Heroes of the Imagination; and *The Seekers: The Story of Man's Continuing Quest to Understand His World,* by Daniel J. Boorstin

Bound for Canaan: The Underground Railroad and the War for the Soul of America, by Fergus Bordewich

Earthly Powers: The Clash of Religion and Politics in Europe, from the French Revolution to the Great War, by Michael Burleigh

A History of New York City to 1898, by Edwin G. Burrows and Mike Wallace

The Chinese in America: A Narrative History, by Iris Chang

Inhuman Bondage: The Rise and Fall of Slavery in the New World, by David Brion Davis

Faith and Treason: The Story of the Gunpowder Plot, by Antonia Fraser

The Cold War: A New History, by John Lewis Gaddis

The Best and the Brightest, by David Halberstam

The Confident Hope of a Miracle: The True History of the Spanish Armada, by Neil Hanson

Bury the Chains: Prophets and Rebels in the Fight to Free an Empire's Slaves and *King Leopold's Ghost: A Story of Greed, Terror, and Heroism in Colonial Africa,* by Adam Hochschild

The Fatal Shore: The Epic of Australia's Founding, by Robert Hughes; and consider *A Commonwealth of Thieves: The Improbable Birth of Australia,* by Thomas Keneally

Edge of Empire: Lives, Culture, and Conquest in the East, 1750–1850, by Maya Jasanoff

Judgment Days: Lyndon Baines Johnson, Martin Luther King, Jr., and the Laws That Changed America, by Nick Kotz

New York Burning: Liberty, Slavery, and Conspiracy in Eighteenth-Century Manhattan, by Jill Lepore

The Arabs in History (and his other work), by Bernard Lewis

The Reformation: A History, by Diarmaid MacCulloch

American Gospel: God, the Founding Fathers, and the Making of a Nation, by Jon Meacham

White Gold: The Extraordinary Story of Thomas Pellow and Islam's One Million White Slaves (and his other work), by Giles Milton

Medici Money: Banking, Metaphysics, and Art in Fifteenth-Century Florence, by Tim Parks

Grand Expectations: The United States, 1945–1974 and *Restless Giant: The United States from Watergate to Bush vs. Gore,* by James T. Patterson

Before the Fallout: From Marie Curie to Hiroshima and *Boxer Rebellion: The Dramatic Story of China's War on Foreigners That Shook the World in the Summer of 1900,* by Diana Preston

Auschwitz: A New History, by Laurence Rees

Lenin's Tomb: The Last Days of the Soviet Empire, by David Remnick

Rough Crossings: Britain, the Slaves and the American Revolution and *Citizens: A Chronicle of the French Revolution,* by Simon Schama

Blood and Thunder: An Epic of the American West, by Hampton Sides

A Distant Mirror: The Calamitous 14th Century, by Barbara W. Tuchman

The Rise of American Democracy: Jefferson to Lincoln, by Sean Wilentz

Historical Biography

A Perfect Union: Dolley Madison and the Creation of the American Nation, by Catherine Allgor

The Defining Moment: FDR's Hundred Days and the Triumph of Hope, by Jonathan Alter

Lindbergh, by A. Scott Berg

My Face Is Black Is True: Callie House and the Struggle for Ex-slave Reparations, by Mary Frances Berry

Martha Washington: An American Life, by Patricia Brady

Andrew Jackson: His Life and Times and *The First American: The Life and Times of Benjamin Franklin* (and his other work), by H. W. Brands

The Path to Power; Means of Ascent; and *Master of the Senate* (and his other work), by Robert A. Caro

Mao: The Unknown Story, by Jung Chang

Titan: The Life of John D. Rockefeller, Sr.; Alexander Hamilton; and *The Warburgs: The Twentieth-Century Odyssey of a Remarkable Jewish Family,* by Ron Chernow

Son of the Morning Star: Custer and the Little Bighorn, by Evan S. Connell

An Unfinished Life: John F. Kennedy, 1917–1963 and *Lyndon B. Johnson: Portrait of a President* (and his other work), by Robert Dallek

The Pirates Laffite: The Treacherous World of the Corsairs of the Gulf, by William C. Davis

Lincoln, by David Herbert Donald

His Excellency: George Washington; Founding Brothers: The Revolutionary Generation; American Sphinx: The Character of Thomas Jefferson; and *Passionate Sage: The Character and Legacy of John Adams*, by Joseph J. Ellis

Georgiana: Duchess of Devonshire, by Amanda Foreman

Love and Louis XIV: The Women in the Life of the Sun King (and her other work), by Antonia Fraser

Princesses: The Six Daughters of George III (and her other work), by Flora Fraser

Nightingales: The Extraordinary Upbringing and Curious Life of Miss Florence Nightingale, by Gillian Gill

Team of Rivals: The Political Genius of Abraham Lincoln (and her other work), by Doris Kearns Goodwin

Malory: The Knight Who Became King Arthur's Chronicler, by Christina Hardyment

A Life in Secrets: Vera Atkins and the Missing Agents of WWII, by Sarah Helm

Benjamin Franklin: An American Life, by Walter Isaacson

Profiles in Courage, by John F. Kennedy

W. E. B. Du Bois: Biography of a Race, 1868–1919 and *W. E. B. Du Bois: The Fight for Equality and the American Century, 1919–1963*, by David Levering Lewis

The Peabody Sisters: Three Women Who Ignited American Romanticism, by Megan Marshall

John Adams and *Truman*, by David McCullough

Samurai William: The Englishman Who Opened Japan, by Giles Milton

Theodore Rex, by Edmund Morris

With Malice toward None: A Life of Abraham Lincoln, by Stephen B. Oates

The Orientalist: Solving the Mystery of a Strange and Dangerous Life, by Tom Reiss

John James Audubon: The Making of an American, by Richard Rhodes

Founding Mothers: The Women Who Raised Our Nation, by Cokie Roberts

Explaining Hitler: The Search for the Origins of His Evil, by Ron Rosenbaum

A Great Improvisation: Franklin, France, and the Birth of America (and her other work), by Stacy Schiff

Stalin: A Biography, by Robert Service

Lincoln's Melancholy: How Depression Challenged a President and Fueled His Greatness, by Joshua Wolf Shenk

Khrushchev: The Man and His Era, by William Taubman

Queen of Fashion: What Marie Antoinette Wore to the Revolution, by Caroline Weber

Queen Isabella: Treachery, Adultery, and Murder in Medieval England (and her other work), by Alison Weir

The Professor and the Madman: A Tale of Murder, Insanity, and the Making of the "Oxford English Dictionary" (and his other work), by Simon Winchester

Revolutionary Characters: What Made the Founders Different, by Gordon S. Wood

The Pirate Hunter: The True Story of Captain Kidd, by Richard Zacks

History of War and Military History

This is an area of the collection where sufficient detail and coverage is important. The works below cover five wars of high interest simply to give a sense of the variety and scope of war titles. It is not intended to be a representative list of all viewpoints or all wars. Readers' advisory librarians should note the content of their collections, looking for both broad overviews and works on specific battles and personalities; appendix A can serve as a guide. Books on wars since Vietnam are listed in chapter 11.

AMERICAN REVOLUTION

First American Army: The Untold Story of George Washington and the Men behind America's First Fight for Freedom, by Bruce Chadwick

Washington's Crossing, by David Hackett Fischer

Washington's Secret War: The Hidden History of Valley Forge, by Thomas Fleming

1776, by David McCullough

The Glorious Cause: The American Revolution, 1763–1789, by Robert Middlekauff

Washington's Spies: The Story of America's First Spy Ring, by Alexander Rose

Iron Tears: America's Battle for Freedom, Britain's Quagmire: 1775–1783, by Stanley Weintraub

AMERICAN CIVIL WAR

The Army of the Potomac trilogy (and his other work), by Bruce Catton

Sea of Gray: The Around-the-World Odyssey of the Confederate Raider Shenandoah, by Tom Chaffin

The Civil War: A Narrative trilogy (and his other work), by Shelby Foote

Battle Cry of Freedom: The Civil War Era (and his other work), by James M. McPherson

Chancellorsville (and his other work), by Stephen W. Sears

The Sword of Lincoln: The Army of the Potomac, by Jeffry D. Wert

WORLD WAR I

The Pity of War: Explaining World War I (and his other work), by Niall Ferguson

The First World War (and his other work), by John Keegan

A World Undone: The Story of the Great War, 1914 to 1918, by G. J. Meyer

The First World War: Volume I: To Arms (a projected three-volume set); see also the one-volume overview *The First World War,* by Hew Strachan

The Guns of August (and her other work), by Barbara W. Tuchman

WORLD WAR II

A Woman in Berlin: Eight Weeks in the Conquered City, by Anonymous, translated by Philip Boehm

Band of Brothers: E Company, 506th Regiment, 101st Airborne from Normandy to Hitler's Eagle's Nest and *D Day: June 6, 1944: The Climactic Battle of World War II* (and his other work), by Stephen E. Ambrose

An Army at Dawn: The War in Africa, 1942–1943, by Rick Atkinson

Flags of Our Fathers, by James Bradley, with Ron Powers, and *Flyboys: A True Story of Courage,* by James Bradley

The Rape of Nanking: The Forgotten Holocaust of World War II, by Iris Chang

Hiroshima, by John Hersey

The Second World War, by John Keegan

The Bedford Boys: One American Town's Ultimate D-Day Sacrifice and *The Longest Winter: The Battle of the Bulge and the Epic Story of WWII's Most Decorated Platoon,* by Alex Kershaw

Ivan's War: Life and Death in the Red Army, 1939–1945 (and her other work), by Catherine Merridale

Miracles on the Water: The Heroic Survivors of a World War II U-Boat Attack, by Tom Nagorski

Ghost Soldiers: The Forgotten Epic Story of World War II's Most Dramatic Mission, by Hampton Sides

Bitter Ocean: The Battle of the Atlantic, 1939–1945, by David Fairbank White

VIETNAM WAR

A Rumor of War, by Philip Caputo

Dispatches, by Michael Herr

We Were Soldiers Once . . . and Young: Ia Drang—The Battle That Changed the War in Vietnam, by Harold G. Moore and Joseph L. Galloway

Bury Us Upside Down: The Misty Pilots and the Secret Battle for the Ho Chi Minh Trail, by Rick Newman and Don Shepperd

Tiger Force: A True Story of Men and War, by Michael Sallah and Mitch Weiss

Pivot Points

Nelson's Trafalgar: The Battle That Changed the World, by Roy Adkins

Undaunted Courage: Meriwether Lewis, Thomas Jefferson, and the Opening of the American West (and his other work), by Stephen E. Ambrose

Empire Express: Building the First Transcontinental Railroad, by David Haward Bain

Agincourt: Henry V and the Battle That Made England, by Juliet Barker

Wide as the Waters: The Story of the English Bible and the Revolution It Inspired, by Benson Bobrick

1812: The War That Forged a Nation, by Walter R. Borneman

Sailing the Wine-Dark Sea: Why the Greeks Matter; How the Irish Saved Civilization; The Gifts of the Jews: How a Tribe of Desert Nomads Changed the Way Everyone Thinks and Feels; and *Desire of the Everlasting Hills: The World Before and After Jesus* (and his other work), by Thomas Cahill

1912: Wilson, Roosevelt, Taft and Debs: The Election That Changed the Country, by James Chace

Adams vs. Jefferson: The Tumultuous Election of 1800, by John Ferling

1968: The Year That Rocked the World, by Mark Kurlansky

The Name of War: King Philip's War and the Origins of American Identity, by Jill Lepore

American Scripture: Making the Declaration of Independence, by Pauline Maier

1759: The Year Britain Became Master of the World, by Frank McLynn

Mayflower: *A Story of Courage, Community, and War,* by Nathaniel Philbrick

Lusitania: *An Epic Tragedy,* by Diana Preston

Warriors of God: Richard the Lionheart and Saladin in the Third Crusade, by James Reston Jr.

Inventing America: Jefferson's Declaration of Independence (and his other work), by Garry Wills

Social and Cultural History

Voices from Chernobyl, by Svetlana Alexievich

The Wreckers: A Story of Killing Seas, False Lights, and Plundered Shipwrecks, by Bella Bathurst

Ghost Hunters: William James and the Search for Scientific Proof of Life after Death, by Deborah Blum

Parting the Waters: America in the King Years, 1954–63; Pillar of Fire: America in the King Years, 1963–65; and *At Canaan's Edge: America in the King Years, 1965–68,* by Taylor Branch

The Greatest Generation, by Tom Brokaw

1215: The Year of Magna Carta, by Danny Danziger and John Gillingham

Embracing Defeat: Japan in the Wake of World War II, by John W. Dower

At the Hands of Persons Unknown: The Lynching of Black America, by Philip Dray

A Pickpocket's Tale: The Underworld of Nineteenth-Century New York, by Timothy J. Gilfoyle

A Nation under Our Feet: Black Political Struggles in the Rural South from Slavery to the Great Migration, by Steven Hahn

The Children, by David Halberstam

Sons of Mississippi: A Story of Race and Its Legacy, by Paul Hendrickson

Postwar: A History of Europe since 1945, by Tony Judt

1491: New Revelations of the Americas before Columbus, by Charles C. Mann

Salonica, City of Ghosts: Christians, Muslims and Jews, 1430–1950 (and his other work), by Mark Mazower

Seize the Fire: Heroism, Duty, and the Battle of Trafalgar (and his other work),
    by Adam Nicolson

The Birth of America: From before Columbus to the Revolution, by William R. Polk

Lost Battalions: The Great War and the Crisis of American Nationality, by
    Richard Slotkin

Disaster History

Rising Tide: The Great Mississippi Flood of 1927 and How It Changed America
    and *The Great Influenza: The Epic Story of the Deadliest Plague in History*,
    by John M. Barry

*The Worst Hard Time: The Untold Story of Those Who Survived the Great
    American Dust Bowl*, by Timothy Egan

The Children's Blizzard, by David Laskin

The Terrible Hours, by Peter Maas

Curse of The Narrows: The Halifax Disaster of 1917, by Laura M. Mac Donald

The Circus Fire: A True Story of an American Tragedy, by Stewart O'Nan

The Colony: The Harrowing True Story of the Exiles of Molokai, by John Tayman

Triangle: The Fire That Changed America, by David von Drehle

Krakatoa: The Day the World Exploded—August 27, 1883 and *A Crack in the
    Edge of the World: America and the Great California Earthquake of 1906*, by
    Simon Winchester

Micro History

*The Measure of All Things: The Seven-Year Odyssey and Hidden Error That
    Transformed the World*, by Ken Alder

Zarafa: A Giraffe's True Story, from Deep in Africa to the Heart of Paris, by
    Michael Allin

*The Lighthouse Stevensons: The Extraordinary Story of the Building of the Scottish
    Lighthouses by the Ancestors of Robert Louis Stevenson*, by Bella Bathurst

The Medici Giraffe, and Other Tales of Exotic Animals and Power, by Marina
    Belozerskaya

*Wittgenstein's Poker: The Story of a Ten-Minute Argument between Two Great
    Philosophers*, by David Edmonds and John Eidinow

At Day's Close: Night in Times Past, by A. Roger Ekirch

Coal: A Human History, by Barbara Freese

Zipper: An Exploration in Novelty, by Robert D. Friedel

A Thread across the Ocean: The Heroic Story of the Transatlantic Cable, by John Steele Gordon

A Perfect Red: Empire, Espionage, and the Quest for the Color of Desire, by Amy Butler Greenfield

The Basque History of the World: The Story of a Nation, by Mark Kurlansky

Measuring America: How an Untamed Wilderness Shaped the United States and Fulfilled the Promise of Democracy, by Andro Linklater

Crying: A Natural and Cultural History of Tears, by Tom Lutz

The Tulip: The Story of the Flower That Has Made Men Mad, by Anna Pavord

One Good Turn: A Natural History of the Screwdriver and the Screw, by Witold Rybczynski

Zero: The Biography of a Dangerous Idea, by Charles Seife

A History of the World in Six Glasses and *The Turk: The Life and Times of the Famous Eighteenth-Century Chess-Playing Machine,* by Tom Standage

The Earth Moved: On the Remarkable Achievements of Earthworms, by Amy Stewart

Difference Engine: Charles Babbage and the Quest to Build the First Computer, by Doron Swade

Big Cotton: How a Humble Fiber Created Fortunes, Wrecked Civilizations, and Put America on the Map, by Stephen Yafa

Resources and Awards

It is not hard to keep up with history and historical biography. Indeed, it is often more difficult not to feel swamped by all the titles, subjects, and review sources. In addition to professional review journals and major newspapers and magazines, National Public Radio often has features on history titles, as does C-SPAN. There are some series worth monitoring as well, chief among them the Eminent Lives series by HarperCollins and Atlas Books and two series by Oxford University: Pivotal Moments in American History, and the Oxford History of the United States. All three series feature major authors and cover important and popular historical topics.

Although all the reviews and book buzz is great for title awareness, it does not help when you are trying to decide if one work is more authoritative or central than another. Therefore, in addition to scanning a variety of review sources, readers' advisory librarians (and collection development librarians) should track the major awards in the subject area. This helps ensure that the best writing is being identified in the midst of all the choices, that it is added to the collection, and that your list of key authors and titles continues to include the best writing of each year.

PULITZER PRIZE

The Pulitzer Prize is a critical award for this subject area, and winners and short-listed titles should be kept up with and added to any reading plan or suggested reading list you keep. The history award is for books of American history, and there is a separate award for biography. The general nonfiction Pulitzer Prize is important to monitor as well, since it is often a work of history. See http://www.pulitzer.org.

NATIONAL BOOK AWARDS

The nonfiction National Book Award winner and short list are vital to track each year. History books of one type or another are frequently short-listed and often win. See http://www.nationalbook.org/nba.html.

NATIONAL BOOK CRITICS CIRCLE AWARD

The National Book Critics Circle Award has a general nonfiction category that is sometimes won by a history title. The short-listed titles are also worth scanning. The awards, judged by a distinguished group of book critics, also include a category for biography. See http://www.bookcritics.org/page2.html.

NOTABLE BOOK LIST

The ALA's Notable Books Council typically includes history and biography works in its list of most notable books for adults. This list is particularly useful for readers' advisory librarians, since the books are selected for their appeal to the general reader. See http://www.ala.org/ala/rusa/rusaprotools/rusanotable/notablebooks.htm.

COSTA BOOK AWARDS

The Costa Book Awards, formerly known as the Whitbread, have a category for biography. Both the winning title and the short list are worth monitoring. See http://www.costabookawards.com.

11

GENERAL NONFICTION

In preceding chapters we review eight of the most popular subdivisions of nonfiction individually to give readers' advisory librarians a thorough understanding of the subject areas of nonfiction and their key authors and titles. But there is much more to the nonfiction world than what is in those eight chapters. There are wonderful books that do not easily fit into one of the subject-specific sections, and there are interesting and intriguing subjects for which there is not a large body of nonfiction work published.

In this chapter we consider such additional titles by highlighting their appeal to readers and offering both benchmark titles and suggested further reading. Any author listed should be considered worthy of further investigation, and every general nonfiction book award previously discussed should be considered a possible source for more good titles.

It is possible, of course, to fit almost any of the titles listed here into one of the other specific subject chapters, but listing them individually highlights the unique appeals of their subject nature (remember, subject is often what first draws a reader to a nonfiction title) and avoids the awkwardness inherent in trying to force a book into a tangential subject area.

Benchmark Books to Read and Suggest

In this chapter we look at six general subject areas:

- Arts, Literature, and Philosophy
- Essays
- Humor
- Religion and Spirituality
- Economic, Political, and Social Sciences
- War (Memoir, Reporting, and Analysis)

The benchmark title examples below serve as an introduction to the variety of works included in this more general chapter. They represent different writing styles, address a broad range of subjects, and illustrate how the different nonfiction elements shape a reading experience. Use them to review the ways connections can be made between titles and subject areas, how important narrative drive is when considering suggestions for readers, the effect of type on the reading experience, and how appeal elements influence reader enjoyment.

Arts, Literature, and Philosophy

Books about the creative life can be fascinating and hold rich rewards for readers. Common types for this subject include biographies, essays, and explanatory or micro history. The appeals of those types apply generally to this subject area, with the appeals of character, learning/experiencing, detail, and language dominating.

The character-driven nature of biographies allows readers to feel that they know someone they have long admired, studied, or read. Biographies also provide a sense of the culture, times, and society, which can be important in building a contextual understanding of a body of writing, art, or philosophy. Typically these biographical works also include a mix of story and research that readers enjoy.

Detail and learning/experiencing are other points of appeal for many. The feeling of understanding and competence one gets from these books is satisfying. Readers want to know how colors became popular, how artists and writers met each other, how one influenced another, and how to interpret paintings and texts. These books increase the readers' knowledge of the subject and provide insights into works they have long loved.

Language is a large appeal point as well. Describing art, explaining a philosophy, or capturing the creative process of writing is in itself an intensely language-demanding task. Many writers rise to the occasion and pen works that are lucid, elegant, and insightful. Writing style effects tempo, and many of these books feel leisurely to moderately paced.

Will in the World: How Shakespeare Became Shakespeare, by Stephen Greenblatt

Greenblatt, editor of the *Norton Shakespeare*, takes the frustratingly opaque bits of Shakespeare's biographical trail and, with a bright and engaging style, blends them with close reading, literary theory, and historical explanation.

The result is a biography that illuminates the entire world of sixteenth- and seventeenth-century England and Shakespeare's place within it. Greenblatt acknowledges up front that the known details of Shakespeare's life are well documented—as allusive and as unhelpful as they may be—and he does not really have much more to offer in terms of new discoveries. What he does have is an amazing insight into Shakespeare's work as it relates to his biography. He uses quotes from plays and sonnets to trace the development of Shakespeare's life and genius, and he connects it all to the world in which Shakespeare was living. In so doing, Greenblatt provides the reader a way to navigate both the work and the man—in a wonderful blend of literary exploration and historical biography.

Read this book because it is a great example of both biography and literary inquiry and shows how nonfiction subjects range widely. It also illustrates the ways differing narrative states exist within one book (in this case, fact based, moderately narrative, and selections of the world's best fiction and poetry) and how the reader reacts to those states.

Suggest this book to readers interested in learning how to read a text closely, to those who enjoy Shakespeare, and to those who like to read about literature in both a historical and an explanatory context. Greenblatt's achievement is singular, but works such as *Shakespeare: The Invention of the Human,* by Harold Bloom, and *A Year in the Life of William Shakespeare: 1599,* by James Shapiro, work well as supports for Greenblatt's book. Bloom provides close readings of the plays in essays that offers similar explanatory context. Shapiro does the same thing with historical events that Greenblatt does with Shakespeare's biography—uses a close reading to explain a given theory and in so doing helps readers contextualize selected plays from a historical point of view.

Essays

Like biography and memoir, essays are a type of nonfiction all their own. The appeal of essays varies with the author and the intent of the work, so considerations of appeal have to be applied individually to each title. One broad factor does, however, apply to all essays—their brevity. A great deal of nonfiction is long and takes commitment on the part of the reader. Essays are short and require little time to read and hardly any commitment at all. Indeed, part of the great appeal of essays is that they invite readers to browse through their pages at leisure without the obligations of beginning, middle, and end.

Essay collections are widely diverse. Some gather the work of a single author and show the range and interests of that writer over time; others are thematic and collect the best essays on a given subject. Essays tend to be first published in magazines and newspapers, which is why most of the subject chapters in this book point to important serials to skim for key authors and topics. Many major nonfiction authors have published essays at some point in their careers, so reading essays is a great way to discover authors and track their development over time. That way, by the time their first book is published, you already know something of these writers and to whom they will appeal. Collections are also a wonderful way to help readers discover authors to enjoy. By offering either a range of single-author essays or one or two collections consisting of the work of many authors, you can introduce readers to a variety of styles. If you and your reader are only starting to explore the possibilities of nonfiction, then essays are a great way to get your bearings.

There are essays collections in many of this book's subject-specific chapters, so if a patron is interested in a particular subject, be sure to look there for good suggestions as well.

Being Perfect, by Anna Quindlen

Anna Quindlen uses the image of a backpack full of bricks to describe the burden of the urge to be perfect. In this brief essay she explores the crutch of perfection, the comfort it offers, and the empty promise it delivers. Her lesson is simple, almost the stuff of bumper sticker wisdom, but she elevates her message—that the true work of life is to become yourself—with a fine command of language, a lovely and wry point of view, and a perfect pace.

Read this book because it exemplifies the form and illustrates what many readers look for in essays—brevity, insight, and a tight command of language.

Suggest this book to readers looking for a short, friendly shot in the arm. Quindlen has written another similar short essay, *A Short Guide to a Happy Life,* which readers might enjoy, as well as several collections of essays including *Living Out Loud* and *Thinking Out Loud: On the Personal, the Political, the Public and the Private.* She has also written novels, a literary travel book, *Imagined London: A Tour of the World's Greatest Fictional City,* and an ode to the joys of reading, *How Reading Changed My Life.* Since part of the appeal of essays can be the connection a reader has to the author, all of Quindlen's work, including her novels, should be suggested to readers. Another author who might speak to readers on a similar level (but in a different voice) is Anne Lamott. *A Room of One's Own,* by Virginia Woolf, might also work for readers who enjoy Quindlen's perspective and want to read more about women forging their own way.

Humor

Humor is a frequent vehicle for authors to make their point or tell their stories, and there are funny books in many of the subject-specific chapters as well as the shorter subject overviews in this chapter. *A Man without a Country*, by Kurt Vonnegut, is dark and savagely funny and is listed in the essay bibliography below. *Kitchen Confidential*, by Anthony Bourdain, is an irreverent riot listed in chapter 3 on food. *A Year in Provence*, by Peter Mayle, is sweet, funny, and charming and is listed in chapter 8 on travel. This section contains books whose subjects are too diverse to fit anywhere else. Thankfully, humor is everywhere.

Humor books share many appeal elements with memoirs and essays. As with memoirs, character is important. Humor books are often personal and offer the reader a connection with authors and a chance to experience their take (often wacky and bent) on the world. The chance to identify with an author and share experiences is often a huge draw as well. The author as character is often a stand-in for the reader. Many readers find it both affirming and cathartic to have some of their worst, hardest, or most embarrassing life moments, even if only tangentially related to the ones described by the author, glossed by the perspective and wit of a gifted humorist. Conversely, many readers simply like to observe the strange and compelling characters found in humor books. The odder the character, the more insane the situation, the better.

Language and pace matter a great deal in humor books. The buildup of a joke or the long running riff of situational comedy is a special skill which, when employed correctly, can reduce readers to laughter-induced tears. Because of the pacing required for comedy to work, humor books tend to be fast reads.

The tone of these books is also important. They can be funny, witty, droll, bitingly sarcastic, dry, ironic, irreverent, caustic, or endearing. They give readers permission to be similarly expressive and offer a release and an escape for many.

Similar to essays, humor books tend to be short, or at least constructed in such a way that readers can dip in and out of them. Combined with their fast pace, this makes humor books easy to read and quite engaging. Also like essays, the appeal of each author is individual and based on style, subject, and authorial intent. Both reader and readers' advisory librarian will have to experiment to find the tone and voice they most enjoy. But that should hardly be a hardship.

Dress Your Family in Corduroy and Denim, by David Sedaris

In this collection of stories about his life, Sedaris does what he does best— offer readers a mix of observant satire, self-deprecation, and flat-out-funny writing. His voice is pitch perfect as he tells of pilfered Halloween candy, being locked out of his house and his brilliant plan to get back in by arranging the death of his six-year-old sister, his relationship with Hugh, and his life as cleaner, writer, brother, lover, and son. It is a great mix of stories: sharp, tender, intimate, and, as always, very funny.

Read this book because Sedaris is a master of the mix of humor, essay, and memoir.

Suggest this book to readers who enjoy humorous essays with an ironic, often caustic, twist. Sedaris has several other works, including the riotous "SantaLand Diaries," which launched his career (they are in *Barrel Fever* and *Holidays on Ice*), *Naked*, and *Me Talk Pretty One Day*. His audio performances are also well worth noting; he is a great reader of his own stories. All comedy is individual, but those looking for something in the same vein might consider David Rakoff's *Don't Get Too Comfortable: The Indignities of Coach Class, the Torments of Low Thread Count, the Never-Ending Quest for Artisanal Olive Oil, and Other First World Problems* or *Fraud: Essays*.

Religion and Spirituality

Readers enjoy books on religion and spirituality for several reasons. The two major appeals are the opportunity for growth and understanding (learning/ experiencing) and the comfort (tone and story line) these books provide.

Readers interested in this subject are often either deeply religious or struggling to believe—whether that belief is traditionally religious or more broadly spiritual. These books help affirm both the belief and the struggle while offering the shared learning experience of others on the same path. These appeals cannot be overstated; the comfort and collective wisdom one gets from many books on this subject are critical to the reader.

Readers also enjoy these books for the same reasons they enjoy memoirs. The personal connection with an individual story made universal lends itself well to sharing a spiritual journey and the consolations of faith. Other readers find that books on spirituality appeal to their curiosity. The opportunity to travel from outsider to participant is intriguing to readers who enjoy seeing how others celebrate their faith. In that same vein, detail is often important as readers learn about the ceremonies and history of a religion or spiritual tradition.

Plan B: Further Thoughts on Faith, **by Anne Lamott**

Lamott writes in a heartfelt but simple voice, exhorting readers to breathe and pray, be and rest, and, perhaps most of all, listen. She uses her own life to describe the path of seeking these things—from the story of her son's first letter to his father to her own message to new graduates. Her work is intensely personal yet offers readers guideposts to navigate their own world through her stumbling discoveries of faith. Though her voice is decidedly liberal—in language, politics, and religion—readers seeking a fellow traveler find tender solace in her stories and comfort and encouragement in her gentle point of view.

Read this book because it highlights the two major appeals of this subject—the sharing of faith and the comfort it brings. Lamott is also a major voice in the subject area and can be used as a touchstone with readers.

Suggest this book to readers looking for gentle stories of faith from an open and universal tradition. Lamott has written other works on faith, including *Traveling Mercies: Some Thoughts on Faith,* a primer on writing, and several novels. Readers who enjoy Lamott's meandering thoughts on faith might also appreciate *Plain and Simple: A Journey to the Amish,* by Sue Bender, or *The Barn at the End of the World: The Apprenticeship of a Quaker, Buddhist Shepherd,* by Mary Rose O'Reilley.

Economic, Political, and Social Sciences

Quirky social science books are one of the nonfiction subjects that helped launch the new awareness by readers' advisory librarians of the richness of nonfiction. Joining them in this category are books on politics and economics. Books in this area range widely. Books by political pundits express the argument of the day—designed to pump up a base or tear down an opponent. Biographies by politicians, be they past presidents or advisors, are platforms to make a case and express a particular point of view. Mixed in with these bluntly political vehicles are works that address politics from a slightly more removed perspective, those that explore social conditions (which are in themselves political fodder), titles that explain why we behave the way we do or how market forces work, and titles that offer inside looks at interesting events (the thrill of winning a Scrabble game) and sorry states (the violence financed by diamonds). These titles get a lot of press attention, which tends to drive readers toward them with a get-on-the-bandwagon mentality. The continuing polarization of our national politics has also created an interest in these titles. Readers watch TV and listen to talk radio and want to either read more about issues or confirm their view. Since our readers know about them and ask us for them, it is important to understand some of the common appeal factors of these books.

The primary appeals are learning/experiencing, tone, and story line as expressed by authorial intent. All other appeal considerations, such as language, detail, and pacing, fall into place based on the primary appeals.

Learning/experiencing is an important appeal element because it works along with subject to draw readers to a particular title. Readers want different things from these books. Some want to understand an intriguing concept, some want to experience an event or life vicariously, and some want to be affirmed in their opinions. Not surprisingly then, essays and reporting (both investigative and immersion) are common types in these subject areas, and the general appeals of those types apply to many of these titles.

Many of these books also have definite authorial intents, which are expressed in story line, language, and tone. Books are written to support a cause, explain a phenomenon, track a social or political development, investigate, or persuade. They can be funny, harsh, vilifying, skewed, reasoned, bolstering, or explanatory.

Although it can be a challenge to provide assistance in this area (after all, you do run out of political titles, just as you do football books or books on quarks), the area offers rich rewards. Many titles are fascinating and well crafted and provide insight and understanding into our collective and individual behavior. Other titles offer inspiration and eye-opening glimpses into lives that need to be noted.

Nickel and Dimed: On (Not) Getting By in America, by Barbara Ehrenreich

In this classic piece of immersion journalism, Barbara Ehrenreich decided to live the life of the working poor. She found that beneath the politics of welfare reform, homelessness, and the minimum wage are real people trying to get by. They do it by sleeping in cars, sharing low-end hotel rooms, and working at least two jobs. In Florida, Maine, and Minnesota, as a waitress, nursing home aid, maid, and Wal-Mart sales clerk, Ehrenreich lived off her meager income, struggled to find housing, and figured out the truth behind the politics: minimum wage is not a living wage; it is barely a survivable wage.

Read this book because it is an excellent example of immersion reporting and of how the appeal of learning/experiencing works in a narrative.

Suggest this book to readers who want to understand what life is like on poverty-based wages, to those who enjoy learning through their reading, especially about social issues, and to readers who like immersion reporting. Ehrenreich has also written *Bait and Switch: The (Futile) Pursuit of the American Dream,* an insider look at the white-collar job search. Readers wanting to learn more about poverty should consider *The End of Poverty: Economic Possibilities for Our Time,* by Jeffrey Sachs, and those looking for other works of sociological immersion reporting might consider *Self-Made Man: One Woman's Journey into Manhood and Back,* by Norah Vincent.

War: Memoir, Reporting, and Analysis

Readers enjoy these books for a variety of reasons. Some enjoy reading about the danger and missions involved with war. Others read for the political statement many of these books make, especially those on the most recent conflicts. Many read to understand the way war works—who decides, how decisions get made, what motivates the decision to go to war, and so on. Still others enjoy reading for the heroic feel some of these books convey or for the memoir aspects many contain. For readers who have never faced battle or have no military experience, these books help illuminate a world that can be fascinating. For readers who have experienced the chaos of war, they can be cathartic.

Why the reader picks up the book to start with greatly determines if the book will be enjoyed. Readers who need their faith in the military affirmed will not enjoy a book that exposes the worst side of soldiers in battle or appreciate a title that points out all the mistakes of military leadership. Others want to read critical works on the military and want investigative accounts. Still others read to understand. The confusion and haze that surround policymaking in general, and battles in particular, drive readers to seek in-depth coverage and explanation. Thus, learning/experiencing is a strong appeal factor. Tone and authorial intent are also important appeal factors, for the same reasons explored in the previous section.

Other appeal elements include pacing, detail, and story line. Books in this area range from fast paced and highly narrative to more leisurely, less narrative explanation. Details are abundant and include such topics as political infighting, policymaking, battle dress, weapons, tactics, and troop movements. The story of war, the battles, the motivations, and the characters also holds strong appeal. All these aspects combine into a vibrant pool of reading choices.

Black Hawk Down: A Story of Modern War, by Mark Bowden

In a work that helped redefine the way war stories are told, Bowden provides readers with a bullet-by-bullet account of the October 3, 1993, battle in Somalia. The soldiers, members of Task Force Ranger, were on a mission to capture two deputies of Mohamed Farrah Aidid, a warlord wreaking havoc on Mogadishu. What was planned to take an hour turned into a much longer battle, with soldiers pinned down, separated from each other in small units, running out of ammo, and injured and dying. In a desperate overnight battle, the men of Task Force Ranger, Rangers, Delta forces, and SEALs all participated in a rescue, but before it was over, eighteen soldiers were dead and dozens more were wounded. On the Somali side, five hundred were dead and more than a thousand injured. Bowden re-creates the chaos of the battle and its aftermath in a stunning achievement of rapid-fire narrative war reporting.

Read this book because it is a modern classic of war journalism, illustrates highly narrative writing, and gives insight into what many readers are looking for in this subject area: a firm grasp of the facts; details about troop movements, weaponry, and tactics; and an insider look at soldiers at war.

Suggest this book to those interested in military subjects, especially those who enjoy battle accounts. *Black Hawk Down* was turned into a movie that makes good parallel viewing (as do the film versions of *Band of Brothers* and *Platoon*). Bowden also wrote *Guests of the Ayatollah: The First Battle in America's War with Militant Islam,* which readers might also enjoy. Other titles to consider include the novel *The Killer Angels,* by Michael Shaara, and the classic war reporting of other wars, including *We Were Soldiers Once . . . and Young: Ia Drang—The Battle That Changed the War in Vietnam,* by Harold G. Moore and Joseph L. Galloway, and *Pork Chop Hill,* by S. L. A. Marshall. Still other you-are-there war narratives include *Not a Good Day to Die: The Untold Story of Operation Anaconda,* by Sean Naylor, and *Thunder Run: The Armored Strike to Capture Baghdad,* by David Zucchino.

Selected Bibliography of General Nonfiction to Read and Suggest

Arts, Literature, and Philosophy

Shakespeare: The Biography (and his other work), by Peter Ackroyd

A Gentle Madness: Bibliophiles, Bibliomanes, and the Eternal Passion for Books (and his other work), by Nicholas A. Basbanes

American Gothic: A Life of America's Most Famous Painting, by Steven Biel

History Play: The Lives and Afterlife of Christopher Marlowe, by Rodney Bolt

Wrapped in Rainbows: The Life of Zora Neale Hurston, by Valerie Boyd

The Portland Vase: The Extraordinary Odyssey of a Mysterious Roman Treasure, by Robin Brooks

Flaubert: A Biography, by Frederick Brown

Orson Welles: The Road to Xanadu and *Orson Welles: Hello Americans,* by Simon Callow

Jean-Jacques Rousseau: Restless Genius, by Leo Damrosch

Strapless: John Singer Sargent and the Fall of Madame X, by Deborah Davis

Melville: His World and Work, by Andrew Delbanco

Byron: Child of Passion, Fool of Fame, by Benita Eisler

Color: A Natural History of the Palette, by Victoria Finlay

Evening in the Palace of Reason: Bach Meets Frederick the Great in the Age of Enlightenment, by James R. Gaines

Living to Tell the Tale, by Gabriel Garcia Marquez, translated by Edith Grossman

Art Lover: A Biography of Peggy Guggenheim, by Anton Gill; and see *Mistress of Modernism: The Life of Peggy Guggenheim,* by Mary V. Dearborn

Vindication: A Life of Mary Wollstonecraft, by Lyndall Gordon

Can't Be Satisfied: The Life and Times of Muddy Waters, by Robert Gordon

Will in the World: How Shakespeare Became Shakespeare, by Stephen Greenblatt

All I Did Was Ask: Conversations with Writers, Actors, Musicians, and Artists, by Terry Gross

Dream Boogie: The Triumph of Sam Cooke, by Peter Guralnick

The Lost Painting: The Quest for a Caravaggio Masterpiece, by Jonathan Harr

Frida: A Biography of Frida Kahlo, by Hayden Herrera

Making the Mummies Dance: Inside the Metropolitan Museum of Art, by Thomas Hoving

Things I Didn't Know: A Memoir; Goya; Nothing If Not Critical: Selected Essays on Art and Artists; and *American Visions: The Epic History of Art in America* (and his other work), by Robert Hughes; see also *Francisco Goya*, by Evan S. Connell

Brunelleschi's Dome: How a Renaissance Genius Reinvented Architecture; Michelangelo and the Pope's Ceiling; and *The Judgment of Paris: The Revolutionary Decade That Gave the World Impressionism*, by Ross King

The Breaking Point: Hemingway, Dos Passos, and the Murder of Jose Robles, by Stephen Koch

Virginia Woolf and *Virginia Woolf's Nose: Essays on Biography*, by Hermione Lee

Eudora Welty: A Biography, by Suzanne Marrs

The Metaphysical Club: A Story of Ideas in America, by Louis Menand

Andrew Wyeth: A Secret Life, by Richard Meryman

Impressionist Quartet: The Intimate Genius of Manet and Morisot, Degas and Cassatt, by Jeffrey Meyers

Savage Beauty: The Life of Edna St. Vincent Millay and *Zelda: A Biography*, by Nancy Milford

The Genius in the Design: Bernini, Borromini, and the Rivalry That Transformed Rome, by Jake Morrissey

The Rape of Europa: The Fate of Europe's Treasures in the Third Reich and the Second World War, by Lynn H. Nicholas; see also *The Amber Room: The Fate of the World's Greatest Lost Treasure*, by Adrian Levy and Catherine Scott-Clark

James Tiptree, Jr.: The Double Life of Alice B. Sheldon, by Julie Phillips

Mark Twain: A Life, by Ron Powers

Girl Sleuth: Nancy Drew and the Women Who Created Her, by Melanie Rehak

Jelly's Blues: The Life, Music, and Redemption of Jelly Roll Morton, by Howard Reich and William Gaines

The Shakespeare Wars: Clashing Scholars, Public Fiascoes, Palace Coups, by Ron Rosenbaum

A Clearing in the Distance: Frederick Law Olmsted and America in the 19th Century (and his other work), by Witold Rybczynski

Vera (Mrs. Vladimir Nabokov), by Stacy Schiff

Duveen: A Life in Art, by Meryle Secrest

Mockingbird: A Portrait of Harper Lee, by Charles J. Shields

Utopia Parkway: The Life and Work of Joseph Cornell, by Deborah Solomon

The Unknown Matisse: A Life of Henri Matisse, vol. 1: The Early Years, 1869–1908 and *Matisse the Master: A Life of Henri Matisse: The Conquest of Colour, 1909–1954*, by Hilary Spurling

For the Love of Music: Invitations to Listening, by Michael Steinberg and Larry Rothe

De Kooning: An American Master, by Mark Stevens and Annalyn Swan

A Writer's Life, by Gay Talese

Where Dead Voices Gather, by Nick Tosches

Still Looking: Essays on American Art, by John Updike

Everything That Rises: A Book of Convergences, by Lawrence Weschler

Born to Kvetch: Yiddish Language and Culture in All Its Moods, by Michael Wex

Essays

The Best American Magazine Writing, compiled by the American Society of Magazine Editors (published annually; includes essays as well as other types of writing)

The Best American Essays, edited by Robert Atwan (published annually)

Notes of a Native Son, by James Baldwin

The Way of Ignorance and Other Essays and *The Long-Legged House*, by Wendell Berry

Wanting a Child, by Jill Bialosky and Helen Schulman

The New New Journalism: Conversations with America's Best Nonfiction Writers on Their Craft, by Robert Boynton

Banvard's Folly: Thirteen Tales of People Who Didn't Change the World, by Paul S. Collins

The Aztec Treasure House: New and Selected Essays, by Evan S. Connell

The Next American Essay, edited by John D'Agata

Orphans, by Charles D'Ambrosio

The Art of Travel, by Alain de Botton

Slouching towards Bethlehem: Essays and *The White Album* (and her other work), by Joan Didion

Book by Book: Notes on Reading and Life and *Bound to Please*, by Michael Dirda

Creationists: Selected Essays, 1993–2006, by E. L. Doctorow

The Best American Nonrequired Reading, edited by Dave Eggers (published annually; contains a mix of fiction and nonfiction)

Ex Libris: Confessions of a Common Reader, by Anne Fadiman

A Temple of Texts, by William H. Gass

Many Circles, by Albert Goldbarth

Approaching Eye Level, by Vivian Gornick

In Fact: The Best of Creative Nonfiction, edited by Lee Gutkind

Love, Poverty, and War: Journeys and Essays, by Christopher Hitchens

The Art of Fact: A Historical Anthology of Literary Journalism, edited by Kevin Kerrane and Ben Yagoda (contains selections from longer works as well as essays)

High Tide in Tucson: Essays from Now or Never, by Barbara Kingsolver

In Short: A Collection of Brief Creative Nonfiction and *In Brief: Short Takes on the Personal*, edited by Judith Kitchen and Mary Paumier Jones

Sex, Drugs, and Cocoa Puffs: A Low Culture Manifesto, by Chuck Klosterman

The Disappointment Artist, by Jonathan Lethem

Getting Personal: Selected Writings, by Phillip Lopate

The Eloquent Essay: An Anthology of Classic and Creative Nonfiction, edited by John Loughery

The Undertaking: Life Studies from the Dismal Trade, by Thomas Lynch

Waist-High in the World: A Life among the Nondisabled, by Nancy Mairs

Up in the Old Hotel, by Joseph Mitchell

Best American Essays of the Century, edited by Joyce Carol Oates and Robert Atwan

The Bullfighter Checks Her Makeup: My Encounters with Extraordinary People, by Susan Orlean

Metaphor and Memory; Fame and Folly; and *Quarrel and Quandary,* by Cynthia Ozick

How Reading Changed My Life; A Short Guide to a Happy Life; and *Being Perfect*, by Anna Quindlen

Reporting: Writings from the "New Yorker," by David Remnick

The Fourth Genre: Contemporary Writers of/on Creative Non-Fiction, edited by Robert L. Root and Michael Steinberg

The Secret Parts of Fortune: Three Decades of Intense Investigations and Edgy Enthusiasms, by Ron Rosenbaum

Literary Journalism, edited by Norman Sims and Mark Kramer

Somewhere in America: Under the Radar with Chicken Warriors, Left-Wing Patriots, Angry Nudists, and Others, by Mark Singer

The Covenant with Black America, edited by Tavis Smiley

Regarding the Pain of Others, by Susan Sontag

The Content of Our Character: A New Vision of Race in America, by Shelby Steele

Off Ramp: Adventures and Heartache in the American Elsewhere, by Hank Stuever

The Gay Talese Reader: Portraits and Encounters, by Gay Talese

The Opposite of Fate: A Book of Musings, by Amy Tan

Too Soon to Tell, by Calvin Trillin

The Last Empire: Essays, 1992–2000 (and his other collections), by Gore Vidal

A Man without a Country, by Kurt Vonnegut

Consider the Lobster and Other Essays and *A Supposedly Fun Thing I'll Never Do Again: Essays and Arguments*, by David Foster Wallace

Shiksa Goddess; or, How I Spent My Forties, by Wendy Wasserstein

Vermeer in Bosnia: Cultural Comedies and Political Tragedies, by Lawrence Weschler

Essays of E. B. White and *One Man's Meat*, by E. B. White

The Woman at the Washington Zoo: Writings on Politics, Family, and Fate, by Marjorie Williams

A Room of One's Own (and her other work), by Virginia Woolf

Humor

Making Friends with Black People, by Nick Adams

Dave Barry's Money Secrets (and his other work), by Dave Barry

The Benchley Roundup, by Robert C. Benchley

Fun Run and Other Oxymorons: Singular Reflections of an Englishman Abroad, by Joe Bennett

Too Much of a Good Thing Is Wonderful, by Regina Berreca

Forever, Erma: Best-Loved Writing from America's Favorite Humorist, by Erma Bombeck

The Sweet Potato Queens' Book of Love (and her other work), by Jill Conner Browne

Magical Thinking: True Stories, by Augusten Burroughs

When Will Jesus Bring the Pork Chops? (and his other work), by George Carlin

Love and Marriage (and his other work), by Bill Cosby

The Funny Thing Is . . . , by Ellen DeGeneres

I Feel Bad about My Neck and Other Thoughts on Being a Woman, by Nora Ephron

Steal This Book: And Get Life without Parole, by Bob Harris

Being Dead Is No Excuse: The Official Southern Ladies Guide to Hosting the Perfect Funeral, by Charlotte Hays and Gayden Metcalfe

The Areas of My Expertise, by John Hodgman

Why Animals Sleep So Close to the Road (and Other Lies I Tell My Children), by Susan Konig

Gutted: Down to the Studs in My House, My Marriage, My Life, by Lawrence LaRose

Pure Drivel, by Steve Martin

The Bear in the Attic, by Patrick F. McManus

How Tough Could It Be? The Trials and Errors of a Sportswriter Turned Stay-at-Home Dad, by Austin Murphy

We Thought You Would Be Prettier: True Tales of the Dorkiest Girl Alive; I Love Everybody (and Other Atrocious Lies): True Tales of a Loudmouth Girl; and *The Idiot Girl's Action-Adventure Club: True Tales from a Magnificent and Clumsy Life* (and her other work), by Laurie Notaro

Holidays in Hell (and his other work), by P. J. O'Rourke

The Most of S. J. Perelman, by S. J. Perelman

The Neal Pollack Anthology of American Literature, by Neal Pollack

Don't Get Too Comfortable: The Indignities of Coach Class, the Torments of Low Thread Count, the Never-Ending Quest for Artisanal Olive Oil, and Other First World Problems and *Fraud: Essays,* by David Rakoff

We're Just Like You, Only Prettier: Confessions of a Tarnished Southern Belle, by Celia Rivenbark

Dress Your Family in Corduroy and Denim and *Me Talk Pretty One Day* (and his other work), by David Sedaris

Seinlanguage, by Jerry Seinfeld

Tiny Ladies in Shiny Pants: Based on a True Story, by Jill Soloway

Naked Pictures of Famous People, by Jon Stewart

The Thurber Carnival, by James Thurber

How to Survive a Robot Uprising: Tips on Defending Yourself against the Coming Rebellion, by Daniel H. Wilson

Religion and Spirituality

Tuesdays with Morrie: An Old Man, a Young Man, and Life's Greatest Lesson, by Mitch Albom

On the Threshold: Home, Hardwood, and Holiness, by Elizabeth J. Andrew

The Great Transformation: The Beginning of Our Religious Traditions; The Spiral Staircase: My Climb Out of Darkness; A History of God: The 4,000-Year Quest of Judaism, Christianity and Islam; and *Islam: A Short History* (and her other work), by Karen Armstrong

In the Wilderness: Coming of Age in Unknown Country, by Kim Barnes

Seeking Enlightenment . . . Hat by Hat: A Skeptic's Guide to Religion, by Nevada Barr

Velvet Elvis: Repainting the Christian Faith, by Rob Bell

Plain and Simple: A Journey to the Amish, by Sue Bender

The Abbey Up the Hill: A Year in the Life of a Monastic Day-Tripper, by Carol Bonomo

The Last Week: The Day-by-Day Account of Jesus's Final Week in Jerusalem, by Marcus J. Borg and John Dominic Crossan

Secrets in the Dark: A Life in Sermons, by Frederick Buechner

The Power of Myth, by Joseph Campbell, with Bill Moyers; and see *The Hero with a Thousand Faces,* by Joseph Campbell

The Tao of Physics, by Fritjof Capra

Scarred by Struggle, Transformed by Hope (and her other work), by Joan D. Chittister

The Book of Secrets: Unlocking the Hidden Dimensions of Your Life, by Deepak Chopra

Salvation on Sand Mountain: Snake-Handling and Redemption in Southern Appalachia, by Dennis Covington

The Universe in a Single Atom: The Convergence of Science and Spirituality (and his other work), by His Holiness the Dalai Lama

Encountering God: A Spiritual Journey from Bozeman to Banaras, by Diana L. Eck

The Collar: A Year of Striving and Faith inside a Catholic Seminary, by Jonathan Englert

Walking the Bible: A Journey by Land through the Five Books of Moses and *Where God Was Born: A Journey by Land to the Roots of Religion,* by Bruce Feiler

The Prophet, by Kahlil Gibran

The Journey: Living by Faith in an Uncertain World (and his other work), by Billy Graham

Driving by Moonlight: A Journey through Love, War, and Infertility, by Kristin Henderson

Father Joe: The Man Who Saved My Soul, by Tony Hendra; and see *How to Cook Your Daughter: A Memoir,* by Jessica Hendra, for a different perspective

Mama Made the Difference (and his other work), by T. D. Jakes

When Bad Things Happen to Good People, by Harold S. Kushner

Traveling Mercies: Some Thoughts on Faith and *Plan B: Further Thoughts on Faith,* by Anne Lamott

The Tulip and the Pope: A Nun's Story, by Deborah Larsen

Mere Christianity (and his other work), by C. S. Lewis

Swimming with Scapulars: True Confessions of a Young Catholic, by Matthew Lickona

Traveling Light: Releasing the Burdens You Were Never Intended to Bear (and his other work), by Max Lucado

Vows: The Story of a Priest, a Nun, and Their Son, by Peter Manseau

Accidental Buddhist, by Dinty W. Moore

Care of the Soul: A Guide for Cultivating Depth and Sacredness in Everyday Life and *Dark Nights of the Soul,* by Thomas Moore

The Energy of Prayer: How to Deepen Your Spiritual Practice, by Thich Nhat Hanh

The Cloister Walk and *Amazing Grace* (and her other work), by Kathleen Norris

The Barn at the End of the World: The Apprenticeship of a Quaker, Buddhist Shepherd, by Mary Rose O'Reilley

Beyond Belief: The Secret Gospel of Thomas (and her other work), by Elaine Pagels

Memory and Identity: Conversations at the Dawn of a Millennium (and his other work), by Pope John Paul II

The Road Less Traveled: A New Psychology of Love, Traditional Values and Spiritual Growth, by M. Scott Peck

Zen and the Art of Motorcycle Maintenance: An Inquiry into Values, by Robert M. Pirsig

Unveiled: The Hidden Lives of Nuns, by Cheryl L. Reed

The Unmistakable Touch of Grace, by Cheryl Richardson

The Death of Adam: Essays on Modern Thought, by Marilynne Robinson

The Holy Longing: The Search for a Christian Spirituality, by Ronald Rolheiser

Rumspringa: To Be or Not to Be Amish, by Tom Shachtman

A Book of Life: Embracing Judaism as a Spiritual Practice, by Michael Strassfeld

Leaving Church: A Memoir of Faith, by Barbara Brown Taylor

The Power of Now: A Guide to Spiritual Enlightenment, by Eckhart Tolle

God Has a Dream: A Vision of Hope for Our Time, by Desmond Tutu

Conversations with God: An Uncommon Dialogue, by Neale Donald Walsch (and the other books in that series, including *Home with God*)

The Simple Feeling of Being: Visionary, Spiritual, and Poetic Writings, by Ken Wilber

Illuminata: A Return to Prayer (and her other work), by Marianne Williamson

What Jesus Meant (and his other work), by Garry Wills

Prayer: Does It Make Any Difference? (and his other work), by Philip Yancey

The Best American Spiritual Writing, edited by Philip Zaleski (published annually)

Economic, Political, and Social Sciences

ECONOMICS

The Long Tail: Why the Future of Business Is Selling Less of More, by Chris Anderson

Barbarians at the Gate: The Fall of RJR Nabisco, by Bryan Burrough and John Helyar

Affluenza: The All-Consuming Epidemic, by John de Graaf, David Wann, and Thomas H. Naylor

The Wal-Mart Effect: How the World's Most Powerful Company Really Works—and How It's Transforming the American Economy, by Charles Fishman

China, Inc.: How the Rise of the Next Superpower Challenges America and the World, by Ted C. Fishman

How Soccer Explains the World: An Unlikely Theory of Globalization, by
Franklin Foer

*The Conquest of Cool: Business Culture, Counterculture, and the Rise of Hip
Consumerism*, by Thomas C. Frank

The World Is Flat: A Brief History of the Twenty-first Century and *The Lexus and
the Olive Tree: Understanding Globalization*, by Thomas L. Friedman

Big Coal: The Dirty Secret behind America's Energy Future, by Jeff Goodell

*The Undercover Economist: Exposing Why the Rich Are Rich, the Poor Are Poor—
and Why You Can Never Buy a Decent Used Car!* by Tim Harford

Freakonomics: A Rogue Economist Explores the Hidden Side of Everything, by
Steven D. Levitt and Stephen J. Dubner

Liar's Poker: Rising through the Wreckage on Wall Street, by Michael Lewis

When Genius Failed: The Rise and Fall of Long-Term Capital Management, by
Roger Lowenstein

The Smartest Guys in the Room: The Amazing Rise and Scandalous Fall of Enron,
by Bethany McLean and Peter Elkind

Confessions of an Economic Hit Man, by John Perkins

*The Travels of a T-shirt in the Global Economy: An Economist Examines the
Markets, Power, and Politics of World Trade*, by Pietra Rivoli

*Fast Boat to China: Corporate Flight and the Consequences of Free Trade, Lessons
from Shanghai*, by Andrew Ross

The Paradox of Choice: Why More Is Less, by Barry Schwartz

*The Wisdom of Crowds: Why the Many Are Smarter Than the Few and How
Collective Wisdom Shapes Business, Economies, Societies and Nations*, by
James Surowiecki

Call of the Mall: The Geography of Shopping and *Why We Buy: The Science of
Shopping*, by Paco Underhill

POLITICAL SCIENCE

Madam Secretary: A Memoir, by Madeleine Albright

All the President's Men, by Carl Bernstein and Bob Woodward

*The Great Deluge: Hurricane Katrina, New Orleans, and the Mississippi Gulf
Coast*, by Douglas Brinkley

Bobos in Paradise: The New Upper Class and How They Got There and *On
Paradise Drive: How We Live Now (and Always Have) in the Future Tense*,
by David Brooks

State of Emergency: The Third World Invasion and Conquest of America (and his other work), by Patrick J. Buchanan

Barbara Bush: A Memoir, by Barbara Bush

Heartbeat: George Bush in His Own Words, by George Bush, edited by Jim McGrath

Blood Diamonds: Tracing the Deadly Path of the World's Most Precious Stones, by Greg Campbell

House of War, by James Carroll

Our Endangered Values: America's Moral Crisis and *Palestine: Peace Not Apartheid,* by Jimmy Carter

Failed States: The Abuse of Power and the Assault on Democracy (and his other work), by Noam Chomsky

My Life, by Bill Clinton; see also *First in His Class: A Biography of Bill Clinton,* by David Maraniss

Living History, by Hillary Rodham Clinton

Godless: The Church of Liberalism (and her other work), by Ann Coulter

Faith and Politics: How the "Moral Values" Debate Divides America and How to Move Forward Together, by Senator John Danforth

Conservatives without Conscience, by John Dean

Bushworld: Enter at Your Own Risk, by Maureen Dowd

Colossus: The Rise and Fall of the American Empire, by Niall Ferguson

What's the Matter with Kansas? How Conservatives Won the Heart of America, by Thomas Frank

The Truth (with Jokes) (and his other work), by Al Franken

Watching the World Change, by David Friend

Journey of the Jihadist: Inside Muslim Militancy, by Fawaz A. Gerges

Enemies: How America's Foes Steal Our Vital Secrets—and How We Let It Happen (and his other work), by Bill Gertz

Winning the Future: A 21st Century Contract with America, by Newt Gingrich

Bias: A CBS Insider Exposes How the Media Distort the News (and his other work), by Bernard Goldberg

Storming the Court: How a Band of Yale Law Students Sued the President—and Won, by Brandt Goldstein

Deliver Us from Evil: Defeating Terrorism, Despotism, and Liberalism (and his other work), by Sean Hannity

Screwed: The Undeclared War against the Middle Class—and What We Can Do about It, by Thom Hartmann

The Unquiet Grave: The FBI and the Struggle for the Soul of Indian Country, by Steve Hendricks

Bushwhacked: Life in George W. Bush's America (and her other work), by Molly Ivins and Lou Dubose

A Matter of Character: Inside the White House of George W. Bush, by Ronald Kessler

American Vertigo: Traveling America in the Footsteps of Tocqueville, by Bernard-Henri Levy

The American Way of Strategy, by Michael Lind

Stupid White Men . . . and Other Sorry Excuses for the State of the Nation! (and his other work), by Michael Moore

The Worst Person in the World, and 202 Strong Contenders, by Keith Olbermann

Culture Warrior (and his other work), by Bill O'Reilly

American Theocracy: The Peril and Politics of Radical Religion, Oil, and Borrowed Money in the 21st Century and *Wealth and Democracy: A Political History of the American Rich* (and his other work), by Kevin Phillips

My American Journey, by Colin L. Powell; see also *Soldier: The Life of Colin Powell*, by Karen DeYoung

My Turn: The Memoirs of Nancy Reagan, by Nancy Reagan

An American Life, by Ronald Reagan; see also *President Reagan: The Role of a Lifetime*, by Lou Cannon

Reason: Why Liberals Will Win the Battle for America, by Robert B. Reich

The Greatest Story Ever Sold: The Decline and Fall of Truth from 9/11 to Katrina, by Frank Rich

Strategery: How George W. Bush Is Defeating Terrorists, Outwitting Democrats, and Confounding the Mainstream Media, by Bill Sammon

Watchdogs of Democracy? The Waning Washington Press Corps and How It Has Failed the Public, by Helen Thomas

The Lemon Tree: An Arab, a Jew, and the Heart of the Middle East, by Sandy Tolan

31 Days: The Crisis That Gave Us the Government We Have Today, by Barry Werth

State of Denial: Bush at War, Part III (and his other work), by Bob Woodward

The Heartless Stone: A Journey through the World of Diamonds, Deceit and Desire, by Tom Zoellner

SOCIAL SCIENCES

Let Us Now Praise Famous Men, by James Agee and Walker Evans

The Fire Next Time (and his other work), by James Baldwin

The Lost Children of Wilder: The Epic Struggle to Change Foster Care, by Nina Bernstein

Living at the Edge of the World: How I Survived in the Tunnels of Grand Central Station, by Jamie Pastor Bolnick and Tina S.

Blues for Cannibals: The Notes from Underground (and his other work), by Charles Bowden

Why Do I Love These People? Honest and Amazing Stories of Real Families, by Po Bronson

Among the Thugs, by Bill Buford

Our Town: A Heartland Lynching, a Haunted Town, and the Hidden History of White America, by Cynthia Carr

Body Brokers: Inside America's Underground Trade in Human Remains, by Annie Cheney

Coyotes: A Journey through the Secret World of America's Illegal Aliens, by Ted Conover

Professor, the Banker, and the Suicide King: Inside the Richest Poker Game of All Time, by Michael Craig

Remember Me: A Lively Tour of the New American Way of Death, by Lisa Takeuchi Cullen

The Serpent and the Rainbow and *Light at the Edge of the World: A Journey through the Realm of Vanishing Cultures,* by Wade Davis

Guns, Germs, and Steel: The Fates of Human Societies and *Collapse: How Societies Choose to Fail or Succeed* (and his other work), by Jared Diamond

Little Money Street: In Search of Gypsies and Their Music in the South of France, by Fernanda Eberstadt

Nickel and Dimed: On (Not) Getting By in America and *Bait and Switch: The (Futile) Pursuit of the American Dream,* by Barbara Ehrenreich

The Spirit Catches You and You Fall Down, by Anne Fadiman

Word Freak: Heartbreak Triumph Genius Obsession World Competitive Scrabble Players, by Stefan Fatsis

Stumbling on Happiness, by Daniel Gilbert

Death's Door: Modern Dying and the Ways We Grieve: A Cultural Study, by Sandra M. Gilbert

The Tipping Point: How Little Things Can Make a Big Difference and *Blink: The Power of Thinking without Thinking,* by Malcolm Gladwell

Articles of Faith: A Frontline History of the Abortion Wars, by Cynthia Gorney

War Is a Force That Gives Us Meaning, by Chris Hedges

Confederates in the Attic: Dispatches from the Unfinished Civil War, by Tony Horwitz

The Dead Beat: Lost Souls, Lucky Stiffs, and the Perverse Pleasures of Obituaries, by Marilyn Johnson

Everything Bad Is Good for You: How Today's Popular Culture Is Actually Making Us Smarter, by Steven Johnson

And a Time to Die: How American Hospitals Shape the End of Life, by Sharon R. Kaufman

The Soul of a New Machine and *Among Schoolchildren,* by Tracy Kidder

There Are No Children Here: The Story of Two Boys Growing Up in the Other America, by Alex Kotlowitz

The Shame of the Nation: The Restoration of Apartheid Schooling in America, by Jonathan Kozol

American Ground: Unbuilding the World Trade Center, by William Langewiesche

Random Family: Love, Drugs, Trouble, and Coming of Age in the Bronx, by Adrian Nicole LeBlanc

American Bee: The National Spelling Bee and the Culture of Word Nerds, by James Maguire

Stuart: A Life Backwards, by Alexander Masters

Positively Fifth Street: Murderers, Cheetahs, and Binion's World Series of Poker, by James McManus

Bringing Down the House: The Inside Story of Six M.I.T. Students Who Took Vegas for Millions, by Ben Mezrich

Cross X: A Turbulent, Triumphant Season with an Inner-City Debate Squad, by Joe Miller

The American Way of Death, by Jessica Mitford

Human Cargo: A Journey among Refugees, by Caroline Moorehead

Enrique's Journey, by Sonia Nazario

Bowling Alone: The Collapse and Revival of American Community, by Robert D. Putnam

Reefer Madness and Other Tales from the American Underground, by Eric Schlosser

Black Planet: Facing Race during an NBA Season (and his other work), by David Shields

And the Band Played On: Politics, People, and the AIDS Epidemic, by Randy Shilts

White Guilt: How Blacks and Whites Together Destroyed the Promise of the Civil Rights Era and *The Content of Our Character: A New Vision of Race in America,* by Shelby Steele

The Sociopath Next Door, by Martha Stout

A Hope in the Unseen, by Ron Suskind

You Just Don't Understand: Women and Men in Conversation (and her other work), by Deborah Tannen

Fear and Loathing in Las Vegas: A Savage Journey to the Heart of the American Dream and *Hell's Angels,* by Hunter S. Thompson

Self-Made Man: One Woman's Journey into Manhood and Back, by Norah Vincent

Urban Tribes: Are Friends the New Family? by Ethan Watters

Mr. Wilson's Cabinet of Wonder: Pronged Ants, Horned Humans, Mice on Toast, and Other Marvels of Jurassic Technology (and his other work), by Lawrence Weschler

Not in Kansas Anymore: A Curious Tale of How Magic Is Transforming America, by Christine Wicker

The Electric Kool-Aid Acid Test, by Tom Wolfe

War: Memoir, Reporting, and Analysis

Note: Books about war since Vietnam are listed here, as are selected works on military subjects. Books on Vietnam and earlier conflicts are listed in chapter 10.

The Lion's Grave: Dispatches from Afghanistan and *The Fall of Baghdad,* by Jon Lee Anderson

Crusade: The Untold Story of the Persian Gulf War and *In the Company of Soldiers: A Chronicle of Combat,* by Rick Atkinson

War Reporting for Cowards, by Chris Ayres

See No Evil: The True Story of a Ground Soldier in the CIA's War on Terrorism, by Robert Baer

Jawbreaker: The Attack on Bin Laden and Al Qaeda: A Personal Account by the CIA's Key Field Commander, by Gary Berntsen and Ralph Pezzullo

Black Hawk Down: A Story of Modern War and *Guests of the Ayatollah: The First Battle in America's War with Militant Islam*, by Mark Bowden

Imperial Life in the Emerald City: Inside Iraq's Green Zone, by Rajiv Chandrasekaran

Raid on the Sun: Inside Israel's Secret Campaign That Denied Saddam the Bomb, by Rodger Claire

Against All Enemies: Inside America's War on Terror, by Richard A. Clarke

Ghost Wars: The Secret History of the CIA, Afghanistan, and Bin Laden, from the Soviet Invasion to September 10, 2001, by Steve Coll

The Warrior Elite: The Forging of SEAL Class 228, by Dick Couch

Shooter: The Autobiography of the Top-Ranked Marine Sniper, by Jack Coughlin and Casey Kuhlman, with Donald A. Davis

The Last True Story I'll Ever Tell: An Accidental Soldier's Account of the War in Iraq, by John Crawford

Charlie Wilson's War, by George Crile

Salvador, by Joan Didion

The Balkan Express: Fragments from the Other Side of War, by Slavenka Drakulic

This Man's Army: A Soldier's Story from the Front Lines of the War on Terrorism, by Andrew Exum

Hello to All That: A Memoir of War, Zoloft, and Peace, by John Falk

Over There: From the Bronx to Baghdad, by Alan Feuer

One Bullet Away: The Making of a Marine Officer, by Nathaniel C. Fick

The End of Iraq: How American Incompetence Created a War without End, by Peter W. Galbraith

Cobra II: The Inside Story of the Invasion and Occupation of Iraq, by Michael R. Gordon and Bernard E. Trainor

We Wish to Inform You That Tomorrow We Will Be Killed with Our Families: Stories from Rwanda, by Philip Gourevitch

Inside Delta Force: The Story of America's Elite Counterterrorist Unit, by Eric Haney

Chain of Command: The Road from 9/11 to Abu Ghraib, by Seymour M. Hersh

Imperial Grunts: The American Military on the Ground, by Robert D. Kaplan

Overthrow: America's Century of Regime Change from Hawaii to Iraq, by Stephen Kinzer

From Baghdad, with Love: A Marine, the War, and a Dog Named Lava, by Jay Kopelman, with Melinda Roth

Rogue Warrior, by Richard Marcinko

Not a Good Day to Die: The Untold Story of Operation Anaconda, by Sean Naylor

The Assassins' Gate: America in Iraq, by George Packer

A Problem from Hell: America and the Age of Genocide, by Samantha Power

Ambush Alley: The Most Extraordinary Battle of the Iraq War, by Tim Pritchard

Fiasco: The American Military Adventure in Iraq, by Thomas Ricks

State of War: The Secret History of the C.I.A. and the Bush Administration, by James Risen

Masters of Chaos: The Secret History of the Special Forces, by Linda Robinson

First In: An Insider's Account of How the CIA Spearheaded the War on Terror in Afghanistan, by Gary Schroen

The Bookseller of Kabul, by Asne Seierstad

Night Draws Near: Iraq's People in the Shadow of America's War, by Anthony Shadid

The One Percent Doctrine, by Ron Suskind

Jarhead: A Marine's Chronicle of the Gulf War and Other Battles, by Anthony Swofford

Company C: An American's Life as a Citizen-Soldier in Israel, by Haim Watzman

No True Glory: A Frontline Account of the Battle for Fallujah, by Bing West

Generation Kill: Devil Dogs, Iceman, Captain America, and the New Face of American War, by Evan Wright

The Looming Tower: Al-Qaeda and the Road to 9/11, by Lawrence Wright

The Battle for Peace: A Frontline Vision of America's Power and Purpose, by Tony Zinni and Tony Koltz

Thunder Run: The Armored Strike to Capture Baghdad, by David Zucchino

12

LEARNING AND MARKETING THE COLLECTION

Learning the Collection and Keeping Up with the Book Buzz

Identifying nonfiction titles that work in a readers' advisory context is a key part of conducting the service. It is important to learn your library's current nonfiction collection and devise a system to track new titles as they are published.

There are several ways to remember titles and keep up with the buzz about new ones. The following list of suggestions is rather long. It might seem that the work of learning about nonfiction and keeping up with the constant stream of new titles is a daunting task—write annotations, take notes, skim these magazines, watch TV, listen to the radio, visit your local bookstore, scan websites, monitor awards, and read, read, read. But, though the list of things to do is long, it is not prescriptive, and the work is fun. What could be better than spending a few hours each week exploring new books or dipping into your collection to find books you have yet to discover?

1. Walk into your nonfiction stacks and start scanning the titles.

Once you have read the individual subject chapters and gained a sense of nonfiction's key authors and a few of its major works, go wander in your stacks. Look at the titles in the subject concentrations that match this book and see what titles you own and which authors you recognize. Pull books for displays, your sure-bet cart, or your personal reading. Get the lay of the land of your own library. Books are selected, cataloged, briefly reside on the new book shelf, get checked out, and then slip into the stacks. If you do not make it a habit of browsing your own collection periodically, you run the risk of forgetting about them.

2. Read nonfiction and read it widely.

You cannot start using a collection you have not read. Aim to read three or four books per subject area. Read both older titles from your collection and newly published titles as well. This helps you learn the collection and keep abreast of the most current titles. As you read the titles, think about the following questions:

- Why is this book popular (author, press, subject, style, story)?
- What are readers (the media, patrons, fellow librarians, etc.) saying about this book?
- What does the author do best?
- Where does the book fall on the narrative continuum?
- What type of book is it?
- Is this book like any other book you have already read?
- Does the book remind you of any other title or author?
- Where does this book fit in terms of what you have already read in the subject area?
- Who would enjoy this book?
- What can you do with the book—put it on display, include it in a specific booklist, add it to your sure-bet cart?

3. Take notes on your reading.

Create annotations for every book you read. If you cannot do that, keep reading notes, reading logs, or just simple lists. All of these tools take time to create, but they pay you back a hundredfold over their lifetime. By keeping track of what you read, be it a book, a review, or the fast skimming of a title, you capture the essence of the work for use in the future.

Jot down titles you want to read, keep a list of titles you have read, fill out annotations for titles you read fully, and keep reading notes, associations, and lists of similar titles. Make lists of just nonfiction, but make lists of fiction and nonfiction titles that work together as well. Sometimes there are fiction and nonfiction books on the same topic, and these make natural lists, but there are always books of nonfiction that support works of fiction, and these should be looked for as well.

Keeping a running list of titles that work together offers both practice and comfort. You force yourself to engage in the habit of nonfiction and prove to yourself that there are connections you can identify.

Whether you write these lists in a notebook, type them on your computer, or write about them on a webpage or blog, keeping track is vital. Do the work once and capture it in some form of annotation to use over and over again.

Only by starting to keep track of nonfiction will we ever get to the same point we are with fiction.

4. Make it a habit to read reviews.

Reading reviews keeps titles in your head, helps you find out about forthcoming books, and starts teaching you the names of the prominent nonfiction writers. When you read a review, do so from a readers' advisory perspective. Look for features that help identify the title's narrative nature, subject, type, and key appeal features. Here are key clues to look for:

Does the review contain any language that addresses the book's narrative nature? If it suggests that the book reads like a novel or is research laden, you have some idea how to place it on the narrative continuum. A review that refers to plot is always worth noting, since this is a strong clue about the narrative nature. Character descriptions are another indicator of high-to-medium narrative work. Look for descriptions of the author's use of language, which can help give a sense of the work's narrative nature (as well as its tone and style). Books with lots of technical language or a scholarly tone are usually less narrative and more fact based. Language clues such as "funny," "breezy," or "romp" tend to indicate that the book is more narrative. If the review recommends the book for certain audiences or types of readers, take this seriously. Any nonfiction book suitable for graduate students is likely to be a book on the nonnarrative end of the continuum.

Is there any indication of type? Some reviews mention explicitly well-known nonfiction types such as essays, biography, or memoir. Other reviews include indications of type in their descriptions of content. Look for words such as "reporting," "investigation," "adventure," or "travelogue."

Words like "saga," "gripping," or "tome" are good indicators of the tone of the work. Also, be on the lookout for any mention of a book's detail or setting, for these too can reveal a great deal about a book's type and content.

Nonfiction reviews sometimes include reference to other seminal work or state that the book being reviewed is sure to become the standard in the field. These seminal titles should always be noted and kept in an ongoing list. If the collection development staff does not do this already, they will certainly be interested in any list the readers' services staff develops. Knowing a work is considered the best in the field can be endlessly useful to collection development staff, reference staff, readers' advisory staff, and readers.

If a review compares the author or the work to others, think about the comparison. Is the other author familiar to you? What is his or her writing like? Is the other author one you have on one of your lists or possibly one you have decided to create a reading guide about? If so, it should be an indication that this might be a book to examine further.

Does the review mention a fiction genre? Can you think of how the book might fit onto a booklist? Can you think of someone who would love to read the title? Is the book sparking any connections to other books?

If you notice any of these elements or can answer any of the questions just posed on the basis of a review, this should be a book you flag for further examination, jot down on your list of books to be considered, or pull from your collection and read.

Although many nonfiction reviews still focus more on arrangement, indexes, and accuracy of fact, and few include important elements such as a title's position on the narrative continuum, its type, or its complete multifaceted appeal, that is beginning to change. Many reviews now include comments on characters, pace, tone, and reader response. Review sources differ, so take some time at the start of your investigations to see how each source approaches nonfiction and what elements they stress.

To see this in practice, consider the following review from *Booklist* magazine:[1]

Carnivorous Nights: On the Trail of the Tasmanian Tiger, by Margaret Mittelbach and Michael Crewdson. Illustrated by Alexis Rockman

The Tasmanian tiger, also known as the thylacine, is a probably extinct carnivore from the island of Tasmania. Doglike in form, the thylacine was a pouched predator. Nature writers Mittelbach and Crewdson fell in love with a taxidermy specimen that they discovered while doing research at the American Museum of Natural History. Their friend, artist Alexis Rockman, grew up roaming the halls of the same museum and also loved the thylacine mount. When they discovered that people still claimed to sight the Tasmanian tiger, and that scientists were attempting to clone one, *the trio decided that they needed to go to Tasmania and look for them* in the wild. *The result is a wonderful romp, part science and part Bill Bryson,* as authors and artist visit museums, studying thylacine remains. Rockman's luminous *illustrations* of the thylacines and other native wildlife illuminate this marvelous search for an elusive, charismatic animal. The *story* will appeal to lovers of both *travel and nature writing.*—Review by Nancy Bent

In this review, Nancy Bent includes several key readers' advisory clues. She tells us the *subject* of the book: a science-tinged road trip in search of the Tasmanian tiger. She tells us the *type* of book: travel story and nature writing. She provides context by mentioning another nonfiction writer—Bill Bryson. This lets us know a great deal about the *tone* of the book, its *language,* and much of its content; it will be funny but informative and nicely written. Bent also supplies information on the *narrative nature* of the book: romps are stories, science is fact based, and thus we can guess that the work is somewhere on the medium to high end of the continuum. We also get a suggestion of *character;* after all, three people decided they had to take a road trip to look for a possibly extinct animal—that indicates fascinating character possibilities. This is a great deal of useful information for one review. It can lead to another read-alike possibility, material for a display or booklist, and a book to pull for our sure-bet carts.

5. If you can't read it, look at it.

You can find out a great deal about a book even if you do not have time to read it.

Read the covers of the book and the blurb.

- How is the book characterized, as a scholarly tome or a popular look at a subject? Which authors endorse the book on the front or back cover? Do you know any of them and their work? Are they comparing this book to any others?

- Do you get a sense of story line from the back and flaps?

Look at the arrangement of the book.

- Is it broken into small sections. Are there lots of bullet points or lists?
- Are there maps, illustrations, charts, or figures?

Open the book to any page and start reading.

- Does the language flow?
- Are you reading a lecture or a story?
- What is your general impression of the book?
- Skim from the front, middle, and end of the book. Does this change your impression of whether it reads like a lecture or a story?
- Can you determine a style and type?
- Is there a sense of pacing?
- Are there characters?
- Is there a setting?
- Does the book remind you of any other author or title?
- Who would want to read this book, and what similar authors would they also like to read?

Answering these questions helps you become familiar with a title without reading the whole thing. Doing this with books helps cement them in your mind, provides a growing body of work for you to build on, and helps place one book in context with another.

6. Talk about the books.

Talk about the nonfiction you read with your patrons and colleagues. Ask them what nonfiction they are reading. Get in the habit of talking about nonfiction in your library.

Talk to your collection development staff. Ask them for titles they think are important, suggest titles to them, and work together to identify titles and authors you need to stay aware of.

7. Tune into the buzz about nonfiction books.

Begin a subject awareness campaign and keep current with what is hot and forthcoming in the world of nonfiction. Here are some tools to help you keep current:

- Pay attention to what is being discussed on morning shows—C-SPAN and National Public Radio in particular, since they tend to focus on nonfiction.
- Read a variety of library review journals, popular magazines, and both local and national newspapers. Scan websites, bestseller lists, and book blogs.
- Visit your local book store and see what is on display and who is coming to talk or sign books. Pay attention to what websites such as Amazon, Barnes and Noble, and Powell's are promoting as well.
- Listen to what library marketing houses have to say. See what they are pushing in the nonfiction world. Get on their e-mail lists and pay attention to their publications. If you have a chance to visit them during national conferences such as ALA or PLA, introduce yourself, tell them what you are trying to do, and ask for title suggestions and advanced reading copies.
- Scan audiobook catalogs. If a work is suitable as an audiobook, odds are that it is a title worth considering from a readers' advisory standpoint.

The buzz of books is particularly strong with nonfiction titles. Readers can take a long time to decide to tackle a book. The bestseller list, word of mouth, what is on TV and radio, what readers see promoted in bookstores, and what their friends are reading all contribute to what they eventually pick up. Not all readers are immediately drawn to a huge biography of a dead president, or the memoir of a writer they do not read, or a science concept they have never heard of. But over time, with the steady drone of the book buzz at work, readers can be seduced to a title, to see what the fuss is all about if nothing else. This gives us a bit more time in the nonfiction world to tune into the buzz ourselves, but it also means that books can never be forgotten either. Learning our current collection and keeping up with new titles is a continuous process, but one that helps us make connections between titles, helps us do our daily readers' advisory work more easily, and allows us to feel more comfortable when working with patrons.

Marketing: Sharing the Collection

The steps listed above help you to learn your collection, but sharing the collection with your patrons is equally important. Remember that your goal is to share the wonders of the collection and to help readers find what they are seeking. It is as simple as that. You do not have to be constrained by a small staff and a nonexistent budget. You just have to look around and find ways to share what you love with readers who love it too.

There are as many ways to promote and share the collection as there are inventive minds in your library. Nothing this book presents is as meaningful as an idea from a staff member who knows her library, her patrons, and her books. But to get the spark of marketing going, here are some ideas that cover all areas of the library.

When you market nonfiction readers' advisory service, you are really just marketing readers' advisory service as a whole and expanding it to include nonfiction. So start by looking at your fiction section. What has been done to make reading more inviting or to offer reading suggestions? Ask yourself if anything you are currently doing can be applied to your nonfiction section. If, for example, you currently have a staff pick section, encourage everyone who participates to start including nonfiction suggestions from time to time. Then see what new things you can do in the following areas:

Nonfiction Stickers

Most libraries use genre label stickers to identify romance, horror, mystery, and others in their fiction stacks to facilitate browsing. There is no reason not to apply that same idea to the Dewey side of the stacks as well. You can decide to sticker titles based on what your readers' advisory staff thinks is most useful—highly narrative nonfiction titles, nonfiction that you believe holds wide appeal, or some other aspect that can help patrons find great books. Although this would take some effort, it offers both patrons and staff a visual clue to book suggestions in the nonfiction area. If you decide to undergo a nonfiction reading study, then by the end of a year you should have a list of authors and titles that are good candidates for these special labels. You can also use the titles highlighted in previous chapters and those listed in appendix B to create a starter set of titles. Most of the major library supply vendors have blank label stock you can design yourself for a high-quality look, or you can print your own labels for smaller operations. If you do decide to label some titles, also consider adding tracings for them in your catalog. If you are not yet into tagging, talk to your cataloging staff about other methods of making these titles searchable as a group through your catalog.

Shelf Talkers

Shelf talkers are small signs that hang down from or sit on a shelf in the stacks. They can be used to list read-alike authors, to suggest other titles or subject areas to explore, or to help readers find other books by the same author.

For example, you can create a shelf talker on Bill Bryson that lists his other titles and suggests three to five similar authors. Readers browsing in the 917.4 area of the collection who come across *A Walk in the Woods* will see the shelf talker and know to look for other Bryson titles with call numbers that range from the nearby (916.762) to the faraway (420.9 and 500). They will also find other authors to consider if it turns out that they enjoyed *A Walk in the Woods*. You can place a shelf talker for Bryson at more than one location, thus helping readers follow his wide-ranging interests more easily. The same approach could work for any author who writes on a wide diversity of subjects.

Another way shelf talkers can be used is to help readers find similar books when the Dewey classification is not helpful. For example, instead of making a shelf talker on an author, you can make a shelf talker on a particular title. *Seabiscuit* is a great example. On the shelves with *Seabiscuit* are other books on horseracing, the history of the Kentucky Derby, and jockeys. These books will not provide readers with the same experience as Hillenbrand's book. Though *Funny Cide* by Sally Jenkins is not too far away in the stacks (depending on the number of other titles you have in your collection), it is interfiled with all the non-applicable titles and might not be found—especially if a reader did not know about it already. Additionally, the many other books that make good reading suggestions for fans of Hillenbrand are nowhere near the horseracing books. A shelf talker that lists read-alikes for *Seabiscuit* can lead readers to the right locations in the stacks.

You can also use shelf talkers to connect nonfiction and fiction or to direct readers from one area of the collection to another through book suggestions. For example, near the travel books you could put a shelf talker that lists core travel narratives. In the cookbook section you could suggest several wonderful food history books. In the Regency history section you could direct readers to the fiction romance collection and suggest some core authors. Just a few well-considered and constructed additions to the shelves can make a huge difference to readers. They will notice that something new is going on in the nonfiction section, and seeing one improvement leads them to look for others. You will be amazed at just how much small things mean to readers.

If you start with two or three shelf talkers, you can create more over time and either use every one you make or switch them in and out, creating an ever-changing marketing opportunity in the stacks and addressing a range of different reading interests.

Displays

If your library has space near the nonfiction books, either at the start of the collection or somewhere nearby, try to make a small, permanent display of books. If you choose to sticker your books, you could easily shelve the books as you sticker them in this location—as sort of a "launch party" for the title before it goes back in the stacks. If you decide not to sticker books, but you have made a list of authors or titles to draw on, you can stock the display with books from your lists. During times of heightened interest, such as an election or local media event, you can stock the area with relevant titles. The idea is simply to allow patrons a chance to browse a smaller collection of nonfiction that holds wide appeal. This accomplishes two things: it shows patrons that there is an atmosphere in the library of sharing and suggesting books, and it entices fiction readers over to the nonfiction section to check out what is on display.

Mix the displays at your library. Put nonfiction titles and fiction titles together whenever you can. You can do this through themed displays, bestseller displays, staff picks, or any other way you can imagine. The more you mix the books, the easier it becomes to see connections between titles, authors, and sections of your collection.

New Book Area

There is even more opportunity to market your collection in the new book area. Many libraries put the new book display as close to the front door as possible. This allows patrons to come into the library to pick up their reserved books, check out the new book area, and leave—never having seen anything else in the library. If you have a readers' advisory desk, move the new book area near it (or vice versa). If you do not have a specific readers' advisory desk, put the new books near the most suitable service desk. The goal is to have patrons near both the staff who are charged with helping them find books and the area of the library that best showcases the library's reader services.

Keeping the new bookshelf near a service desk also makes it easier for staff to keep the display looking good. Whenever you can, straighten out the shelf and turn books face out. If you have space and the books to do so, create mini-displays on the shelf itself. For example, if you happen to have two new cookbooks and either a memoir of a foodie or a history book on food, make space on the shelf to display them face out, or place two of them with spines facing out and put the other on top face out. Even someone not looking for a food book will notice the display and realize that the library is linking books for patrons.

Also consider keeping all your readers' advisory guides near the new book area. By making the new bookshelf the "hot" book place in the library and placing it near the staff who offer readers' services, the library goes a long way, with little effort, to get patrons to think of the library as a place to get book suggestions.

Staff

The library staff is an invaluable resource. If you have not already done so, gather from the staff what they read and see if you have any closet experts in house. Staff suggestions make for fun reading for patrons, and all staff members should be able to make suggestions. The books do not have to be new; in fact, promoting older titles is always a good thing, since both readers and staff tend to overlook them. We often forget that any book readers have not yet read is a new book to them, even if we read it years ago.

Talk to readers. Everyone should get out from behind the desk at least some time on each shift and talk to readers in the stacks. Even if they do not need help, they will appreciate a quick query and offer of assistance. The library staff is the best source of marketing any library has. Only the staff can make the library a welcoming place for readers to get suggestions and talk about books.

Website

Library website design seems to be idiosyncratic and wholly dependent on the skill of the designer. Still, no matter the level of skill and no matter the design, space should be available on the website to promote reader services. Anything your library makes in paper, from booklists to book suggestions, should be on your website. There should be a direct link from your main page to your readers' advisory page, and any special readers' advisory items should be highlighted on the main page as well. Readers' advisory tools such as databases, e-mail services, and links to informative websites should be included on the site. An archive of staff picks should also be included as well as any other in-library book features. Also consider offering online readers' advisory assistance to help those uncomfortable approaching a librarian and discussing what they read in person. Once they experience your assistance in this more private way, they are more likely to talk to you the next time they visit. Your website could well be the first face of your library for readers. Make it usable, useful, and inviting.

Reading Guides

Make guides on nonfiction topics for readers, not just for researchers. Try to create guides that include fiction and nonfiction on the same topic, or in support of one another, as well as guides that cover only nonfiction. Just one reading guide titled something as blatant as "Nonfiction That Reads Like Fiction" can go a long way in marketing the nonfiction readers' advisory service. Consider establishing a ratio of fiction to nonfiction guides. For example, for every two fiction guides, decide to make a nonfiction guide as well. Slowly you will build your collection of guides and introduce readers to a range of nonfiction choices.

The Catalog

The catalog can be a great place to share books with readers. It does not just have to be seen as a finding tool. Catalogs offer a greater richness than that. First, talk to your cataloging department and see if you can find a way to add tracings for all award-winning titles. This helps librarians and patrons spot these books when browsing the catalog and allows them to search on a particular award. There are databases that offer this information, but there is nothing like seeing it in your own catalog connected to your own collection.

Also consider linking from titles in your catalog to the electronic versions of your reading guides. You can also put links in your online reading guides back to your catalog. This helps readers find your titles and readers' advisory guides more easily and makes the catalog a better readers' advisory tool.

When you are helping a patron and see such a link, it reminds you that you have a guide on the topic and can either hand patrons a copy or show them how to get to the electronic version.

Features of Library 2.0 such as blogging, wikis, and tagging can also be incorporated into both the catalog and the website. Opportunities to create electronic forums for book discussions via comments, tags, or other means should be welcomed as a way of extending readers' advisory conversations beyond the walls of the library and its hours of operation.

NOTE

1. Nancy Bent, Review of *Carnivorous Nights: On the Trail of the Tasmanian Tiger,* by Margaret Mittelbach and Michael Crewdson, *Booklist,* April 1, 2005. Emphasis added.

13

WHOLE COLLECTION
READERS' ADVISORY SERVICE

Incorporating nonfiction into readers' advisory work is not the limit of readers' advisory. In fact, it simply lays the groundwork for a broader and more holistic view of the service. Once we are able to offer a mix of fiction and nonfiction, to see the connections within books and between titles, we can begin to consider the widest approach to readers' advisory—whole collection readers' advisory service. This approach includes not just fiction and nonfiction and not just books but everything we own or have access to, in the broadest conception of our collections, including audiobooks, movies, music, art, images, databases, and websites.

Working Holistically

Whole collection readers' advisory service is both a philosophy and method of offering readers' advisory that goes beyond the traditional methods we all know. We are trained in readers' advisory work to use appeal to match a reader to another similar book and to use the read-alike as the primary vehicle to match one title with another. But when we read, be it fiction or nonfiction, we read for more than the appeal of a book. We read for the broader experience the book offers us.

As useful and important as the concept of appeal is, it does not have to be the end of our considerations. Whole collection readers' advisory acknowledges the additional reasons a reader enjoyed a book and contends that there can be additional ways of offering the service.

Often what we want when one book is finished is for that reading experience to be extended—because part of the joy, the sheer exhilaration of reading, is all the different aspects contained within the covers of a book just waiting to fascinate us. And that joy and fascination are not served only by suggesting other similar titles. They are best served by combining similar titles with a huge range of other ways of expanding the reading experience.

There are simply times when readers want something more than a list of similar authors, times when their engagement with a book has led them to desire more materials about a certain element the book explores or when their enjoyment of a title calls for a lingering within its pages—not a move to a different title altogether. For example, when we finish reading *Outlander,* by Diana Gabaldon, an epic romance about a World War II nurse traveling through time to Scotland on the eve of the Jacobite rebellion, we might want to read more about the Scottish uprising, herbal and medical science of the day, or a work that explains the many myths and fairy tales Gabaldon refers to in her novel.

As readers' advisory librarians we can offer fans of *Outlander* many different resources. We can certainly suggest *Knight Errant,* by R. Garcia y Robertson, as a possible read-alike, but the patron might not be ready to leave the world of *Outlander* and therefore find all read-alike suggestions unsatisfying. Applying the philosophy of whole collection readers' advisory, we can find an image of a fairy ring and a map of Scotland online. We can pull a book of clan tartans to find the Fraser pattern. We can give the patron *The King Has Landed: Songs of the Jacobite Risings* on tape or CD so that she can listen to the music of the rebellions. We can suggest titles on Scottish folklore, herbal remedies, and early medical practice, or on witchcraft, World War II nurses, and Scottish history. In addition, we can help the reader find other resources on *Outlander,* including Gabaldon's website, her other titles, and her nonfiction work, *The Outlandish Companion.* All these resources will help the reader explore the aspects of *Outlander* she finds fascinating or allow her to stay inside Gabaldon's world as long as she wishes.

In instances such as these, when readers want to explore the world of the book they are loving now, whole collection readers' advisory offers what they are seeking in ways that are far more satisfying than a list of read-alike titles. Similarly, there are times when the subject of a book is really the overwhelming area of interest for a reader and when read-alikes are simply not the point. A reader who loves *Abundance: A Novel of Marie Antoinette,* by Sena Jeter Naslund, might not really need a list of read-alikes. Instead she might want more on Marie and her world. Books such as *Queen of Fashion: What Marie Antoinette Wore to the Revolution,* by Caroline Weber, *A Scented Palace: The Secret History of Marie Antoinette's Perfumer,* by Elisabeth de Feydeau, *Marie Antoinette: The Journey,* by Antonia Fraser, the Sofia Coppola movie of the same name (based on Fraser's work), *The Knight of Maison-Rouge:*

A Novel of Marie Antoinette, by Alexandre Dumas, *The Hidden Diary of Marie Antoinette,* by Carolly Erickson, and *Farewell, My Queen,* by Chantal Thomas, would please her more (at least at this point in time) than the works of Geraldine Brooks or Sarah Dunant, which would take her far away from the French Revolution to the year of the plague or Renaissance Florence.

This chapter explores two ways of offering whole collection readers' advisory service: the read-around and the reading map. Read-arounds are print resources that lead readers from one title outward to a range of other title suggestions. They can include read-alikes, but they also include other works that support the featured title. In the example below, fiction and nonfiction works on the American Revolution combine with read-alikes for David McCullough to create a read-round for *1776.*

Reading maps are electronic guides to the interior life of a book; they trace the various explorations that can be launched from within a given title. For example, a reading map on *Jonathan Strange and Mr. Norrell* could follow threads on the Napoleonic wars, Wellington, Bryon, Regency England, publishing, magic, British folklore, Venice, York, London, and many other aspects as well.

There are many reasons to make read-arounds and reading maps:

THEY BRING THE WHOLE COLLECTION TOGETHER AND BRIDGE THE DEWEY DIVIDE.

- Readers' advisory really should be about readers and their wide-ranging interests and not about the way we organize our collections. These tools mine the collection for all it contains related to a specific starting work and show the richness of the collection to readers.

- They help narrow the gaps between formats of material and types of books.

- They offer patrons the best we have in terms of resources, expertise, and imagination and allow us to really think about both our collections and the resources to which we have access.

THEY PROVIDE GUIDANCE TO READERS ABOUT WHICH RESOURCES AND TITLES TO TRY NEXT.

- Read-arounds and reading maps provide shape and direction to a vast range of explorations that take into account more than a listing of similar titles can ever accommodate, so they give readers more guidance.

- They offer readers a tool to spark their thinking. Readers are always hungry for more, and these tools give them a new way of thinking about their own reading.

CREATING READ-AROUNDS AND READING MAPS PROVIDES THE OPPORTUNITY FOR BOTH INVESTIGATION AND REFLECTION.

They provide us a chance to think through the myriad ways a title works. Working one's way through all the connections of a book and matching those connections to the collection builds both skill and confidence. It is much easier to face a reader in the stacks and offer readers' advisory service when you have spent time really thinking about how your collection works and how titles interact. It is helpful to realize how far-reaching even the smallest and most focused of works can be.

Perhaps most important, they help readers' advisory librarians context-ualize the collection and practice skills on a deeper level. They give us space to think and connect what we know to the books in our collections and offer us ways to explore the implications of subject, appeal, story, narrative, and type.

Read-Arounds

A read-around starts with a specific initial title and then expands outward to include fiction and nonfiction, read-alikes, and supporting materials such as works that focus on important aspects of the initial title, books that further illuminate central themes, and titles that provide contextual support. Since read-arounds are printed guides, they have both limitations and advantages. They are easier to make than reading maps and require no special skills or software. They do not require permission to use images, and they are self-limiting in terms of how much can be included. The ease of production and the enforced limits on space makes the creation of a read-around a less daunt-ing process than the creation of a reading map, so they are a good place to start when creating guides to your entire collection.

Follow these general steps to make a read-around, and refer to the illus-tration below built around *1776,* by David McCullough:

1. Pick your starting title. Read-arounds work best for titles that have many different aspects to them and for titles in series. At first, select

titles that are multifaceted and have quite a bit of detail, a strong sense of place or time, and strong subject interest.

2. Decide what kinds of things to include. It is best to decide collectively on how standard elements are to be treated so that all of your guides are uniform. The only items that need to be included are read-around titles. You may, however, want to consider read-alikes, a summary of the main title, or a summary of the featured author's work and style as well as a complete bibliography of the featured author, lists of holdings in other formats, and a list of other pertinent read-alikes or read-arounds. Consider including links to web resources such as the author's website or websites directly related to locations, characters, or events in the book. Also, decide if your read-around should be fully annotated or not.

3. Select read-arounds for the title. Consider your initial starting title. Look at all the elements that amplify the book. These are often subjects, famous characters, locations, time periods, or specific details such as cooking, art, or some aspect of history.

4. Identify the most important of these elements. When creating a read-around, you need to strike a balance among what interests the reader, what your collection can support, and how lengthy your guide can be. Printing guides costs money, so decide early on how many pages you can afford to print and use that limit to decide how many elements to include.

5. Select titles to include for each element. Pick these titles as you would any read-alike title. They must be a good match for the element and the initial starting title. Readers need to see how they relate, even if they are not interested in that particular element.

6. If you decide to include them, select read-alikes for the title. Before you create your first read-around, decide how many read-alikes will be standard in each guide. Three to five seems to be a rough standard for many libraries and provides the reader with a sufficient range of choices.

1776, by David McCullough: A Read-Around Guide

David McCullough is one of the nation's best writers of popular and social history. He writes elegant, beautifully conceived, and perfectly paced works with strongly defined characters, gripping story lines, and well-integrated facts. McCullough's books are fascinating not just for the history he conveys but for the stories he tells about both famous and ordinary people and the engaging way he constructs his books. McCullough invites his readers into the story and entertains them with an addictive mix of scholarship, description, and you-are-there immediacy.

Reading about the American Revolution

If you would like to read more about the world of *1776,* try these suggestions:

Angel in the Whirlwind: The Triumph of the American Revolution, by Benson Bobrick. Readers who simply want to learn about the American Revolution, from the start at Lexington to the final victory in Yorktown, may enjoy Bobrick's sweeping story of the events of the war. Employing a great sense of place and a strong narrative drive, Bobrick uses George Washington and Benedict Arnold as the focus of his story. By mapping their fates through the war, Bobrick gives readers a thread to follow through the Revolution and a vehicle to experience the span of battles and encounter the key players of the era. Readers who were intrigued by the way McCullough spun out the sweep of the Revolution will find more to enjoy in the scope of Bobrick's heroic saga.

The Road to Valley Forge: How Washington Built the Army That Won the Revolution, by John Buchanan. Buchanan is an academic writer who manages to blend story with his perceptive interpretation of fact. Although there is a great deal of scholarly theory in this book, there is also a gripping narrative that relays the story of blood, battles, and political intrigue. Tracing the revolutionary army from its horribly rag-tag state in 1776 through its victorious rebirth in 1778 after Valley Forge, Buchanan employs multiple perspectives to explain the change in the army and in the direction of the war. This is military history at its finest, and readers who enjoy details about battles, troop movements, and military strategy will enjoy the fast-paced and intricately plotted portions of this book and may be surprised at how much they also enjoy Buchanan's scholarly segments.

Washington's Crossing, by David Hackett Fischer. Sharing with McCullough the ability to use detail and storytelling to bring history vividly to life, Fischer focuses on an epic moment in the American

Revolution: George Washington's crossing of the Delaware River. Weighed down by defeats in Long Island and New York City, Washington and his officers brilliantly planned and enacted an important victory, the destruction of a Hessian garrison and a British brigade. Similar to Thomas Fleming, Fischer explores the military strategy and leadership of Washington as well as his understanding of the nature of war and his enemies. This engaging story is impressively researched and offers readers insight on revolutionary military history as well as a pivotal moment of the war.

Washington's Secret War: The Hidden History of Valley Forge, by Thomas Fleming. Thomas Fleming is considered one of the leading writers on the American Revolution. In this book he, like David McCullough, sees Valley Forge as a turning point in the war. Fleming focuses on Washington and his development into a new type of leader—one who mixed politics and military strategy equally well and was able to hold the army together, guide the Continental Congress in the direction he needed it to go, and keep the British dangling on the hook of conciliation. Fleming uses short chapters to help guide the reader through the complex maneuvers and writes in an easy and engaging manner.

The Glorious Cause: The American Revolution, 1763–1789, by Robert Middlekauff. Offering a comprehensive overview of the American Revolution, Middlekauff mixes scholarly research with elegant and engaging writing. His descriptions of the events leading to the Revolution are clear and multifaceted, and they put the mood of the fledgling nation and the politics of the British government into context. His descriptions of battles are gripping and immediate. Though this book is not as story oriented as *1776,* readers who want to understand the whole of the American Revolution, from the first grumblings of discontent to the inauguration of the first U.S. president, will find Middlekauff's book illuminating. This is an important work on the American Revolution and was a finalist for the Pulitzer Prize.

Washington's Spies: The Story of America's First Spy Ring, by Alexander Rose. In an intriguing blend of story and scholarship, Rose tells the fascinating tale of the Culper ring of spies. During the war it was important for both Washington and the British leaders to know what was going on, but neither side was skilled in the art of espionage. Groups like the Culper ring invented their own methods of gathering and transferring secrets. Rose uses their correspondence to illuminate their operations, Washington's demands and levels of annoyance at their failures, and their work at improving the spying game, such as disappearing ink and code making. This compelling work mixes moments of pure drama with moments of exacting research as Rose sets the scene of occupied New York and the covert operations happening in the city. This book considers all aspects of the Revolution's espionage including the famous spy stories of Benedict Arnold and Nathan Hale.

A Great Improvisation: Franklin, France, and the Birth of America, by Stacy Schiff. Switching perspectives slightly, this work focuses on the same time period as *1776* but stresses the importance of Benjamin Franklin and the creation of American foreign policy. In December 1776 Franklin landed in France to begin his most important job, gaining the aid of the French in the Revolution. Like McCullough, Schiff offers readers a range of wonderfully diverse perspectives on the events of Franklin's mission and vividly describes the age—French double agents, British spies, secrete negotiations, and high-tension drama.

Rise to Rebellion: A Novel of the American Revolution, and its sequel, *The Glorious Cause,* by Jeff Shaara. Shaara, well known for his historical novels about war, turns his wonderful eye on the American Revolution. In this two-part saga he brings us the events, people, and scope of the war. Shaara has a great gift for detail and brings the overly familiar facts of high school history into singing life. Readers get to follow the intrigue of the Sons of Liberty, see Washington rise from Virginia planter to national leader, and experience, battle by battle, the chaos of war. Along the way readers encounter a rich tapestry of historical characters and are given a vivid sense of the times and locales of the Revolution. The novels perfectly capture the noble and epic struggle to craft a nation.

Iron Tears: America's Battle for Freedom, Britain's Quagmire: 1775–1783, by Stanley Weintraub. In this riveting work, Weintraub dares to consider the question of how the American Revolution was actually won. Was it because of the nerve and skill of Washington and his troops, or was it because England lost the will to fight? This provocative work considers the Revolution from the perspectives of all levels of British society, from the poor rioting in the streets to the aristocracy angered by loss of profits. Readers who enjoyed *1776* for the attention McCullough paid to George III will find Weintraub's perspective equally enthralling.

More Like McCullough: Read-Alike Authors

David McCullough writes story-filled biographies as well as popular histories, including books on pivotal moments and figures in American history other than the Revolution. If you enjoyed **1776** for the way it captures a specific historical moment, then you might also enjoy **The Johnstown Flood; The Path between the Seas: The Creation of the Panama Canal, 1870–1914;** and **The Great Bridge: The Epic Story of the Building of the Brooklyn Bridge.** If you enjoyed the sections of **1776** that focused on the characters of the times, then you might want to try **John Adams; Truman; Mornings on Horseback: The Story of an Extraordinary Family, a Vanished Way of Life and the Unique Child Who Became Theodore Roosevelt;** and **Brave Companions: Portraits in History.**

There are several authors writing engaging popular and social history books. Not all of them write on the subjects that interest McCullough, but their books have the same riveting feel, the anecdotal and character-based history, and the wonderfully enjoyable mixture of scholarship and storytelling. To explore others who write history and biography in the same captivating way as McCullough, try these authors:

Caroline Alexander

If you enjoy McCullough's attention to character and command of history, then Caroline Alexander might appeal as well. Start with **The Bounty: The True Story of the Mutiny on the** Bounty because it is written in the same enthralling and inviting way as many of McCullough's works and deftly mixes fact-based writing with gripping story. The *Bounty* mutiny took pace in the South Pacific, where Lieutenant Bligh was cast out with eighteen crewmen in a 23-foot open boat. Bligh, who had sailed with Capt. James Cook, navigated the tiny boat for forty-eight days in open seas and landed himself and his crew safely. Alexander creates a rich world filled with all the characters surrounding the mutiny and includes their letters, testimony, and journals in her riveting account. Also consider Alexander's character-centered story of leadership and adventure, **The** Endurance: **Shackleton's Legendary Antarctic Expedition.** In this stunning story Alexander unveils the history behind Sir Ernest Shackleton's expedition to cross the Antarctic continent, the destruction of his ship in the ice pack, the stranding of the entire crew, and their epic quest to rescue themselves.

Stephen Ambrose

Like McCullough, Stephen Ambrose writes both biography and history and has the same mastery of detail and description and sense of affection for his subjects. Start with *Undaunted Courage: Meriwether Lewis, Thomas Jefferson, and the Opening of the American West.* Ambrose follows the expedition of Lewis and Clark from its beginnings in the friendship of Lewis and Thomas Jefferson, through the expression of manifest destiny inherent in the journey, to the exploration's epic yet tragic conclusions. Using a deft hand with character, story, and atmosphere, Ambrose captures the sense of the times in the same compelling way as McCullough. In *Band of Brothers: E Company, 506th Regiment, 101st Airborne from Normandy to Hitler's Eagle's Nest,* Ambrose uses the same anecdotal construction as McCullough and captures the same sense of the heroic that seems to infuse all of McCullough's writing. This character-centered history of World War II follows one unit of men over the course of the war. Horrifying and brutal, this history uses the stories of Easy Company to illustrate the arc of the war and its wide-ranging effects.

Ron Chernow

Ron Chernow, like McCullough, writes sweeping biographies that illuminate the lives and times of his subjects as well as their impact on history. Chernow also shares McCullough's knack for melding solid scholarship with riveting prose. Begin with *Alexander Hamilton* to get another viewpoint on the American Revolution. Hamilton, an arch-enemy of Thomas Jefferson and John Adams, rose from a horrible childhood to become a trusted confidant and aide-de-camp to George Washington, coauthor of *The Federalist Papers* and the man who mapped out much of what America was to become. Chernow is best known for his financially oriented works, and *Titan: The Life of John D. Rockefeller, Sr.* is among his best. This elegantly written biography shares with McCullough's biographies the strong focus on characters, the illumination of an age, and the use of pivotal moments to explain larger sweeps of history. Rockefeller rose from a poor childhood to become the richest man in the world and the owner of the most feared monopoly, Standard Oil. His dramatic story is well captured in Chernow's character-focused and detail-oriented saga.

Joseph J. Ellis

Joseph J. Ellis is an elegant and graceful writer and has penned several highly regarded works on the American Revolution. He shares with McCullough an attention to character and a gift for making dry facts come to fascinating life. Ellis is a master, as is McCullough, of providing fresh context and meaning to supposedly well-known historical personages and events. To continue the story begun in *1776,* try *His Excellency: George Washington.* This portrait of the first U.S. president takes the mythic and revered character of Washington off the dusty shelves of history and exposes a complex, conflicted, and heroically real man who not only fought and won the Revolutionary War but continually fought an internal war with himself—one of ambition and pride. This consideration of the man behind the legend is both illuminating and beautifully descriptive of the age. In *Founding Brothers: The Revolutionary Generation,* Ellis does what he and McCullough do best, contextualize the meaning of history. Here he studies six moments of the revolutionary era and considers the wide implications of each. Conceiving Alexander Hamilton, Aaron Burr, Thomas Jefferson, Benjamin Franklin, George Washington, John Adams, and James Madison as the core founding "brothers," Ellis considers the duel between Burr and Hamilton, Washington's Farewell Address, the importance of the Adams's administration and the role of his wife Abigail, the politics of the placement of the nation's capital, Franklin and Madison's battles over efforts to force Congress to address slavery (and the failure to do so), and the sad history of enmity between Jefferson and Adams and their eventual reconciliation.

Nathaniel Philbrick

Nathaniel Philbrick shares with McCullough an elegant style, attention to detail, and compulsive mix of history and adventure. Start with **Mayflower: *A Story of Courage, Community, and War*** because it considers some of the same issues as *1776:* the construction of a national identity, the individual stories that create collective history, and the force of personality on determining events. Philbrick is best known for books that have connections to the sea. Try *In the Heart of the Sea: The Tragedy of the Whaleship* Essex, which relates the exciting and harrowing account of the *Essex,* a whaleship sunk by an 80-ton sperm whale. Herman Melville heard about the fate of the *Essex* and the eight men who survived and was inspired to write his classic novel *Moby Dick.* In *Sea of Glory: America's Voyage of Discovery, the U.S. Exploring Expedition, 1838–1842,* Philbrick writes about one of the last great voyages of exploration. Charles Wilkes, almost uniformly despised by his crew, leads the Ex-Ex on a voyage that discovered Antarctica, charted Oregon and Washington, collected thousands of new species, and formed the foundation for the Smithsonian Institution.

More on McCullough

Find out the latest news from David McCullough on his website, which gives information about each of his books, including a synopsis, wonderful images, and reviews: http://www.electriceggplant .com/davidmccullough/.

McCullough's publisher's website also has a great deal of interesting information, including a podcast, links to historical sites, and much more: http://www.simonsays.com/content/destination.cfm? tab=1&pid=328883.

Readers interested in more ideas from McCullough might enjoy his 2003 Jefferson Lecture in the Humanities: http://www.neh.gov/ whoweare/mccullough/lecture.html.

There are several great interviews with McCullough. Try the following for a range of topics:

> Powell's Bookstore interview: http://www.powells.com/authors/ mccullough.html.
>
> National Endowment for the Humanities interview: http://www .neh.gov/whoweare/mccullough/interview.html.
>
> Academy of Achievement interview: http://www.achievement .org/autodoc/page/mcc2int-1.

Reading Maps

Reading maps are visual journeys through books that allow readers to inhabit the world of the book and then follow reading itineraries beyond it. They are in a web-based format, but they are not just web versions of read-arounds. They have a different purpose. Read-arounds are intended to augment a book with other reading choices that go beyond basic read-alikes; reading maps capture the world of the book with other titles, pictures, music, links to websites, and additional hypertext material, charting both the internal world of the book itself and all the threads of reading interest that stem from it.

In addition to all the reasons listed above to create such tools, reading maps are both fascinating and practical. They are fascinating because they are visually interesting and, depending on their technical sophistication, have the potential for a huge wow factor and endless variety. Offering readers something so different and intriguing captures their imaginations and can transform how they think about your library and your readers' advisory service. They are practical because they are less expensive to produce than paper reading guides, offer richer content than can be printed on paper, can have a much higher production value, do not take up space on the counter or shelves or need special holders, and, most critical, can be updated immediately.

Reading maps can be elaborate, fanciful, and wide ranging. They can be simple and track a journey to one location, or they can be directly connected to one book but branch off in many different directions. Reading maps do not have to be intricate to be effective, and they are not hard to create; in fact, they are a great deal of fun.

How to Make a Reading Map

Reading maps are web-based creations, so you either need to know how to create a webpage with a fair degree of comfort and skill or work with someone who does. The following are general steps to creating a reading map. For an example based on *Jonathan Strange and Mr. Norrell,* by Susanna Clarke, see http://www.overbooked.org/neal_wyatt_reading_maps/.

1. Once you have a method of production, consider how patrons will access the map. It is best to offer as many access points as possible, so consider linking your maps from your library's readers' advisory webpage and also linking to them from the catalog record of each item mentioned in the map.

2. To create a reading map, you first need a place to start. This can be a topic or a specific book (or film or sound recording). It is easier the first time you make a map if you pick an area about which you have great interest and knowledge so that the elements of the map come readily to mind. Also, plan to build a simple map for your first project.

3. Use your first map as a trial run to establish guidelines for future maps. Decide which elements to include in every map you make. Items such as annotations, read-alikes, read-arounds, book discussion questions, reviews, links into your catalog, links to electronic resources, links to electronic texts, and interviews with the author are all elements you

might include in your maps. As you make your first map, you will think of others.

4. Now consider the central book. Think about the subject of the book and its appeal factors. Here are the key appeal elements for creating reading maps:

Character. Real-life characters are perfect to match to other books, as are series characters from fiction titles. Mythical characters lend themselves to all sorts of explorations, both fiction and nonfiction.

Story line. The various levels used to construct a book can be pulled apart to set up directions to explore in a reading map, and the book's plot can be used to inform the content of the map.

Setting. Readers often want to read more about a location they find intriguing. Using the settings of the book is an ideal way to begin to structure a map. Once the settings are in place, many different elements can be added to each locale—starting a domino effect of maps within maps.

Detail. Readers, once hooked on one aspect of detail, naturally seek more information on that topic; therefore, including detail elements in all reading maps is critical.

Subject. If the subject of the work was not developed during your exploration of the details of the book, then it is important to bring it into the reading map as an element of its own. The subjects of a book often drive reader interest and allow for a wide range of branches (side trips) for a map to trace.

5. Brainstorm the book. List all the associations from the book—places, historical people and events, themes, key appeal aspects, read-alikes, read-arounds, ideas explored, and anything that strikes you about the book and captures your interest. Brainstorm ideas for the elements of the map and directions you wish to follow. Be as free and as wide ranging in your thinking as possible. The goal is to map the landscape of the book as completely as you can. At this point, nothing is off limits, and no idea is too subtle or obscure.

6. Share with your colleagues all your ideas to see if they can suggest other directions or elements worth including.

7. Break the list of associations into working groups and start expanding each group with titles, authors, and ideas. Use the entries in each group to brainstorm other elements to include. Keep expanding a group until

you feel you have fleshed out its idea or theme and then move on to the next group. Often as you work on one section, ideas will come to you for another. Keep moving through all the elements of what amounts to the book's storyboard until you feel you have represented the scope of the title.

8. Now, stand back and look at what you have done. Which groups are fundamental to the book? Which groups are the most fully developed? Those areas with the richest content, along with the elements you choose to be standard in any reading map, should be the initial elements you create. Focus on these aspects first, and then you can go back and decide to include or not include areas for which you had less content.

9. Decide what opening element you wish to follow. This choice determines what kind of map you will make. All the other elements flow from this first step, so consider it carefully. If there is a central focus to the book, then start with that. If not, then consider how the book breaks down into larger elements. Is it a book about time and place? Is it a book about characters? Is it a book about a journey? Find a unifying theme to all the groups you identified and make that your opening element.

10. You can build the map in any manner you like, but try to match the journey to the form of the map. If you are creating a meandering path through many disparate aspects, then consider placing the starting title in the center and working outward to represent visually the many directions a reader could follow. If instead you are creating a linear progression through time—say the development of the mystery novel or the chain of events of World War II through books—you might want to consider a more linear arrangement.

11. Try to include as much texture and different elements as you can. Play with font, color, mouse movements, jacket images, pictures, sound files, video files, and deeper resources such as recipes, excerpts from key works, quotes, and other items that bring visual interest to the page. As you find these elements, ask for permission to use them from the owner and credit sources in your map, or use what your library already owns in terms of clip art and photo databases, jacket cover rights, annotations, and the like. Also consider digital image websites that allow use of content as long as it is credited, your own (and your friends') photos, local history collections, links to images, and other copyright-free visual content.

Map Ideas

There are no limits on the subjects or titles you can turn into reading maps. You could get started by creating a map on your favorite title or your favorite trip. You could select a short poem filled with allusions and map it, or create a map on one of your hobbies. Because there is no end to wonderful and fascinating books, there is no end to the number of maps that can be made. To spark your thinking, here is a list of topics that are particularly rich in mapmaking possibilities:

Regency England	Lewis and Clark
Shakespeare	Moon exploration
The Crusades	Painters (Vermeer, for example)
The Templars	Studies of places, ideas, themes
Chocolate	Development of a genre or subgenre, or reading tour to a genre or subgenre
Pirates	
Arthurian legend	Reading tour to any location (including your library or your city)
Darwin	
Stanley and Livingstone	Programs at your library: author visits, the summer reading program, book groups
Food books	

I began this book by suggesting that nonfiction is a new realm and that we need a way to chart the landscape of these books. I conclude by urging you to see all of readers' advisory service—fiction, nonfiction, audiobook, music, movies, and the rich world of our online resources—as an even larger landscape in need of exploration. By offering whole collection readers' advisory service and by looking beyond traditional concepts, we can expand what it means to offer readers' advisory service to our readers. This new journey will redefine not only our current methods of offering the service but the service itself.

HOW TO BUILD A NONFICTION SUBJECT GUIDE

Part of the goal of this book is to present popular nonfiction subjects in manageable subdivisions so that readers' advisory librarians can classify and sort through the huge array of nonfiction titles published each year. Classifying books into general subjects, and within a general subject into types, makes suggesting nonfiction easier. We do this with fiction all the time. Once we know a reader enjoys romance, we can then figure out what type of romance and finally what type of author to suggest. There is a bedrock comfort in having a sense of control over our collections.

This book introduces popular broad subject areas and lists suggested books and key authors, but there is nothing like actually working with your own collection or within your own particular subject interest to make the information in this book concrete. If you have the time, creating your own subject guide is the best way to start working with nonfiction. It gets you into your collection, lets you see what you have and what is popular at your library, helps you evaluate your collection by identifying items to weed and areas that need to be built up, and is invaluable in building your skills as a readers' advisor.

By following this plan, and changing it to suit your needs, you can build your own subject guides based on your collection.

1. Pick a subject.

Select one subject that interests you; it is best to start practicing in an area in which you are already familiar.

2. Find out who is writing and what they are writing about.

- Look at your collection. See how the subject ranges, paying attention to concentrations by one author or in one micro subject area.

- Browse through your catalog and see how subjects are classified.

- Find out if an award is given in the subject area and who won in the past five years.

- Check the national awards and lists: the Pulitzer Prizes, the National Book Award, the National Book Critics Circle, ALA Notable Book Council books, the Alex Awards, the Book Sense Book of the Year Award and the Book Sense Book Picks, *Booklist* Editor's Choice, *Kirkus* Special Reports, New York Public Library's Books to Remember, the Costa Award (formerly the Whitbread), the Los Angeles Times Book Prizes, the "best" lists created by *New York Times Book Review,* the starred reviews listed in Overbooked.org, the Lukas Prize, the Samuel Johnson Prize, the William Saroyan International Prize for Writing, ALA Black Caucus Awards, and any others that are relevant to your location or your particular subject (see below for URLs).

- Look at the *Best American* series (*Best American Science Writing, Best American Essays,* etc.) and other collections.

- Search the Internet for collected lists of the best titles of the year or a compendium of the best titles ever published on your particular topic. Often newspapers or magazines sponsor such lists and have famous writers compile them.

- Skim popular magazines on the subject area.

- Scan audiobook catalogs for nonfiction titles in your subject area. Books that work well in audio format usually have a strong narrative sense and often make good suggestions.

- Talk to your nonfiction collection development librarian.

- Talk to friends and coworkers who read in the subject area.

- See if the professional media have published core lists, lists of best books, or something similar.

- Gather up all you have found and start building a list of authors and titles. Keep adding to and refining this list.

3. Look at the books.

Check the circulation of the authors on your list to find out who is popular at your library. You can use this information to help guide the rest of your work. You should be able to tell, as you go through the process, what types of books, what subjects, and what appeal points create a popular title in your library.

From the list you are building, pick five to seven authors and examine their books to see if they

- are on the same topic or if the topics vary. If they vary, how widely?

- are the same type. Are they explorations, memoirs, biographies, investigations?

- fall on the same point in the narrative continuum. Are they highly story based, more fact based, or somewhere in the middle? Are they all the same in terms of narrative or do they vary, and if so, how widely?

Read all the reviews you can find on each title.

4. Think about the intertwined aspects of nonfiction (narrative nature, subject, type, and appeal).

Select a book to read all the way through. As you are reading, ask yourself the following questions:

- How is this different from fiction?
- How is it the same?
- What is the subject of the book?
- What am I enjoying about this book?
- What am I not enjoying?
- What is the tone of the book?
- Does the tone enhance the narrative of the book? How or how not?
- Who would like to read this and why?
- Does it remind me of any other book? If so, what?
- Does it remind me of any other author? If so, who?

- What type of book is this? Is it a type I have already encountered or something new?

Run the book through the nonfiction matrix:

- Where is the book on the narrative continuum? Is it highly narrative (reads like fiction), highly fact based (has few or no narrative moments), or a mix (combines highly narrative moments with passages of fact-based prose)?
- What is the subject of the book?
- Articulate the book's appeal:

    What is the pacing of the book?

    Describe the characters of the book.

    How does the story feel?

    What is the intent of the author?

    What is the focus of the story?

    Does the language matter?

    Is the setting important and well described?

    Are there details and, if so, of what?

    Are there sufficient charts and other graphic material? Is it useful and clear?

    Does the book stress moments of learning, understanding, or experience?

    Why would a reader enjoy this book (rank appeal)?

    1.
    2.
    3.
    4.
    5.

Repeat this process with two more books and then compare the books.

1. Are your answers to the questions the same? If so, how?
2. Are they different? If so, can you pinpoint the difference to the type of book?

3. What does the comparison tell you about the narrative nature, subject, appeal, and types of books in the subject you are examining and the differences between authors within the subject?

5. Create a subject summary.

You now have enough information to being outlining the subject. Consider the range of subjects, different approaches, types of books, appeal of each type, and key titles and authors for each subject type.

- Briefly outline the subject and its range. Are there any things of particular note to be aware of—trends, problems, etc.
- List the types of books present in the subject.
- Capture the appeal of the books and state why readers enjoy them.
- List books and magazines that can be used to get a sense of the subject.
- Pull out some examples and annotate them briefly so everyone can have the same reference point.
- Build a list of core authors.
- List the key awards in the subject area.

The subject summary can and should be added to as you work more and more in nonfiction and as new books are published and new authors emerge.

6. Integrate what you now know into your work.

You should know enough to begin to incorporate your knowledge into your work. Consider mixing fiction and nonfiction together as well as making pure nonfiction suggestions. Challenge yourself within the subject:

- Keep reading the books and create annotations for them.
- Create a booklist.
- Make a display.
- Share and suggest titles with patrons and coworkers.
- Pick one of the books for your next book group.

Nonfiction Awards and Lists

Most of these awards are annotated in chapters 3–10, but I repeat the URLs here to make creating your own subject guides easier.

ALA Black Caucus Awards
http://www.bcala.org/awards/literary.htm

ALA Notable Book Council books
http://www.ala.org/ala/rusa/rusaprotools/rusanotable/thelists/notablebooks.htm

ALA Stonewall Book Awards
http://www.ala.org/ala/glbtrt/stonewall/stonewallbook.htm

Alex Awards
http://www.ala.org/ala/yalsa/booklistsawards/alexawards/alexawards.htm

Book Sense Book of the Year Award
http://www.booksense.com/index.jsp (and click on "Book of the Year Winners")

Book Sense Picks
http://www.booksense.com/index.jsp (and click on "Picks")

Booklist Editor's Choice, selected each January and published in *Booklist* magazine

CASEY Award
http://www.angelfire.com/oh5/spitball/award.html

Costa Award (formerly the Whitbread)
http://www.costabookawards.com

Crime Writer's Association (British)
http://www.thecwa.co.uk

Edgar Allan Poe Awards
http://www.mysterywriters.org/pages/awards/index.htm

Glenfiddich Food and Drink Awards
http://uk.glenfiddich.com/events/date.html

IACP Awards (International Association of Culinary Professionals)
http://www.iacp.com

James Beard Foundation Award for Writing on Food
http://www.jamesbeard.org

Kirkus Special Editions
   http://www.kirkusreviews.com/kirkusreviews/magazine/special_editions.jsp

Los Angeles Times Book Prizes
   http://www.latimes.com/extras/bookprizes/winners.html

Lukas Prize Project for Nonfiction
   http://www.jrn.columbia.edu/events/lukas/winners/

National Academies
   http://www.keckfutures.org

National Book Award
   http://www.nationalbook.org/nbawinners.html

National Book Critics Circle
   http://www.bookcritics.org/?go=awards

National Outdoor Book Award
   http://www.isu.edu/outdoor/bookpol.htm

New York Public Library's Books to Remember
   http://www.nypl.org/branch/books/booklists.cfm

New York Times Book Review "Best" lists, selected at various times of the year
   http://www.nytimes.com/pages/books/

Pulitzer Prize
   http://www.pulitzer.org

Royal Society Prizes for Science Books
   http://www.sciencebookprizes.com/home_welcome.htm

Samuel Johnson Prize for Nonfiction
   http://www.bbc.co.uk/bbcfour/books/features/samueljohnson/

Society of American Baseball Research (SABR)
   http://www.sabr.org

Thomas Cook Travel Book Awards
   http://www.thomascookpublishing.com/travelbookawards.htm

William Hill Sports Book of the Year Award
   http://www.williamhillmedia.com/sportsbook_index.asp

William Saroyan International Prize for Writing, http://library.stanford
   .edu/saroyan/index.html

In addition to a general listing of starred reviews from *Booklist, Kirkus, Library Journal,* and *Publisher's Weekly,* there are special sections on memoirs, sports, travel, true crime, and nature titles at http://www.overbooked.org.

B

A NONFICTION READING PLAN:
THE TEN BOOKS FROM EACH SUBJECT
AREA TO CONSIDER READING

If this book inspires you to explore nonfiction, consider this list the gazetteer for any road trip you may take. These titles form a foundation for each subject area and are works that illustrate the intertwined aspects of nonfiction: narrative nature, subject, type, and appeal. So throw a dart at the list and take off—fascinating destinations await.

Food

Candyfreak: A Journey through the Chocolate Underbelly of America, by Steve Almond

Kitchen Confidential: Adventures in the Culinary Underbelly, by Anthony Bourdain

Heat: An Amateur's Adventures as Kitchen Slave, Line Cook, Pasta-Maker, and Apprentice to a Dante-Quoting Butcher in Tuscany, by Bill Buford

Home Cooking: A Writer in the Kitchen, by Laurie Colwin

An Omelette and a Glass of Wine, by Elizabeth David

The Olive and the Caper, by Susanna Hoffman

Cod: A Biography of the Fish That Changed the World, by Mark Kurlansky

Tender at the Bone: Growing Up at the Table, by Ruth Reichl

Fast Food Nation: The Dark Side of the All-American Meal, by Eric Schlosser

Alice, Let's Eat, by Calvin Trillin

Memoir

All Over but the Shoutin', by Rick Bragg

Running with Scissors, by Augusten Burroughs

The Road from Coorain, by Jill Ker Conway

A Heartbreaking Work of Staggering Genius, by Dave Eggers

Don't Let's Go to the Dogs Tonight: An African Childhood, by Alexandra Fuller

The Liars' Club, by Mary Karr

Walking with the Wind: A Memoir of the Movement, by John Lewis

Angela's Ashes: A Memoir, by Frank McCourt

Five-Finger Discount: A Crooked Family History, by Helene Stapinski

This Boy's Life: A Memoir, by Tobias Wolff

Science

The Elegant Universe: Superstrings, Hidden Dimensions, and the Quest for the Ultimate Theory, by Brian Greene

Arctic Dreams: Imagination and Desire in a Northern Landscape, by Barry Lopez

Annals of the Former World, by John McPhee

Carnivorous Nights: On the Trail of the Tasmanian Tiger, by Margaret Mittelbach and Michael Crewdson

A Beautiful Mind: The Life of Mathematical Genius and Nobel Laureate John Nash, by Sylvia Nasar

Monster of God: The Man-Eating Predator in the Jungles of History and the Mind, by David Quammen

Stiff: The Curious Lives of Human Cadavers, by Mary Roach

A Primate's Memoir: A Neuroscientist's Unconventional Life among the Baboons, by Robert M. Sapolsky

Longitude: The True Story of a Lone Genius Who Solved the Greatest Scientific Problem of His Time, by Dava Sobel

The Right Stuff, by Tom Wolfe

True Crime

Midnight in the Garden of Good and Evil, by John Berendt

In Cold Blood, by Truman Capote

Blue Blood, by Edward Conlon

Newjack: Guarding Sing Sing, by Ted Conover

A Civil Action, by Jonathan Harr

The Other Side of the River: A Story of Two Towns, a Death, and America's Dilemma, by Alex Kotlowitz

The Devil in the White City: Murder, Magic, and Madness at the Fair That Changed America, by Erik Larson

Donnie Brasco: My Undercover Life in the Mafia, by Joseph D. Pistone

Ballad of the Whiskey Robber: A True Story of Bank Heists, Ice Hockey, Transylvanian Pelt Smuggling, Moonlighting Detectives, and Broken Hearts, by Julian Rubinstein

Green River, Running Red: The Real Story of the Green River Killer—America's Deadliest Serial Murderer, by Ann Rule

Sports

Friday Night Lights: A Town, a Team, and a Dream, by H. G. Bissinger

Sowbelly: The Obsessive Quest for the World Record Largemouth Bass, by Monte Burke

Joe DiMaggio: The Hero's Life, by Richard Ben Cramer

Next Man Up: A Year behind the Lines in Today's NFL, by John Feinstein

Still Life with Brook Trout, by John Gierach

Wait till Next Year: A Memoir, by Doris Kearns Goodwin

The Teammates, by David Halberstam

Seabiscuit: An American Legend, by Laura Hillenbrand

The Boys of Summer, by Roger Kahn

Moneyball: The Art of Winning an Unfair Game, by Michael Lewis

Travel

A Walk in the Woods: Rediscovering America on the Appalachian Trail, by Bill Bryson

The Road to Ubar: Finding the Atlantis of the Sands, by Nicholas Clapp

River Town: Two Years on the Yangtze, by Peter Hessler

Blue Latitudes: Boldly Going Where Captain Cook Has Gone Before, by Tony Horwitz

Video Night in Kathmandu, and Other Reports from the Not-So-Far East, by Pico Iyer

Balkan Ghosts: A Journey through History, by Robert D. Kaplan

A Year in Provence, by Peter Mayle

The Great Railway Bazaar: By Train through Asia, by Paul Theroux

Behind the Wall: A Journey through China, by Colin Thubron

The River at the Center of the World: A Journey Up the Yangtze, and Back in Chinese Time, by Simon Winchester

True Adventure

The Bounty: *The True Story of the Mutiny on the* Bounty, by Caroline Alexander

Amazon Extreme: Three Ordinary Guys, One Rubber Raft and the Most Dangerous River on Earth, by Colin Angus

The Perfect Storm: A True Story of Men against the Sea, by Sebastian Junger

Skeletons on the Zahara: A True Story of Survival, by Dean King

Into Thin Air: A Personal Account of the Mt. Everest Disaster, Jon Krakauer

Shadow Divers: The True Adventure of Two Americans Who Risked Everything to Solve One of the Last Mysteries of World War II, by Robert Kurson

The River of Doubt: Theodore Roosevelt's Darkest Journey, by Candice Millard

Sea of Glory: America's Voyage of Discovery, the U.S. Exploring Expedition, 1838–1842, by Nathaniel Philbrick

Alive: The Story of the Andes Survivors, by Piers Paul Read

Wind, Sand and Stars, by Antoine de Saint-Exupery

History

Undaunted Courage: Meriwether Lewis, Thomas Jefferson, and the Opening of the American West, by Stephen E. Ambrose

An Army at Dawn: The War in Africa, 1942–1943, by Rick Atkinson

Parting the Waters: America in the King Years, 1954–63; Pillar of Fire: America in the King Years, 1963–65; and *At Canaan's Edge: America in the King Years, 1965–68*, by Taylor Branch

Washington's Crossing, by David Hackett Fischer

Georgiana: Duchess of Devonshire, by Amanda Foreman

King Leopold's Ghost: A Story of Greed, Terror, and Heroism in Colonial Africa, by Adam Hochschild

1968: The Year That Rocked the World, by Mark Kurlansky

New York Burning: Liberty, Slavery, and Conspiracy in Eighteenth-Century Manhattan, by Jill Lepore

John Adams, by David McCullough

Mayflower: *A Story of Courage, Community, and War,* by Nathaniel Philbrick

General Nonfiction

Because there are so many subsections in this area, I list only five books from each.

THE ARTS

Will in the World: How Shakespeare Became Shakespeare, by Stephen Greenblatt

The Lost Painting: The Quest for a Caravaggio Masterpiece, by Jonathan Harr

The Judgment of Paris: The Revolutionary Decade That Gave the World Impressionism, by Ross King

A Clearing in the Distance: Frederick Law Olmsted and America in the 19th Century, by Witold Rybczynski

A Writer's Life, by Gay Talese

ESSAYS

The Aztec Treasure House: New and Selected Essays, by Evan S. Connell

Being Perfect, by Anna Quindlen

Reporting: Writings from the "New Yorker," by David Remnick

A Man without a Country, by Kurt Vonnegut

Consider the Lobster, and Other Essays, by David Foster Wallace

HUMOR

Dave Barry's Money Secrets: Like: Why Is There a Giant Eyeball on the Dollar? by Dave Barry

When Will Jesus Bring the Pork Chops? by George Carlin

We Thought You Would Be Prettier: True Tales of the Dorkiest Girl Alive, by Laurie Notaro

Holidays in Hell, by P. J. O'Rourke

Dress Your Family in Corduroy and Denim, by David Sedaris

RELIGION AND SPIRITUALITY

Walking the Bible: A Journey by Land through the Five Books of Moses, by Bruce Feiler

Traveling Mercies: Some Thoughts on Faith, by Anne Lamott

Mere Christianity, by C. S. Lewis

Beyond Belief: The Secret Gospel of Thomas, by Elaine Pagels

Leaving Church: A Memoir of Faith, by Barbara Brown Taylor

SOCIAL, ECONOMIC, AND POLITICAL SCIENCES

Nickel and Dimed: On (Not) Getting By in America, by Barbara Ehrenreich

The World Is Flat: A Brief History of the Twenty-first Century, by Thomas L. Friedman

Freakonomics: A Rogue Economist Explores the Hidden Side of Everything, by Steven D. Levitt and Stephen J. Dubner

Positively Fifth Street: Murderers, Cheetahs, and Binion's World Series of Poker, by James McManus

Fear and Loathing in Las Vegas: A Savage Journey to the Heart of the American Dream, by Hunter S. Thompson

WAR REPORTING

Black Hawk Down: A Story of Modern War, by Mark Bowden

Ghost Wars: The Secret History of the CIA, Afghanistan, and Bin Laden, from the Soviet Invasion to September 10, 2001, by Steve Coll

Salvador, by Joan Didion

Chain of Command: The Road from 9/11 to Abu Ghraib, by Seymour M. Hersh

Jarhead: A Marine's Chronicle of the Gulf War and Other Battles, by Anthony Swofford

C

ANNOTATION FORM

It is a vital habit of readers' advisory work to annotate what you read. Writing an annotation is the best way to guarantee that the book you just finished reading will be useful to you, your patrons, and your colleagues a year from now. Here are the elements that should be included in all annotations:

Author

Title

Publication date   This helps put the content of the book into context with the times and informs readers of its relevance. Some areas of nonfiction become dated quickly, such as politics and some science titles, and readers need to know dates to guide them in their choices. It also helps in areas that are less affected by time, such as cooking, memoirs, and travel, simply to help readers place books in their contemporary settings. Knowing the date of a book can also aid the readers' advisory librarian in remembering more about the title.

Number of pages   Some readers base selections on length, and others can scan this field to see if the length of the book matches their mood.

Geographic setting   For travel and true adventure this is essential. It also helps with other titles, such as memoirs, where place might matter. When annotating a book that is not location dependent, such as some science titles and cooking titles, feel free to leave this element blank. Keep it on the form, however, since all annotations should be standard to help readers use them and librarians create them.

Time period   Again, this matters more for some books than others. History is a prime example of period being essential. History in retrospect is also heavily related to time. If it does not apply, simply leave blank.

Subject headings Use a controlled vocabulary. It is easiest to simply copy your library's catalog subject headings into this section. Subject headings also aid in finding a forgotten book.

Type Include type classifications in this section.

Series notes Nonfiction is not often published in series, but there are notable examples such as multipart biographies or sets of memoirs. When needed, use this space to indicate all the titles in the series. If it is not applicable, leave it blank.

Book summary Keep this focused on readers and entice them to read the book by stressing the narrative context, subject, type, and appeal. The summary should be long enough for readers to get a sense of the work and for librarians who have read the work to have their memories jogged. Include words that give the reader clues about tone, language, violence, and sex. Also include appeal terms as part of the description. It is helpful to think in terms of appeal when writing the summary; if the tone is key to the novel, then describing it in appeal terms—creepy thrills—can only help the reader decide if the book is one to read.

Reading elements This section is the heart of the annotation. It is here, and in the next section, where the annotation becomes a tool for readers' advisory work. Include terms that highlight the major appeal elements of the title: pace, characterization, story line, detail, learning/experiencing, language, setting, and tone. It is also helpful to include references to narrative context, subject, and type here if you did not do so completely in the summary section. Start with the strongest appeal elements and work down to the incidental elements. Most works have a strong major appeal and secondary appeal; few are strong in all areas of appeal. If appeal elements are ranked, readers can identify early the driving appeal elements of the book. If you ran the book through the readers' advisory matrix, many of the elements you identified in that process should be included here.

1–3 Annotation Use this space to create a short, one- to three-sentence annotation that can be pulled to create an annotated booklist quickly or provide a reader with a quick explanation of the title. These are easy to create once you have done all the rest of the work of the annotation.

Similar works By including other titles or authors with the same range of narrative content, subject, type, and appeal in the annotation, you help both staff and browsers find additional books to consider. It also augments the annotation more broadly—a sort of "Oh, that's what you mean" if the text itself is not as descriptive as you hope. Including this information forces you (as did the reading elements section) to think of why a reader would enjoy the book, not just what the book is about.

Name of annotator   Including this allows other staff to ask questions of the annotator.

If you are not familiar with creating annotations and would like more detail on the process, I strongly recommend Joyce Saricks's chapter on keeping notes on what you read in *Readers' Advisory Service in the Public Library*.[1] She helped invent the idea of an annotation form and discusses it and a whole range of other note-taking skills. If you would like to see some examples of the book summary part of the annotation, then look at Nancy Pearl's work in *Now Read This* and *Now Read This II*[2] and check out the wide range of book summaries from a variety of advisors in the "What We're Reading" section of *NoveList*, where you can see a huge scope of different approaches.

NOTES

1. Joyce G. Saricks, *Readers' Advisory Service in the Public Library*, 3rd ed. (Chicago: American Library Association, 2005).

2. Nancy Pearl, *Now Read This: A Guide to Mainstream Fiction, 1978–1998* (Englewood, Colo.: Libraries Unlimited, 1999); and *Now Read This II: A Guide to Mainstream Fiction, 1990–2001* (Englewood, Colo.: Libraries Unlimited, 2002).

Author	
Title	
Publication date	
Number of pages	
Geographic setting	
Time period	
Subject headings	
Type	
Series notes	
Book summary	
Reading elements	
1–3 Annotation	
Similar works	
Name of annotator	

D

READING NOTES

Annotations are the ideal, but the sad reality in most libraries is that readers' advisors simply do not always have the time to write full annotations. Despite time pressures, it is vital to keep track of your reading and work toward making some record of your impressions—either while you are reading the book or shortly after.

Reading notes can be seen as shorter versions of annotations. They are much less structured and can be used to capture vital information while it is fresh in your mind, to record your impressions in a way that is useful enough to aid in the eventual creation of an annotation, and to jog your memory about a title. They are really a slightly formal way of making notes for yourself—so use them that way and use the "shorthand" that works best for you.

84, Charing Cross Road, by Helene Hanff, makes for a good introduction to a reading note since it is widely known by many readers' advisors and offers clear and strong examples of many of the reading note elements.

Title *84, Charing Cross Road*	**Author** Helene Hanff
Date read 7/2006	**Date published** 1975 **Number of pages** 97
Geographical setting NYC and London	**Time period** 1949–1969

Series notes *84, Charing Cross Road* is part of a loose trilogy. The other books are *The Duchess of Bloomsbury Street* and *Q's Legacy*.
Narrative context (High (strong story))   Medium   Low (more fact based)

Subject Booksellers and bookselling—Great Britain— Correspondence *(also, literature, friendship, love of books, WWII)*	**Type** Memoir in epistolary form

APPEAL NOTES

Pacing Fast	(Medium)	Slow	**Comments** It is a short, quick read.

Character Strong characters, lots of characters, Helene's and Frank's voices are strong and distinct. She is a bit brisk, but smart and interesting too. Readers may identify with her. He is calm and formal. The supporting cast of characters is great—quirky, fun, and good foils to the main characters.
Story line Helene and Frank exchange letters as she buys books from his store. Over time they share personal information and comments about the books. It is strongly narrative in its story line, the focus is on the relationship and the books, and the intent is to share the experience.
Detail Lots—of books, reading, shopping, NYC, London during the war, her reading tastes, and looking for and buying books.
Learning/experiencing The main appeal of the book, or at least the main point of the author. There is a lot to experience here—reading pleasures, growing through reading (us and her), friendships, wartime London, and lots to learn about as well including reading plans and the antiquarian book business.
Language Lovely. It is correspondence, which adds a bit to the whole feel of the book and how it reads, but both of them are good writers, and even in the more prosaic parts the language is elegant, evocative, and deeply enjoyable.
Setting NYC and London—inside her apartment and around NYC and inside the store and their homes as well as around London. It is not that evocative. Certainly setting is not one of the strongest appeals.
Tone Warm, cozy, uplifting, and reassuring.
Similar books *Used and Rare: Travels in the Book World,* by Lawrence Goldstone and Nancy Goldstone—more about loving and finding books. Not the same in terms of story line, but similar in subject and learning/experiencing. *Dear Exile: The True Story of Two Friends Separated (for a Year) by an Ocean,* by Hilary Liftin and Kate Montgomery—also a book of correspondence. Much more modern and nothing to do with books, but the letters capture time and place very well and there is a lot about a modern woman finding her place in the city (NY) and the wider world and about friendship. It is an odd match, but I think for the right reader it would work. *Touchstones: Letters between Two Women, 1953–1964,* by Patricia Frazer Lamb and Kathryn Joyce Hohlwein. Also a book of letters, strongly narrative, and the tone is close and the feel is right. These are missing the focus on literature, but readers can get more of that in Hanff's two other books, and all the "bookish" titles lack the right kind of story line.

READING NOTES

Title	Author	
Date read	Date published	Number of pages
Geographical setting	Time period	
Series notes		

Narrative context High (strong story) Medium Low (more fact based)	
Subject	Type

APPEAL NOTES

Pacing Fast Medium Slow	Comments
Character	
Story line	
Detail	
Learning/experiencing	
Language	
Setting	
Tone	
Similar books	

E

THE READERS' ADVISORY MATRIX

Whenever you read a book, use this matrix to run the book through all the intertwined aspects of working with nonfiction. The simple practice of thinking through a book's various elements helps you understand the book better, reinforces readers' advisory skills, helps you remember a title, and prepares you to talk about the book with readers. The intent of the matrix is to guide you in a mental review of all the key elements of a book. It takes just a second to think through, either after you have finished it or while you are reading. Make using the matrix a habit, and you will find that your readers' advisory skills increase steadily.

The matrix is not intended to be a written exercise, but here is an example of how brief you can be when thinking about titles.

THE READERS' ADVISORY MATRIX FOR *84, CHARING
CROSS ROAD*, BY HELENE HANFF

1. Where is the book on the narrative continuum? ☑ Highly narrative (reads like fiction) ❏ A mix (combines highly narrative moments with periods of fact-based prose) ❏ Highly fact based (has few or no narrative moments)
2. What is the subject of the book? *The literary life—the book is really about loving literature and the relationships between the main characters.*
3. What type of book is it? *A memoir in epistolary form.*
4. Articulate appeal **What is the pacing of the book?** *It reads quickly but the pace is leisurely.* **Describe the characters of the book.** *It is a character-focused story. The two main characters are Helene Hanff, a woman living in NYC who is on a particular reading path, and Frank Doel, a manager in an antiquarian bookshop in London.* **How does the story feel?** *Warm, cozy, uplifting, and reassuring.* **What is the intent of the author?** *To share her experience.* **What is the focus of the story?** *The lives of the main characters in their particular times and the importance of books and how they affect and shape a life.* **Does the language matter?** *Yes.* **Is the setting important and well described?** *The settings are only important in that they are real and the time period of the war matters. But they are not well described and not really important to the story.* **Are there details and, if so, of what?** *Lots of details: about books and about looking for and buying books.* **Are there sufficient charts and other graphic materials? Are they useful and clear?** *None.* **Does the book stress moments of learning, understanding, or experience?** *All three, learning through literature and about the book trade, understanding what life was like at that time in London, and experiencing the warmth of their friendship.*
5. Why would a reader enjoy this book (rank appeal)? 1. *Learning/experiencing*   2. *Detail*   3. *Tone*

THE READERS' ADVISORY MATRIX

1. Where is the book on the narrative continuum?

❑ Highly narrative (reads like fiction)

❑ A mix (combines highly narrative moments with periods of fact-based prose)

❑ Highly fact based (has few or no narrative moments)

2. What is the subject of the book?

3. What type of book is it?

4. Articulate appeal

What is the pacing of the book?

Describe the characters of the book.

How does the story feel?

What is the intent of the author?

What is the focus of the story?

Does the language matter?

Is the setting important and well described?

Are there details and, if so, of what?

Are there sufficient charts and other graphic materials? Are they useful and clear?

Does the book stress moments of learning, understanding, or experience?

5. Why would a reader enjoy this book (rank appeal)?

1.   2.   3.

INDEX

Authors, titles, and subjects are interfiled in one alphabet.
Authors print in roman, titles in italics, and subjects in boldface.

Neal Wyatt, a collection development and readers' advisory librarian, is the editor of the "Reader's Shelf" column for *Library Journal* as well as the compiler of the *LJ* online feature "Wyatt's World." She is the editor of the *Reference and User Services Quarterly* "Alert Collector" column, a contributor to *NoveList*, and a reviewer for *Booklist*. She is active in ALA and has served as chair of both CODES and the Notable Books Council and as a member of the RUSA Executive Board and ALA Council. Ms. Wyatt designed and teaches the Web CE course on Readers' Advisory Services for RUSA and is a frequent speaker on readers' advisory topics, having designed and presented programs at PLA and ALA as well as at many local and regional library events. She earned her MSLS from the Catholic University of America and also holds an MA in Literature.